WILD
swimming
COAST

Explore the secret coves
and wild beaches of Britain

Daniel Start

Wild Swimming: Coast

First edition published in the
United Kingdom in 2009 by

Punk Publishing Ltd, 3 The Yard,
Pegasus Place, London SE11 5SD

A catalogue record of this book is
available from the British Library.

ISBN: 978-1-906889-01-2

10 9 8 7 6 5 4 3 2

www.punkpublishing.co.uk

www.wildswimming.co.uk

Contents

Swims by Region

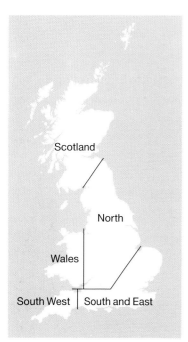

Scotland

North

Wales

South West | South and East

South West

South and East

How to find the swims:

Once you have decided which region you are interested in, turn to the swim map at the start of that section. There you'll find the main swimming locations (1–175) plus additional swims nearby (marked A, B, C). There's also a summary of the regional highlights.

The swim panels for each region contain the descriptions, detailed directions and difficulty ratings of the numbered swimming locations. You can also look through 'Swims at Glance' to give you inspiration for a particular type of swim or day out, or why not just open the book anywhere for a refreshing and fascinating dip into Britain's idyllic saltwater swimming holes.

Wales

North

Scotland

Introduction

That first summer the sun beat down every day. The scent of gorse and heather filled the air, the whiteness of the sand was almost blinding and the ocean shimmered like a pool.

I had just moved to the far west of Cornwall and was meant to be studying, but the heat was so stifling I ended up going swimming every day, looking for secret swimming coves and interesting places to snorkel. Poring over my map in the evenings, I was amazed at the places waiting to be discovered with just a bit of scrambling and exploring off the beaten track: a little beach that no one knew about, a natural rock pool large enough to swim in or a deep inlet for jumping.

That amazing summer was the beginning of an aquatic odyssey as I embarked on a journey around Britain, searching for its most wild and wonderful coves, caves, beaches and islands. Ten years on and I have travelled thousands of miles on foot, by bike, kayak and camper van. I have twisted ankles, drowned camera bags and suffered from hypothermia and heatstroke. But I found solace, too, in the wonders of our foreshores – a secret slice of beach, an archway to swim through or a sea cave encrusted with pink coralline.

Our island race has long been enchanted by the sea and tales of Cornish mermaids and Scottish selkies are symptoms of our fascination with its watery underworlds. But our fondness for swimming and bathing for health and leisure is a relatively recent affair. Not until the end of the sixteenth century did the fashion for 'taking the waters' begin to develop. Much of this popularity was spurred on by the attendant health benefits. When Dr Richard Russell wrote about the restorative qualities of bathing at the tiny Sussex fishing village of Brighthelmstone in 1783 the Prince Regent was quick to visit and rented a small farmhouse there. The Prince enjoyed it so much that he bought the building and converted it to the flamboyant Brighton Pavilion we know today.

Sea-based activities – kayaking, surfing and coasteering – are some of the fastest-growing sports in Britain. With new access laws opening up large swaths of coast, and water quality better than at any time in living memory, there has never been a better time to swim and explore the natural wonders of our coastline.

The more austere Royal Sea Bathing Infirmary in Margate was constructed at about the same time and opened its doors around 1791, offering treatment for complaints such as tuberculosis, skin conditions or jaundice. Patients were not only instructed to immerse themselves in the sea but, sometimes, to drink it too. Professional 'dippers' were employed to thrust patients under the waves, though if you were wealthy you would enter the sea from the privacy of a bathing machine: the ritual immersions were always performed naked.

Today we have a better understanding of the health benefits of sea bathing – and nakedness is definitely optional. Swimming is not only an excellent all-round activity for building fitness and strength, but cold-water dipping also has restorative effects. A plunge dilates the blood vessels and expels toxins from the body while at the same time releasing endorphins that elevate mood, creating an urge to dive straight back in. Regular dipping across a season leads to 'cold adaptation', which can strengthen the immune and cardiovascular systems, as well as increasing libido and improving our spirits.

The combination of a watery pick-me-up and some risqué excitement meant the sea-bathing craze was set to spread. Soon the Victorians were coming to the beach resorts simply to have fun and watch the bathing spectacles. A spate of new railways – plus the introduction

*Our 8,000-mile foreshore
with its remote inter-tidal zone
is perhaps Britain's greatest
wilderness area today.*

of public holidays – accelerated the growth of the seaside resorts familiar to many of us. The seaside was leading a revolution in leisure, social progress and outdoor enjoyment.

The coast has long been central to our literary heritage as well. Daphne du Maurier's *Rebecca* and *Frenchman's Creek* were based on her childhood haunts around Fowey and Helford; Virginia Woolf's *To the Lighthouse* was inspired by holidays at Godrevy; and the wild undercliffs and remote beaches of the Jurassic coast were beloved by Jane Austen. Arthur Ransome set his *Secret Island* tales of the Swallows and Amazons at locations on the Essex shore and Scotland was home to the real Robinson Crusoe, its uninhabited islands firing the imagination of Robert Louis Stevenson, author of *Treasure Island*.

Our coastline has many ancient associations. Tintagel is the home of Arthurian legend, while from many small islands holy men spread the Christian message: communities and monasteries, churches and abbeys were established at Bardsey Island in Wales, Iona in Scotland, Holy Island on the Northumberland coast and St Peter-on-the-Wall in Essex. Today these places continue to offer a spiritual retreat, a place to swim and immerse oneself in nature and reflect on our fascinating history.

Many parts of our coast reveal clues to our industrial past, too. There are old quarries breached by the sea, such as the Blue Lagoon in Wales. In Portland and the Purbecks you can enjoy the perfect lagoons and inlets that were left behind after quarrying for the great stones of St Paul's cathedral. On a hot day with calm seas, at locations such as Dancing Ledge or Durdle Door, you could be on Crete or any other Greek island as you watch people skin-dive in the perfect blue waters, leap from ledges and sunbathe on the golden rocks.

Whether you are exploring the sea caves of the Witch's Cauldron near Cardigan or playing with seals in the Isles of Scilly; collecting oysters and samphire in East Anglia or basking in the ethereal blue glow of the Outer Hebrides' shallow lagoons, wild swimming offers a spectacular introduction to our island's natural history. Britain is as rich in wilderness and secret places as ever and, if you can pick a sunny day, the swimming is out of this world!

Getting Started

Britain's coastline is one of the most beautiful in the world and offers some exceptional wild swimming. Here's how to get going.

Ten ways to be wild and safe

1 Never swim alone and keep a constant watch on weak swimmers.
2 Never use inflatables – they can drift on currents and wind.
3 In surf conditions avoid swimming where rip currents can form: along the edge of coves, at river mouths and near groynes and piers.
4 If caught in an offshore rip, don't swim against it. Simply swim parallel to the beach for 20m then return in on the surf.
5 Avoid steeply shelving beaches in the surf – the waves will 'dump' you.
6 Do not swim from rocks in breaking surf.
7 Never jump or dive into water unless you have checked it for depth and obstructions.
8 Swim within the shelter of coves and bays unless you understand the tidal streams that operate at headlands and in the open sea.
9 Wear a wetsuit if you know you'll be in the water for more than 15–20 minutes.
10 If you get into difficulties, lift your arm to attract help.

More information on pp.252–253

Staying warm It takes a few minutes to get used to British sea temperatures so persevere and you'll be amazed how warm it can feel! Regular dipping makes you less sensitive to cold and has health benefits. Unless you are an experienced swimmer, however, 20 minutes is enough for most people; never allow yourself to start shivering. Come out for a rest, put on lots of layers and exercise to warm up. The sea is at its warmest in September and when the tide has come in over large expanses of warm sand or mud. Swimming in the late afternoon, a few hours before high tide, is often the best time.

Footwear and kit Few of the swims in this book require kit but footwear is always useful. Jellies, surf shoes and beach footwear are cheap and available at seaside stores or in supermarkets. These will protect you from sharp rocks as well as weeverfish that bury themselves in the wet sand at low water (if stung, immerse your foot in hot water for 20 minutes to relieve the pain). Goggles are great fun and good for navigating while swimming among rocks. Wetsuits will help you stay in longer and, should you get into difficulties, they will protect you from hypothermia. For the intrepid, a 'dry' bag (sold in kayak and sailing shops) is a good option – for sandwiches and dry clothes too.

Tides and currents You need to understand the tides, so buy yourself a small tide timetable at any local seaside shop or download one from www.bbc.co.uk/weather/coast/tides. The tide repeats itself twice a day, advancing 45 minutes day-on-day. 'Spring' (does not refer to the season) tides repeat every two weeks and occur at every full or new moon throughout the year. These tides are much stronger and higher than regular tides. In between, at half-moons, are 'neap' tides, which are much weaker. Tides create slow currents in the open sea, but you need only worry about these if you are outside the protection of a cove or a bay. Rip currents are completely separate from tides and are created in surf conditions where there are breaking waves. They are localised and possible to avoid and escape from. Read pp.252–253 to find out more.

How to use this book

Finding the swims
You'll find 175 main swimming locations numbered through this book in the swim boxes. Another 175 additional swims, close to the main swims, are also listed (A, B, C). Every location contains a grid reference, postcode and directions. The postcode leads to the nearest road access and can be used with a SatNav or a route-planning website such as Google Maps or AA Route Planner. The adjustment tells you how far the swim is from the postcode (for example, walk 200m N). The 8-digit Ordnance Survey grid reference is the most accurate reference, down to the nearest 100m. Type it into www. multimap.com, click the OS Map button, zoom in and you can view and print out detailed 1:50,000 and 1:25,000 walking maps.

www.wildswimming.co.uk
gives full instructions on using and printing these maps, plus tips on finding your own locations with maps.

Walk difficulty
In each box panel we've graded the difficulty of access to the cove, beach or swimming place as easy, moderate or difficult, and estimated how long the approach walk is from the nearest road. The most difficult routes may involve climbing down steep, poorly marked paths or scrambling over wet slippery rocks – hazardous for younger children or for the unsteady. Wear good footwear and take your time.

Swim difficulty
Locations inside a sandy cove or bay pose very few dangers in calm seas and these are classed as easy. If a beach is rocky, is known to develop particularly strong rip currents in surf conditions, or if you are swimming from an exposed coastline or headland that is open to tidal currents, either one $\triangle$ or two $\triangle\triangle$ hazard symbols are added to indicate the swim is moderate to difficult. Do refer to pp.252–253 to make a proper assessment of the tides and risks.

Food, camping, transport
Recommended pubs, cafés ⑪ and campsites ▲ have been allocated symbols. We also indicate National Trust properties (NT), Sustrans national cycle routes (www.sustrans. org.uk) and train stations.

Tides
Some places are tide dependent and these have been indicated as LT, MT, HT, AT for low, mid, high or all tides.

Directions
N, NE, E, SE, S, SW, W and NW refer to the points of the compass, L and R to left and right. 'Dir' means 'follow in the direction of'. 1km = 0.6 miles, 1 mile = 1.6km, and 1m = 1.1 yard. Walking 1km takes 20 minutes on rough ground.

Access
Stick to rights of way or open access land. The foreshore and any land below high water are common ground. It is likely that new legislation will open up the whole coast to walkers, so keep up to date at www.wildswimming.co.uk

Swims at a Glance

Beach Camping * wild camping

Paddle in the sunset, pitch your tent, wake up with a splash

Cosy Pubs

A pub within reach, for *après*-swim warmth and refreshment

Sunset Views

West-facing coves; perfect for watching the sun go down

Sea Food

From curry to crab sandwiches, cream teas to big breakfasts

Secret Islands

Uninhabited islets and lagoons: be Robinson Crusoe for a day

Skinny-dipping * semi-official naturist beach

Beautiful naturist beaches and remote locations

Swims at a Glance

Caves and Arches

Temples of the ocean. Swim through arches and explore sea caves

4a	Piper's Hole	101	St Non's Bay
13B	Thurlestone Rock arch	105	Barafundle Beach Arches
26A	Tintagel Haven	109	Draught sands and caves
33A	Baggy Point sea caves	123	North Landing
47	Durdle Door	144A	Fingal's Cave
48	Stair Hole, Lulworth	165	Brei Holm, Papa Stour
95A	Carreg-y-Ty	166	Bow Fiddle, Portknockie
96	Witch's Cauldron, Ceibwr	168	Bullers of Buchan
100A	Ram's Nose	171	The Garran

Great for Families and Picnics

Off the beaten track, but less than ten minutes from the car

10A	Porthluney	88b	Porth Oer
21A	Trevaunance Cove	94	Mwnt
22A	Porthcothan	104B	Broad Haven
30A	Sandy Mouth	105	Barafundle Beach arch
53	Studland Bay	137	Bamburgh Castle sands
57	East Head, West Wittering	140	Football Hole
63	Camber Sands, west	147	Calgary Bay
68	Botany Bay, Broadstairs	162	Achmelvich cove
85	Rhoscolyn Arches	170	Lunan Bay

Plunge Pools

Deluxe rock pools, warmed by the sun and big enough to swim in

12B	Polperro tidal pool	92	Borth-y-Gest
20A	Porthtowan	101B	Ogof Golchfa
23	Treyarnon rock pool	102	Porth-y-Rhaw
28A	The Greenaway	110	Bluepool Corner
34B	Tunnels Beach	137A	Harkess Rock Pools
36A	Woody Bay	141A	Craster plunge pool
51	Dancing Ledge	153	Talisker Bay
70B	Tollesbury	171	The Garran
79	Stiffkey, Freshes Creek	175	St Abb's Head

Best for Jumps

Traditional places to jump and dive. Always check the depth

Leave the Car at Home

Swims and beaches an hour or so's walk from a train station

Literature and Legend

Atmospheric haunts of artists, writers and adventurers

South West

Along Devon and Cornwall's dramatic coastline, sandy coves and smugglers' inlets are set amid rugged scenery. The south coast is gentle with several meandering estuaries while the north is wilder and bears the full brunt of south-westerly swells. The region, which has inspired writers and artists from Daphne du Maurier to Barbara Hepworth, has become very popular, but there are plenty of secret places if you want to escape the crowds.

South West Highlights

36 38 39

Minehead

Exeter

Torbay

Dartmouth

C

13 18 B A

A B A A 17 B

Prawle Point

16

1 Pedn Vounder Sands is one of the most spectacular tidal beaches in Britain with shallow sandy lagoons, Logan Rock and a cliff-top theatre nearby.

4 The Isles of Scilly are Britain's own tropical archipelago with the clearest waters and miles upon miles of dazzling white sandy beaches.

5 Serpentine cliffs and extraordinary rock formations dominate the west side of the Lizard, from spectacular Kynance to Mullion Cove.

16–17 The coves around Prawle Point are some of the most remote and beautiful in the whole of this region.

20 The adventurous can explore the base of Chapel Porth cliffs at low tide and even enter the old sea caves beneath the famous Wheal Coates engine house.

22 The great rock stacks at Bedruthan Steps are legendary, but take this approach to the beach and avoid the crowds.

23 Treyarnon is a wonderful pool set in the rocks by the cove.

26 King Arthur's castle towers above Tintagel Haven with access to Merlin's caves below. Or continue on to find the Rocky Valley waterfall plunge pools and dramatic Bossiney Haven beach.

29–32 The Hartland peninsula is one of Devon's forgotten corners, dominated by dramatic folded cliffs. Speke's Mill Mouth is its jewel, with a giant waterfall plunging down into pools on the beach below.

36 A delightful walk beside a wooded stream leads to Heddon Mouth shingle beach where German U-Boats once docked.

Logan Rock and Pedn Vounder Sands at low tide

Land's End, Penwith and the Isles of Scilly

Granite outcrops and burial cairns rise up among heather and gorse. Far below a turquoise sea shifts, throwing up spray in the hot morning sun. The craggy granite peninsula of Land's End, at the furthest tip of England, is studded with secret coves, and further out on the Isles of Scilly archipelago are some of the finest white sand beaches.

For me, Nanjizal Bay is the real Land's End. One of the most inaccessible beaches in Penwith, the two-mile walk is a pilgrimage to a mystical and wild place. At the north end three sandstone caves are hunched like gnarled dinosaur feet. At the south a tall eyelet rock arch – Zawn Pyg, the 'Song of the Sea' – shields a low-tide, sandy plunge pool. The sand from Nanjizal, completely displaced by a violent storm in 1953, is slowly returning and there is a good stretch at low tide.

The sands that Nanjizal lost, Pedn Vounder some three miles east has gained. This dramatic bay is protected by towering granite outcrops; sandbars and lagoons form between them and shallow pools warm up in the sun. Bathers can swim in among little inlets or wade over to the Logan Rock headland, where a cantilevered rock once stood until some local lads tipped it into the sea as a challenge nearly a hundred years ago.

Pedn Vounder is mainly used by local people, campers and nudists and there's a great pub and cliff-top campsite above. The beach is reached

4

1A

4A

by a flower-lined track but a tricky descent keeps the crowds away. If you're staying in the area, try to catch a performance at the open-air Minack Theatre, continue up the lane to the church at St Levan, and perhaps also visit lesser-known Porth Chapel Beach.

Heading north from Nanjizal and Land's End a sleepy stream runs down through Cot Valley. Here the path leads down past great marble boulders to sands at low tide. The tiny Brisons islands stand half a mile offshore and each year an annual swimming race takes place between them and nearby Priest's Cove, with a flotilla of rowing gigs organised by the Cape Cornwall Slipway Association following on behind to pick up the stragglers. From here the north coast becomes steeper and rockier with breaks at little-known Portheras Cove and, at spring low tides, at the sands of Gurnard's Head and eventually Zennor, which has a great pub and a legendary mermaid.

Looking west from Penwith on a clear day you can sometimes make out the white shimmer of the Isles of Scilly, 28 miles offshore. The sea between covers the ancient mythical kingdom of Lyonesse and, according to Arthurian legend, when the final storm covered the land a knight rode out on a white horse. The sand on Scilly is iridescent, mixed with pulverised white sea-shells brought in from the Caribbean by the Gulf Stream. The crystal water is a diver's paradise. Stay on one of the off-islands to really soak up island life. Tresco's Pentle Bay is spectacular, while St Martin's has Great Bay. A single-track road to its tiny bakery is lined with stalls filled with garden tomatoes and orchard-fruit jam, with honesty boxes for payment.

The constant revealing and concealing of sea caves and causeways is part of the adventure of Scilly. A low-tide scramble over to White Island from St Martin's reveals deep inlets that are good for snorkelling and jumping, and a dark sea cave named Underland Girt. At the north end of Tresco you can explore Piper's Hole, a freshwater lake in a cavern that visitors often light with candles (see p.253). And on a few special low spring tides each year this shallow archipelago almost joins itself back together as the seas recede and you wade for miles through turquoise water, from one beautiful island to the next.

Song of the Sea arch and pool, Nanjizal

Land's End, Penwith and the Isles of Scilly

1 Pedn Vounder Sands

Grid ref. SW393223
Postcode TR19 6LF
Walk 15 mins, diff
Train Penzance, 15km

Superb tidal sands and lagoons between Logan Rock and popular Porthcurno beach. Part-nudist.

Join B3315 at Newlyn (near Penzance) and continue 15km to Treen village and Logan Rock Inn (01736 810495). Park by post office and follow track past campsite (Treen Farm Camping ⛺ 01736 810273) to coast path (800m), then R and L to rock headland and down tricky path for rock scramble to beach. Beach covered at HT.

A Porth Chapel Beach 2km W of Pedn Vounder on coast path or L off B3315, past Porthcurno Beach, past Minack Theatre, then path on L 300m before St Levan church. (SW382219, TR19 6JU).

B Spectacular **Nanjizal (Mill Bay)** with tidal sands, caves and eyelet rock arch with pool. On coast path: 2km S from Land's End or 3km N from Porthgwarra (SW357236).

2 Portheras Cove

Grid ref. SW389358
Postcode TR19 7TU
Walk 10 mins, mod
Train Penzance, 14km

Remote and little-known cove with white sand at all tides. Cliff walk E from Pendeen lighthouse (1km). Or via track below Lower Chypraze Farm – turn L off B3306 2km after Pendeen just as you enter Morvah.

A Continue N (9km) for spectacular coastal drive to Zennor's Tinner's Arms 🍴 (TR26 3BY) and tidal 'Mermaid' **Pendour Cove** below headland (SW448390).

3 Cot Valley

Grid ref. SW356309
Postcode TR19 7NR
Walk 3 mins, easy
Train Penzance, 14km

Tidal sands at base of pretty valley. From St Just centre head to school and bear L down lanes. Annual swimming race in July to Priest's Cove (1km N) from the Brisons organised by Cape Cornwall Slipway Association.

4 St Martin's, Scilly

Grid ref. SV925162
Postcode TR25 0QN (400m E)
Walk 20 mins, mod
Train Penzance, 3 hours by boat

A low-key, organic-food-friendly island. Great Bay is a sheltered white sand beach with access to White Island at low tide.

From St Martin's Hotel 🍴 (excellent cocktail bar) walk 1km up road and at community hall/reading rooms turn L across moors and continue 400m down to bay. At far N end White Island can be accessed at MT/LT by stone causeway. On NE side find deep inlets and a long sea cave (Underland Girt, SV926175).

A Tresco island: spectacular **Pentle Bay** (SV900143) is W of priory. At far NE tip of island find underground pool in **Piper's Hole**, an old sea cave just above HT line, hidden at top of an inlet (SV887166).

B **Rushey Bay** is sheltered sand bay on S side of wild and rugged Bryher. Scilly's longest sea cave (High Rock Cave) is found at SV874155.

5 Kynance Cove and Asparagus Island

South Cornwall: The Lizard and Helford River

Spectacular Kynance Cove on the Lizard was immortalised by the Romantic poets and painters of the eighteenth century. Shiny black serpentine rocks tower up in pinnacles around the beach and green and purple minerals colour the water.

This National Trust beach is very well known but the walk from the car park limits visitor numbers. The hidden parts are on the far beach by Asparagus Island, only accessible on a falling tide. Here the Devil's Letterbox blowhole hisses and bellows and several deep pools appear among the rocks. Daredevils jump from the high black crags and snorkellers explore overhangs and caves.

The dramatic serpentine scenery continues for six miles north up to Mullion Cove, which is surrounded by black cliffs and islands and features an old quay that is popular for jumping. Here I met a band of young local swimmers who regularly explore this coastline. I joined them on an expedition, scrambling along the south shore and around steep headlands to find sea caves and a tiny wedge of white sand. Jubilant, we waded ashore like modern Robinson Crusoes and lay exhausted in the sun, the towering cliffs condensing the evening light to heat on our bodies.

Heading south, the indented shoreline is full of secret places and has long been associated with the contraband trade. The head of the

5 **Kynance Cove, west side**

7

6

area's most famous pirate family was John Carter, the self-styled 'King of Prussia', who was part-fisherman, part-merchant and part-Robin Hood. At Prussia Cove you can still see the worn ruts of ancient cart tracks leading to the old smuggling slipway. With flat rocky ledges for sunbathing and sand at low tide this, and adjacent Piskies Cove, is an excellent spot for swimming, exploring and diving.

Find even more hideaways as you continue eastwards around the remote Lizard coast. At cute and tiny Cadgwith you can visit the Devil's Frying Pan, an impressive blowhole that is best viewed from the coast path and into which local lads attempt to swim. A long walk from the surfing beach at Kennack Sands or from pretty Coverack brings you to the coves of Lankidden and Downas. They shelter beneath wooded copses, streams and moorland along a stretch of virtually untouched Cornish coastline.

At the Manacles rocks, towards St Keverne, you'll find a coral reef and one of Britain's best-known diving sites. A trip from the dive centre at Porthkerris may yield sightings of cushion and spiny starfish and, in summer, you may even spot a pod of dolphins cruising by or commune with sunfish and giant basking sharks.

By the time you reach the Helford River estuary, which is filled with little tidal inlets, the coast has softened. There are several secret wooded coves along the river with silver-shale beaches, perfect for exploring by kayak or on foot – Bosham is my favourite. Self-drive boats can be hired from Helford Quay and a small ferry will take you across the water to Trebah Manor with its gardens and beach. Gear Farm, at the head of the estuary, is a wonderful place to camp, explore and swim. The owners sell cider, cured meat and superb pizza. But the most atmospheric place is Frenchmans' Pill or Creek, still as silent as it must have been when Daphne du Maurier wrote the book of the same name some 50 years ago. Navron, the strange yellow house, is down a track at the head of the wooded pill. Hidden from sunlight and seemingly trapped in time, the creek, which many say is haunted, is given a jungle-like air by the overhanging trees and green waters. This is a place to explore by open canoe in the dawn mist, or at dusk.

Mullion Cove and old quay, Lizard

South Cornwall: The Lizard and Helford River

5 Kynance Cove

Grid ref.	SW685133
Postcode	TR12 7PJ
Walk	10 mins, mod
Train	Camborne, 29km

Popular but spectacular NT cove, attracting artists for centuries. Deep plunge pools. Discreet NT tea room.

Signed R off A3083 16km S of Helston, dir Lizard. At LT head round to N beach to find pools on far R into which people jump. You can snorkel around Asparagus Island, but only in flat seas due to rip currents.

A 5km before Kynance, turn L (B3296) through Mullion to **Mullion Cove** (6km). Jump from the quay, snorkel among the offshore rocks. Serious wet-suited adventurers swim 500m S to find secret cove of Laden Ceyn, opposite Mullion Island (SW665175, TR12 7ES). △ △

B 20 min walk N from Mullion Cove on coast path leads to sandy **Polurrian Cove**. Or drive from Mullion (turn L by church) and park at busy but charming Poldhu Cove (1km N) or Church Cove (2km N).

6 Lankidden Cove

Grid ref.	SW756166
Postcode	TR12 6SH
Walk	30 mins, mod
Train	Camborne, 25km

A remote pair of tiny LT sand coves. Great snorkelling. Wooded valley.

3km walk on coast path E of popular Kennack Sands (Kuggar, R off B3293 to Coverack). Or 1km walk from Pensongath village, 3km W of Coverack. Lankidden is tucked into E corner of Carrick Luz headland. Downas Cove is 1km E, at bottom of wooded stream valley.

A Cute and tiny **Cadgwith** with its small swimming cove and dramatic Devil's Frying Pan blowhole 300m W (6km S of Coverack, SW722144, TR12 7JX)

B Excellent snorkelling around Drawna Rocks at **Porthkerris** (TR12 6QJ), 3km NE of St Keverne (Dive Centre 01326 280620). Or explore isolated coast N from nearby Porthoustock (TR12 6QW, free parking) via Pencra Head (SW810223) and abandoned mines, to connect with Porthkerris.

7 Prussia Cove

Grid ref.	SW557279
Postcode	TR20 9BA
Walk	15mins, easy
Train	Hayle, 10km

Famous smugglers' cove, good for snorkelling and sunbathing. Coast path leads W 600m to Piskies Cove with caves, or E 500m to Kennegy tidal sands. Turn R at Falmouth Packet Inn (Rosudgeon) off A394, 8km E of Penzance, and continue down lane 2km. Cottage accommodation (01736 762014).

8 Bosahan Cove, Helford

Grid ref.	SW774263
Postcode	TR12 6LB
Walk	30mins, mod
Train	Camborne, 25km

Secluded shingle sand coves backed by woods, 2km E of Helford village on coast path. 2km W leads to Frenchman's Pill. Also coves between Durgan and Mawnan on N Helford bank via ferry (SW781271, TR11 5HZ). Pizza and camping at Gear Farm 🍴🏕 2km E of Mawnan (SW723249, TR12 6DE, 01326 221364), off B3293.

Lansallos Cove, home of smugglers

South Cornwall: Roseland, Fowey and Polperro

The luxuriant gardens and subtropical palms of stylish St Mawes on the unspoilt Roseland peninsula seem worlds away from the dramatic rocks and serpentine cliffs of the Lizard.

The church at St Just is Roseland's jewel. A path winds down through ivy-clad mausoleums and vibrant rhododendrons to a jade-green tidal creek with an Edwardian boathouse. From here the south Cornwall coast opens out into Veryan Bay and the lanes are so deep, narrow and twisted they seem to swallow cars and cycles whole.

Just to the west of Portholland on the coast path, I found a truly hidden wild beach near May's Rock, known only to a few locals who hide their surfboards here in the bushes. If you're alert you'll spot the goat track off to the left. It quickly opens up into a wide, roped path with steps down through low-growing hawthorn. Back in the village, John, who runs the café, explained that they strim the route every year to keep it open, but stop 50 yards short of the coast path to ensure it remains hidden.

Gardens offering cream teas, wooded castles and low-key family coves are spied through hedgerows, and bumble-bees and butterflies twirl and zip through the cow parsley as you head on to dramatic Dodman

9

12 Palace Cove with old quay

10

Point. Once round this headland, you come to the long naturist strand of Vault Beach and perfect little Hemmick Cove, its rocky ledges stretching into the sea. Porthluney Cove is a busy family beach, set beneath imposing Caerhays Castle and chosen by Alfred Hitchcock as the setting for his adaptation of Daphne du Maurier's *Rebecca* in 1941.

If you want to visit the real Manderley you'll need to head east to nearby Fowey, huddled around its riverside creeks. Daphne du Maurier spent her most formative childhood years around Fowey and Gribbin Head, and it was here that she learned to sail. Du Maurier lived at Readymoney Cove, but it was to remote Polridmouth Cove that she went to bathe naked, and it was here she developed her infatuation with Menabilly – Manderley in *Rebecca* – the house where she spent her final years. Both coves are still popular swimming venues. Readymoney, set beneath St Catherine's Castle and just a short walk from Fowey, has a bathing platform tethered in the middle of the cove – great fun to swim to and dive from. A half-hour's walk from Fowey you'll find the Menabilly estate, which has gardens running right down to the beach. Further along is the harbour cove of Polkerris; the Rashleigh Inn is 'Kerrith' in *Rebecca*.

The coast eastwards from Fowey to Polperro, one of the most beautiful and timeless parts of Cornwall, has a long association with smuggling. At the end of the eighteenth century, when the Napoleonic wars were raging and French goods were heavily taxed, landing brandy, tobacco and lace was a major local enterprise. Once on the beach the illicit goods would quickly disappear, to be hidden in caves or transported inland along well-trodden paths to secret hiding places. Generations of seafarers brought contraband goods ashore and you can find out much more about this at the Polperro museum, situated near the harbour mouth, where there is a beautifully restored, natural tidal plunge pool.

'Last night I dreamt I went to Manderley again…'
Daphne Du Maurier's *Rebecca*, inspired by Menabilly and Polridmouth Cove

For a real glimpse of the smuggling coves, however, visit beautiful Lansallos, which has an organic farm shop and campsite. From here a wooded glade leads to a tiny beach with a smugglers' passage, complete with cart tracks worn into the stone. Or you can swim from adjacent Palace Cove – its old 'quay' is just steps hewn from the rock.

10A Hemmick Beach, Dodman Point

South Cornwall: Roseland, Fowey and Polperro

9 St Just-in-Roseland

Grid ref.	SW847358
Postcode	TR2 5JD
Walk	10 mins, easy
Train	Truro, 10km (via ferry)

Shingle estuary beach by lush waterside church and tropical gardens. Turn R off A3078 (dir St Mawes). Descend through church gardens to water, L through gate and woods 200m to shingle beach on R.

10 Cellar Cove, Porthluney

Grid ref.	SW953408
Postcode	TR2 5PU (700m W)
Walk	15 mins, mod
Train	St Austell, 13km

Follow coast path W from West Portholland, up hill then L downhill at junction. 100m after path bears R find hidden path L cutting back and down, becoming v clear with ropes after 50m N.

A Follow lanes E (dir Gorran Haven) to find popular **Porthluney** (SW974413), peaceful **Hemmick** (SW994405) and naturist **Vault** beaches (SX012409).

11 Polridmouth (Menabilly)

Grid ref.	SX103504
Postcode	PL24 2TN (600m S)
Walk	15 mins, easy
Train	Par, 4km

Daphne du Maurier's favourite swimming cove and inspiration for *Rebecca*. Sometimes weedy. Concrete breakwater.

From Fowey (A3082, dir St Austell) turn L after 3km. Pass road to Polkerris (R) and continue to road end – Menabilly with field parking. Walk past farm down to cove.

A **Readymoney Cove** is 2km E of Polridmouth on coast path, or well signed 1km S from Fowey. Bathing platform. Wooded walk leads up to St Catherine's Castle ruins (SX118510, PL23 1JH).

B **Polkerris Cove** is fun and popular with beach-side Rashleigh Inn 🍽 (01726 813991, PL24 2TL). Rocks for snorkelling and jumping beyond quay. Follow coast path 1km N to find secret beach on way to Par Sands. Follow path 1km S (in woods above) to find tiny sandy coves.

12 Lansallos, Lantivet Bay

Grid ref.	SX166512
Postcode	PL13 2PX
Walk	20 mins, mod
Train	Bodmin Parkway, 20km

Secret smugglers' cove with passage, waterfall, snorkelling. NT village.

From Polperro car park turn R by Crumplehorn Inn, continue up lanes 3km, turning R then L, signed Lansallos. Take path by church down through woods 1km to cove. 500m W find **Palace Cove**. Camping at Highertown Farm 🏕 (01208 265211) or Barton Farm tea house 🍽 (01726 870375).

A **Lantic Bay** (SX148509, PL23 1NP, 1km W) two stunning beaches set beneath high cliffs. NT car park 2km E of Polruan on lanes. Cross fields on path and descend. Rip currents in rough conditions. △△

B **Polperro tidal pool**: carved steps lead to pool among rocks at harbour mouth, W side (SX210508, PL13 2QY). From harbour climb steps by Blue Peter Inn to join coast path. Drop down L by bench, then R before white hut shelter (not L to old warehouse).

South Devon: Plymouth to Salcombe

I first swam out to the Thurlestone Rock arch when I was 12 years old. To my brother and myself back then it seemed an awfully long way – about 200 yards of shallow water, bladderwrack floating like a forest beneath us.

A 'thirled' stone is an Old English term for a stone that has been naturally pierced and is therefore imbued with supernatural powers. We climbed through the arch and it felt exciting, like a rite of passage. You need a high tide to actually swim through the hole and by the time we headed back the ebbing waters were revealing the weedy rock ledge that connects the stack to the beach. We arrived back to our towels, shivering but full of our adventure.

West from Thurlestone beach you'll find peace and tranquillity at Cowry Cove beneath the golf course and coast path. The shells on this wild beach are beautiful and down beneath the cliff you are well away from Devon's hustle and bustle. There are views to glorious Bantham Sands and tiny art deco Burgh Island. During the roaring 1920s and indiscreet 1930s the island's hotel was a sophisticated 'party pad' where London society, most famously Agatha Christie, came to enjoy seaside life. When playwright Noel Coward visited

15A

14A

13B

for three days in the 1930s he loved it so much he stayed for three weeks. According to local folklore, floating bars were moored in summer at various points offshore for swimmers and there is still an annual round-island swimming race with cocktails served to the winner by waiters in black tie. Today you can cross the sands to the island and explore Herring Cove just to the north. Afterwards, have a refreshing drink at the Pilchard Inn.

Another hotel, also founded in the 1920s, can be found on the steep grassy slopes that lead down to tiny, sandy Soarmill Cove. This is a wild and empty piece of coast. As I strolled through fields butterfly orchids nodded among the heather and purple moor-grass and yellow rattle were flourishing by the wayside. The cove has a small island and caves for exploring, a few hundred yards to the left. From here a three-mile walk takes you to Bolt Head at the south of Salcombe Harbour. Starehole Bay sits far below, its tiny, double sandy coves sheltered beneath the pinnacles of Sharp Tor and the wooded inlets of Salcombe beyond.

At low tide you can see three masts from the older wrecks submerged in this bay. In nearby Sharpitor you'll come across Overbeck's, an elegant Edwardian house with luxuriant subtropical gardens and featuring a range of the most curious artefacts and inventions, many of nautical bent. A hostel and excellent tea shop provide accommodation and refreshment with views over the sand flats of the harbour. Why not hire a little boat at Whitestrand Quay in Salcombe and explore Stink Cove and Splatcove Point, or land on the sandbars of Sunny Cove on the harbour shore opposite.

If you are looking for liquid refreshment in this part of Devon you are definitely spoilt for choice. To the west of Bigbury and Burgh Island you can visit the thirteenth-century Journey's End Inn above the silver rocks and shale of remote Aymer Cove. Two miles further, at Kingston, is the well-loved, oak-beamed Dolphin with a track down to the sparkling sands of the Erme Mouth Estuary. Finally, at Newton Ferrers you'll find Wadham Rocks and Devon's most hidden cove with its wonderful rock formations.

South Devon: Plymouth to Salcombe

13 Cowry Cove, Thurlestone

Grid ref.	SX665428
Postcode	TQ7 3JS
Walk	20 mins, easy
Train	Ivybridge, 15km

Quiet coves beneath Thurlestone golf course and village.

Thurlestone is signed, 6km W of Kingsbridge off A381. Park at beach car park, beyond golf club and village. Take coast path 1.5km NW, to reach Yarmer (Delver) beach (for families) then Cowry (Loam Castle) beach for naturists. Head for the green changing hut at end of golf course and drop down just before it.

A Continue N 1km for great views of Burgh Island and on to wonderful but busy **Bantham Sands** (SX662438, TQ7 3AL), wade across to Burgh Island at LT and round to **Herring Cove** (SX646441).

B Cross to Thurlestone Sands from beach car parks. At HT **Thurlestone Rock arch** (SX674416) is a simple 300m swim, with a great sense of accomplishment, but dries to rock reef at LT. Good snorkelling. **Δ**

14 Soarmill Cove, Salcombe

Grid ref.	SX698376
Postcode	TQ7 3DS
Walk	15 mins, easy
Train	Ivybridge, 20km

Isolated NT cove below Soarmill Cove Hotel. Little island to swim around at HT.

From Malborough (A381, 2km W of Salcombe) follow signs for Soar and hotel. £3 parking or eat at hotel 🍴 (01548 561566). Caves to explore 200m L (SE).

A From Soarmill walk 4km E on coast path (dir Salcombe) via glorious Bolt Head, and drop down to **Starehole Bay** (SX727365), a double LT cove beneath Sharp Tor. Or park in East Soar NT car park and walk down 2km via farm. Or park at NT Overbeck's House (TQ8 8LW, 01548 842893) and follow coast path under and around Sharp Tor (2km).

B Sandy **Sunny Cove** (SX738370) and **Mill Bay** (East Portlemouth, opp bank of river), access by ferry from South Sands. Or hire self-drive boat from Whitestrand Quay, Salcombe (TQ8 8ET, 01548 843818).

15 Wadham Rocks

Grid ref.	SX579469
Postcode	PL8 1HG (500m S)
Walk	10 mins, mod
Train	Ivybridge, 12km

Silver sand LT cove with coloured rock formations, clear water. Part naturist.

Entering Newton Ferrers on B3186 turn L before church, dir Bridgend, Membland. After 2km turn L at T-junction. Park in lay-by R after 800m. Cross gate, follow track downhill to R, cross two fields and stiles.

A Continue on lane. Turn R to Mothercombe after 2km. Coast path leads S to sand flats of **Erme Mouth** (SX611473, PL8 1LB). Rips can form by river mouth **Δ** (Dolphin Inn 🍴, Kingston TQ7 4QE, 01548 810314).

B Aymer Cove (SX640455) near Ringmore (Journey's End 🍴 pub TQ74HL, 01548 810205). 15min walk from NT car park (off road to Challaborough).

C Wembury Marine Centre and family beach with rock pools, PL9 0HP, 01752 862538. 4km S of E Plymstock, (Plymouth).

Venerick Cove near Prawle Point

South Devon: Prawle Point, Dartmouth and Torbay

It was the late afternoon of a hot summer's day and the sun was casting a soft, golden glow over the rocky landscape. Our group set off down the remote vale, picnics stuffed into bags, towels trailing in the long grass.

Prawle Point is a wild and rugged headland with tiny white coves strung along the coastline like pearls. Marsh fritillaries and silver-studded blue butterflies flitted on the warm breeze, meadow pipits and skylarks darted among the heather, while kestrels and buzzards circled above searching for unwary voles and lizards. As we neared Venerick Cove we could see the Bronze-Age field ridges along Deckler's Cliff. Down below a solitary figure was braving the blue surf, his wet body glinting in the sun and the spray.

A track leads down the cliff-side and you drop on to the beach with the help of a rope. Several offshore rock islands make this a fun place to play. It's remote and clothes are definitely optional. The beach surface is made up of tiny round white beads of quartz, smooth and wet under foot, that blind you in reflected light and grind as the surf chases them up the beach and back down into the sea.

That afternoon we continued on to remote Gammon Head and Elender Cove – easy to miss if you come from the west – nestled deep in the east side of Prawle Point headland. As we arrived the afternoon shadows were already stretching across the sands and the tide was rapidly

16A **Elender Cove**

18C **Whitsand Cove**

17 **Raven's Cove cave**

reclaiming the beach. To the west of Venerick you'll find the excellent beach under Gara Rock, though this area is currently the site of a new hotel development.

This exposed coastline picks up any Atlantic swell so you need to be careful in the surf. The lighthouse at Start Point, five miles to the east, is testament to the number of shipwrecks and the force of the sea. There's a beautifully remote beach below Start Point (Great Mattiscombe Sands) but nowhere is the sea's power more evident than at Hallsands to the north. Here an entire village was washed away by storms in 1917. Today only 2 of the original 37 houses remain, together with the foundations of the sixteenth-century chapel. The villagers, however, blamed not the storms but the dredging operators who had been extracting hundreds of thousands of tonnes of shingle to expand Plymouth's harbour. Over time the village beach had been lowered until it was eventually washed away altogether, leaving the community totally exposed to the sea.

At the north end of Start Bay in Dartmouth restorers are working to re-open Castle Cove, also damaged by the sea. This dramatic shingle cove sits in the shadow of the castle and café, owned by English Heritage, at the mouth of the estuary. It has several caves, great views and was a favourite sea-bathing spot. Now funds are being raised to repair the bathing ledge along its east side. From here the coast path leads to Compass Cove, plunging down a steep grass embankment and then snaking through trees. It's best to swim in Compass Cove at high tide to avoid the slimy green rocks that are revealed at low water. Another mile brings you to little-known Western Combe Cove near the Dancing Beggars, with steps, shingle, an island and caves at the south end. Again, seaweed is a problem, so swim at high tide.

North of Dartmouth near Kingswear, Scabbacombe and Man Sands are two hidden gems with long bays featuring sheltered coves. Further on, the developments of Torbay begin in earnest. On the north side of Torbay we are almost at the limit of the West Country. Before you leave, try the red cliffs of Watcombe Head, hung with tropical vegetation. Adventurers in wet suits or with boats can swim and scramble north and find great slabs of red rock and extraordinary sea caves beneath the cliffs.

Scabbacombe Sands near Kingswear.

South Devon: Prawle Point, Dartmouth and Torbay

16 Venerick Cove, Prawle

Grid ref.	SX762363
Postcode	TQ7 2BU (2km W)
Walk	20 mins, mod
Train	Totnes, 25km

Series of remote wild sandy coves on dramatic Prawle Point coast, most southerly in Devon. There can be heavy swell. △

Entering East Prawle (dir A379) turn R at water tower 1km before village (on cycle route 2). Turn R after 700m then park at corner (600m) and descend on bridleway 1.2km, through gates, keeping close to stream. Venerick Cove (known locally as Moor Sands) is below R. Good food and real ales at the Providence Inn 🍴, East Prawle (01548 511208).

A Turn L on coast path for small tidal sandy **Elender Cove** on E side of Gammon Head (SX767357). Or continue W beyond Venerick 1km to beach beneath new Gara Rock hotel (TQ8 8PH). Continue on lanes via hotel 2km W, then via track through woods (1km), to **Mill Bay** and **Sunny Cove** (swim 14B) opp Salcombe.

17 Start Point, Mattiscombe

Grid ref.	SX817369
Postcode	TQ7 2ET (600m S)
Walk	15 mins, mod
Train	Totnes, 25km

Beautiful remote cove on dramatic Start Point (Great Mattiscombe Sands). Interesting Two Stones conical rocks.

From Stokenham (A379 Torcross, nr Slapton Sands) follow signs to Start Point and lighthouse (just past Hallsands). After 4km of narrow lanes pass two transmitters and Start Farm to find car park. Take path in R corner (SW) down through fields to beach (700m). Walk E 500m, around headland, to find tiny shingle **Raven's Cove** – small cave and snorkelling.

A Continue 1.5km W to **Lannacombe** sand and shingle cove (TQ7 2NH, SX802371). Seasonal camping 🏕 at the B&B. Also accessible via lanes, 2km, though limited parking. Walk 500m W for more coves.

B Pleasant family shingle beach at **Hallsands**. From here walk 500m S (via track or LT beach) to view ruined village.

18 Castle Cove, Dartmouth

Grid ref.	SX887502
Postcode	TQ6 0JN
Walk	2 mins, easy
Train	Totnes, 22km

A traditional swimming cove with caves and bathing ledge beneath Dartmouth Castle.

A Continue on lower coast path 1km to remote **Compass Cove** (down grass slope then steps, LT rocks) and 2km to **Western Combe Cove** with secret steps (just before Dancing Beggars, rocky, SX882485). Castle is 2km S of town (B2305 via Warfleet, Castle café 01803 833588).

B Leave Kingswear N on B3205, turn R after 2km then L at T junction. Park after 1km for **Scabbacombe Sands** (SX920520, naturist) or 2km (after Woodhuish Farm) for Man Sands (SX923535), both 1km descent on tracks from car parks. △

C Dramatic red cliffs back Watcombe Cove (A379, 2km N of Torquay. Café. 10min walk.) Swim/scramble around headland to **Whitsand Cove** or swim with wetsuits 500m N to **Bell Rock** sea caves. △△

Venerick Cove, Prawle

21A Trevaunance Cove, St Agnes

North Cornwall: St Ives to St Agnes

The coast is harsh on Cornwall's northern seaboard. From St Ives to St Agnes are soaring cliffs, tin-mine tunnels and caves, as well as evidence of two women's saltwater passions: Lady Basset's bathing pools and Virginia Woolf's lighthouse.

During Woolf's childhood her family made frequent visits to their holiday home on the edge of St Ives, a place where she spent possibly the happiest days of her life. The elegant octagonal Godrevy lighthouse stood on the horizon, a constant beacon and the inspiration for her philosophical musings in *To the Lighthouse* – the story of a boy's dream to sail to the offshore island. The best viewpoint today is Navax Point, which also conceals the stunning Fishing Cove, set deep beneath the rock face and so well hidden that even some local people don't know it exists.

East from here the cliffs rise to giddy heights for at least five miles. In my search for swims there seemed little chance of finding a way down to the still blue waters. That night I camped, despondent, on the coast path on the high Carvannel Downs but woke early to see thick blankets of morning mist pouring down through a nearby gully on to the beach below, vaporising as they hit the purple sea. By following the narrow coombe I finally found a way down to Porth-cadjack Cove, via a steep path with a

20 **Wheal Coates engine house**

21A

20A

'Probably nothing we had as
children was quite so important
to us as our summers in
Cornwall…to hear the waves
breaking…to dig in the sands;
to scramble over the rocks and
see the anemones flourishing
their antennae in the pools.'
Virginia Woolf in *Moments of Being*

handy rope tied for support. The shady cliffs loomed above and the stacks of Samphire Island stood just offshore. Wondrously alone and unseen, my heart thumping, I plunged into the sea just as the first morning rays broke over the cliff and touched the water.

If you fancy a long foreshore scramble and the tide is on your side, Basset's Cove, a sandier beach to the west of Porth-cadjack, is a possible destination. It was once possible to descend to this cove from the high cliff above via a winch that Lady Basset had installed in 1800 to enable her to bathe here. She also had six multi-level bathing pools cut into the rock on the west side of Portreath Beach. Two are still just visible. There is another rock pool by the harbour wall; it was used until 1970 for swimming lessons.

This tumultuous coast has several bathing pools, mainly built as safe places to swim when the sea is dangerous. The most hidden, at Porthtowan, was built during the Second World War; the beach had been heavily mined by German bombers seeking to destroy the surrounding airfields. The pool had its own access steps cut into the cliff so people could reach it in safety via the coast path without crossing the beach.

A couple of miles to the north the spectacular Wheal Coates engine house is just one of many mining relics in the area and a reminder of the harsh working conditions in the tin mines of the nineteenth century. This engine pumped water from mines 70 fathoms deep with tunnels that extended almost a mile out under the sea. Today, on spring low tides, sand extends for a few miles along the cliff base between Porthtowan, Chapel Porth and Wheal Coates. The intrepid can access the numerous old sea caves, including one that connects with the old lift shaft and flooded mine workings. At high tide, on the cliff above, you may well hear the thunderous boom of waves entering the caves far below.

A tiny working remnant of the tin industry exists at Blue Hills Tin, where traditional tin jewellery is made. The old, ruined mine buildings are dotted among gnarled oaks and waterfalls. Trevellas Cove, below, is the rough neighbour of sandy Trevaunance and, on summer days, you can join local lads jumping from the sea stacks or, if the tide is low, try your hand at skin-diving for the delicious fat mussels growing on the jagged rocks.

Fishing Cove near Godrevy

19 Fishing Cove, Navax Point

Grid ref. SW596429
Postcode TR27 5EE (300m NE)
Walk 15 mins, mod
Train Camborne, 7km

A part-naturist sandy cove on Navax Point near Godrevy lighthouse. North facing under steep cliffs.

Follow B3301 coast road from Hayle 8km to find parking at top of hill (2.5km after Gwithian). Follow coast path 300m L (W) towards headland, then find path R winding down through gorse to cove (200m). Adjacent cove is a 50m swim to L.

A For a real adventure continue on coast road 4km E and turn L down long unsigned track to car park above sheer cliffs and Basset Cove. Walk 400m E on coast path, then drop down into obvious gulley L. Steep scramble with aid of rope leads to shingle **Porth-cadjack Cove** (SW641447) and Samphire Island L. Wild and remote. Explore LT access along cliff base L. △△

B Remains of **Lady Basset's pools** to W of Portreath Beach (SW652453). Another small tidal pool under harbour wall.

20 Chapel Porth, St Agnes

Grid ref. SW698495
Postcode TR5 0NS (500m W)
Walk 1 min, easy
Train Redruth, 11km

Popular but isolated NT cove with lifeguards. Rips when rough.

Turn L (just after museum) as entering St Agnes on B3277 from S. 2km. If calm seas swim L 50m to arches and 'shooting caves'. △△ At LT walk R to sea caves 250m and 500m N, possibly wading or swimming seasonal channel in sand. The furthest is directly under **Wheal Coates** engine house. Enter to find sloped embankment leading to deep flooded down-shaft and light of up-shaft above. Choose a spring LT to allow plenty of time. △△

A 1.5km S at popular **Porthtowan** surfing beach find secluded part-concrete tidal pool from 1940s (SW691484) hidden 300m to N of main beach under cliffs. Access via LT walk on beach or via coast path N: pass popular Blue beach bar ▯ (01209 890329), climb hill then find eroded steps to L after 300m. At LT it is possible to walk N 1.5km to Chapel Porth on sands. Take care.

21 Trevellas Cove, St Agnes

Grid ref. SW726520
Postcode TR5 0XP
Walk 5 mins, easy
Train Redruth, 13km

Shingle beach set at bottom of wild coombe among mine ruins.

Downhill from St Agnes church, dir Perranporth, pass Quay Road on left (leads to Trevaunance Cove) then take immediate L up narrow, steep, one-way hill (Wheal Kitty Lane). Continue 1.3km and turn L down track at bottom of hill after. Shingle cove to L or continue along cliff to stacks. Adjacent Blue Hills artisanal tin works (TR5 0YW, 01872 553341). Local people's HT alternative to popular Trevaunance Cove but rocky at LT. Watch kids cliff-jumping, snorkelling and mussel-collecting from dramatic stacks.

A **Trevaunance Cove** is beautiful and sandy with cafés, hotel (SW720518, directions above). Explore coast path on L side (W) to find stacks for snorkelling. Don't miss St Agnes Beacon for amazing views, and dramatic coastal walks 2km NE to Cligga Head with collapsed cave and old WW2 radar stations and airfield.

North Cornwall: Newquay, Bedruthan and Padstow

From Newquay to Padstow the Cornish coast bears the full brunt of westerly storms and swells. Great caves have been pummelled into the cliffs and blowholes forced up through the ground.

Nowhere quite captures this drama like Bedruthan Steps, a mile-long stretch of tidal sand dotted with rock stacks and 'statues', some pinnacled in sharp points, others with crooked apertures. According to local folklore, the 'steps' were the stacks that the giant Bedruthan used as stepping stones, but they are more likely to be the perilous steps hewn out of the cliff-face in the late eighteenth century when Bedruthan was a stopping point for poets and artists of the Romantic school. The original rock steps were washed away and replaced by a concrete set in the 1970s and still attract many visitors. Rip currents on this beach can be fierce, however, with large swells arriving unchecked from the Atlantic. At low tide these sandy pools are a good place for children to paddle; adults should only swim in the sea here when it is very calm.

The Victorians, who were always keen to conquer nature's wonders, also built steps down to the beach at Pentire, a continuation of Bedruthan to the north and an approach that is little known. You can walk here on the sands at low tide by the rock arch of Diggory's Island, or approach by road via the beautiful Pentire Farm. The old Victorian switchback track can still be seen but it now ends abruptly where the cliff has collapsed. Instead a

25

24 Hawker's Cove

23 Diving into Treyarnon pool

'Rude flights of steps, cut into the profile of the cliffs, and fortified here and there by a crazy iron or timber hand rail… The steps are ancient beyond knowledge, and have given a name to the place.'

Charles G. Harper,
The Cornish Coast, 1910

faint footpath offers a route for the intrepid. The large, empty beach has no stacks and therefore fewer rips, but you should, nevertheless, always take great care when swimming in high swells in this remote location.

A similar scramble leads to the hidden and unvisited northern end of Watergate Bay, the famous sands just north of Newquay. This alternative approach to the bay takes in fantastic cliff scenery and the alluring Beacon Cove, a deeply recessed beach with caves and cliffs that traps the afternoon sunlight like a prism. The approach to the cove is treacherous; descend a steep grass embankment to find a steel cable that leads you down into a large cave. Nimble-footed adventurers will no doubt relish the challenge. I swam here alone as the tide ebbed and an early evening sun broke from beneath storm clouds, body-surfing in perfect hollow waves, the white sand churning into blue below.

For a far more sedate swim nothing can beat the exquisite rock pool at Treyarnon, perched on a ledge above the sea like a great infinity pool. It's about 30 feet long and 8 feet deep with a wonderful array of bladderwracks and the occasional starfish. Treyarnon Bay is just one of the (somewhat overdeveloped) super-coves on the way to Padstow, one of north Cornwall's prettiest and most upmarket seaside towns. Situated in the Camel estuary, Padstow's sands are both a delight for swimmers and a hazard for boats. The infamous Doom Bar creates a beach for St George's and Hawker's coves, but has wrecked many a vessel.

If you head further out of Padstow, make your way to Trevose Head. Start at the dramatic new lifeboat station and work south towards the caravan parks of Mother Ivey's Bay. Wedges of white sand fill the inlets and places like Long Cove provide perfect opportunities for diving, jumping and exploring away from the crowds. Or, if you really want to get right away and test your rock scrambling and swimming skills, why not explore the famous Round Holes. These collapsed caves are like massive craters in the land with eerie passages out to the sea. One can be found on the west side of Trevose Head and on a flat calm day you can descend to the rocks about a hundred yards south and swim into the entrance. Another is east of nearby Trevone Bay and a steep, slippery descent into the hole itself provides access to the great ocean beyond.

Treyarnon rock pool, above the beach

22 Pentire Steps, Bedruthan

Grid ref.	SW849704
Postcode	PL27 7UU (500m SW)
Walk	15 mins, diff
Train	Newquay, 10km

Northern bay of Bedruthan Steps with sandy beach, little visited.

From Newquay on B3276 turn L 1km after second Bedruthan Steps car park (road descends, green sign 'Pentire Farm'). Park at track end, bear L through gate. At coast path look L and see path down on R. Rocky scramble at end. Connects to Bedruthan beach at LT for circular walk. Δ

A Porthcothan, 1.5km N beyond turning above. A quietish narrow cove with safe swimming. On S side, below last house, find tiny secret sand cove (SW853721).

B Entering Trevarrian, 1km S of Mawgan Porth, turn L and park. Take hidden track by Shrub Cottage (TR8 4AQ, near Kernow Trek B&B). After 700m cross stile, bear R up hill, to **Beacon Cove** (SW844668). Very difficult descent on cove's N side (grass banks then L traverse into cave, steel rope) or follow coast path L (S) 1km to reach path down to **Watergate Bay** N (SW843661). Δ

23 Treyarnon rock pool

Grid ref.	SW855744
Postcode	PL28 8JP (500m W)
Walk	5 mins, mod
Train	Newquay, 17km.
Cycle	Route 32

Swimming-pool-sized natural rock pool in rocks above sea. YHA café 🍴 behind. Deep section for jumping. Constantine Bay 500m to N is a classic surf beach and leads on to Trevose Round Hole (swim 25A).

24 Doom Bar, Padstow

Grid ref.	SW912771
Postcode	PL28 8HR
Walk	5 mins, easy
Train	Newquay, 25km
Cycle	Route 32

Turn R off B3276 (dir Newquay) 1km outside Padstow. Signed Hawker's Cove. After 2.5km turn R down track into field. Mainly shallows over Doom Bar – watch estuary currents Δ. Walk 1km S to ancient well and deeper swimming at St George's Cove (SW919765), also accessible 1.5km N of Padstow on coast path, past war memorial. Also good walks N to Stepper Point and Pepper Hole.

25 Long Cove, Trevose Head

Grid ref.	SW860763
Postcode	PL28 8SL (200m NW)
Walk	15 mins, mod
Train	Newquay, 20km

A tiny narrow cove with great rocks for jumping. Visit other hidden sandy inlets and impressive lifeboat stations on this otherwise busy coastline.

From Padstow B3276 (dir Newquay) turn R after 2km, through Harlyn, then sharp R (dir Trevose Head), then first R (400m). Continue 2.5km (private toll road £3.50) to lighthouse car park. Walk 1.5km N, around headland or on road, to lifeboat station, then 300m S, after white art deco house, scrabble down to Long Cove.

A Trevose Round Hole collapsed cave (SW851761). Adventurous swim, calm seas only. 200m S from above car park. Launch from rocks 200m S of hole. ΔΔ

B Trevone Round Hole (2km W Padstow, SW890763), 500m on coast path NE (R) from beach. Scramble leads down inside and out. Dead calm seas only. ΔΔ

Bossiney Haven at low tide

North Cornwall: Polzeath, Port Isaac and Tintagel

I first visited Tintagel castle late one summer night. A full moon was beating down on a still sea and the castle ruins were laced with milky shadows. We climbed down to the rocky haven below the castle and scrambled into the deep, dark cave that runs beneath the headland.

According to legend, when young King Arthur was washed up here after a shipwreck the wizard Merlin nursed him back to health and tutored him in the ways of magic and 'wyrd'. You can still explore the caves, clambering through with torches, feeling and touching your way over slippery dark pools and emerging by a narrow chamber into the opposite cove. The sloping rocks and many caves of Tintagel Haven are an ethereal setting for a swim in the crystal-clear sea. From here a mile-long dramatic walk eastwards leads to narrow Bossiney Haven, hidden among the cliffs and featuring a rock arch shaped like an elephant's trunk, a great sweep of low-tide sand and secret sunbathing rocks. Another mile and you're at Rocky Valley where waterfalls and giant plunge pools fall into the sea. Arthur is said to have baptised his knights upstream at St Nectan's Kieve before they set off on their long and arduous quest for the Holy Grail.

28A

27B **East of Port Gaverne headland**

28

For more cave adventures head south to Port Quin and Lundy Bay. Port Quin was abandoned in the nineteenth century after its entire male population, all fishermen, was drowned at sea one stormy night. Now this tiny, timeless hamlet is owned by the National Trust. On the cliffs above you'll see Doyden Castle folly. Beneath is a rocky inlet where you can swim and flat rocks for scrambling and jumping. If you bear west on the coast path you'll quickly come to the low-tide sands of Lundy Bay. A short swim from the beach leads into great Lundy Hole with its massive skylight and various tunnels branching off to the right. On the other side of the cove a long dark cave leads through the headland to adjacent Epphaven Cove.

Neighbouring Port Isaac, to the east, had more luck with fishing than Port Quin and is one of the better-preserved traditional Cornish villages. Its whitewashed streets and alleys still bustle with fishmongers and pubs alongside the ubiquitous fudge and pottery shops, but neighbouring Port Gaverne has the best swimming. Steps lead down from its little headland to a rocky inlet with wonderfully blue water. From here, if you are feeling strong and the sea is calm, swim around through the narrow pass beneath the spot where local lads jump and enter the lagoon in the far right corner. There are also huge caves in the cliffs a little further on. The Port Gaverne Inn is a gem of a pub with log fires for drying out after your swim.

Heading west again, nearby Polzeath is known for its surf, loud bars and good times. Its tiny church of St Enodoc, lost in the dunes, is a world away. For hundreds of years the church was buried in the sand but once a year the vicar and parishioners descended into the sanctuary through a hole in the roof to perform the annual ceremony required for the tithes. The church has since been unearthed and poet laureate John Betjeman is buried there. The beach lying to the south is one of the best on the estuary. On a flood tide the waters cross the warm sands of the Doom Bar, creating extensive shallows with gentle ripples, and small rocky bays from which to swim or dive. North of here, below the large houses of the Greenaway, purple rock pools with hues of maroon and blue offer a different plunging experience, and there are inlets to snorkel and explore, like an eel.

Port Gaverne headland and stack

North Cornwall: Polzeath, Port Isaac and Tintagel

26 Bossiney Haven, Tintagel

Grid ref.	SX066894
Postcode	PL34 0AZ (400m N)
Walk	10 mins, mod
Train	Bodmin Parkway, 36km

LT N facing cove with cliffs and Elephant Rock arch. Amazing Rocky Valley waterfall pools 1km E or Tintagel 2km W.

Bossiney village is 1km E of Tintagel. Park on L by campsite and transmitter. Cross field 400m to find coast path and steep steps to cove. (NB Continue 700m down road and park by road junction on R to start with Rocky Valley stream walk.)

A Continue W on coast path to **Tintagel Haven** (SX051892). Swim from rocks opposite castle or LT rocky beach below. Caves lead through headland. △

B 2km S of Tintagel, via Trecknow, low key **Trebarwith** (LT) sands with café, lifeguards, surf, cliffs and Gull Rock (SX048864, PL34 0HB). Coast path 2km S leads to dramatic **Tregardock** beach (SX041842, PL33 9ED). Also via lanes S of Delabole, second R, but difficult parking. △

27 Port Quin, Doyden Cove

Grid ref.	SW968806
Postcode	PL29 3SU
Walk	5 mins, easy
Train	Bodmin Parkway, 26km

Rocky inlet in quaint NT Port Quin with Lundy Bay caves and sands to explore. △

From Polzeath, dir Port Isaac, turn L after 2.5km, signed Port Quin. 300m on W side of harbour, drop down to rocky inlet and stream beneath Doyden Point folly.

A LT sands at **Lundy Bay**, 1.5 km W of Port Quin. Second cave on R connects through to Epphaven Cove (100m E). Or swim round to L (W) 100m to land in Lundy Hole (SW959799). △△ Coasteering and accommodation with Cornish Coast Adventures (Sam Williams, 01208 880280).

B From Port Isaac (off B3314 coast road) drop down R to **Port Gaverne**. From beach walk 100m up R side of headland to find steps L to rocky inlet. Swim R through channel, around headland to lagoon, far R, and caves in cliffs E beyond. SX002810, PL29 3SQ. Port Gaverne Inn 🍴 (01208 880244).

28 Daymer Bay South

Grid ref.	SW927769
Postcode	PL27 6SA (1km S)
Walk	20 mins, mod
Train	Roche, 30km

Beautiful sands and flats with warm tidal waters and safe swimming behind St Enodoc (John Betjeman's burial place) and dunes.

Daymer Bay is signed on the L entering Trebetherick and Polzeath from Rock (2km). From car park head S down beach, around Brea Hill, either L via St Enodoc or R via coast path to south beach (600m).

A From Daymer Bay car park head N 500m to the **Greenaway** and drop down beneath second house to find several small scattered LT purple rock pools (SW926781).

B From New Polzeath turn L after 1km to NT Pentire Farm and park. Bear L through farm into field and, after 300m, turn R down to coast path. Turn L and find immediately on R rough path leading down to cliff edge, through hedge tunnel down to rocks between LT sands of **Pentire Point** coves (SW937806, PL27 6QY 1km NW).

North Devon: Hartland Point to Crackington Haven

Hartland's buckled, contorted, waterfall-washed cliffs form one of the least-visited yet most spectacular shores in the South West. Sand and access are at a premium here, but when you do reach the sea the sense of grandeur is immense.

The switchback striations of shales and mudstone, folded and compressed into geometric chevrons and pinnacles, were created by tectonic collisions 320 million years ago. This same band of hard rock stretches right out to Lundy Island offshore, a constant landmark on the near horizon.

One of the most popular places to view the scenery is the lone pub and hotel at Hartland Quay, once a large bustling port that was destroyed by ferocious storms. Take time out for a pint of Wreckers ale and visit the Shipwreck Museum to read accounts of wreckers luring ships on to the rocks. Not everyone had evil intentions, however; the church tower at nearby Stoke was built to be the tallest in Devon and serve as a hazard warning to ships. This stretch of coastline, one of the most dangerous in the country, was also one of the most bountiful for the local residents who collected wood, rope and other booty for free from the beach.

Twenty minutes south down the coast path brings you to Speke's Mill Mouth. This bay has the tallest waterfall in the South West with

30

29B

31 The Mermaid Pool, Crackington

precipitous plunge pools, a wide bay and fingers of rock reaching out to sea. Sand here is precious, as in most of Hartland, and where it collects it drifts into the folds of the wave-cut platforms – the stumps of old seamed cliffs worn down to ground level by the constant gyrations of sea, pebbles and storms. Warm water also collects in these long channels, creating shallow pools that are perfect for paddling in at low tide.

Four miles north of Hartland Quay is the aptly named Shipload Bay, reminding us again of the great cargoes and lives lost on this coast. There were stairs to the bottom of this remote wild bay but a recent storm washed away the bottom steps. It is still possible to get down, but take care. Six miles to the south at Welcombe Mouth beach there is easier access and a sandier reception with a modest beach-side car park located down a bumpy track, and a small waterfall.

Over the county border to the south the eccentric pastor Robert Hawker was the self-appointed guardian of those drowned on the Hartland coast. In the charming Cornish village of Morwenstow he was well known for wearing a seaweed wig and scribing the Cornish anthem, 'Trelawny' or 'The Song of the Western Men'. He built a lookout hut on the cliff made entirely of salvaged timber and retreated there either to compose poetry, indulge his opium habit or converse with Tennyson. When the *Caledonia*, a grain brig from Arbroath, was wrecked on rocks at Morwenstow in 1842, he not only buried its dead but also managed to rescue the figurehead – a Scottish girl brandishing a cutlass – which stands in the graveyard today. Remains of the *Caledonia* can still be found at remote Stanbury Mouth.

South from Morwenstow the cliffs retreat and the coast softens and flattens as the coves become sandier. Duckpool has a freshwater pool at the beach head, Sandy Mouth a National Trust café and car park, and Bude and Widemouth offer long surfing bays. At Millook Haven the cliffs rise up again, displaying the same extraordinary chevron fault lines and pinnacles witnessed in Hartland. Finally, at Crackington Haven the cliffs reach 500 feet and snorkellers jump and swim in the rocky Mermaid Pool under towering Pencarrow Head.

31 Crackington Haven – sunset at low tide

North Devon: Hartland Point to Crackington Haven

29 Speke's Mill Mouth

Grid ref.	SS225236
Postcode	EX39 6DU (1.2km S)
Walk	30 mins, mod
Train	Barnstaple, 38km

Dramatic waterfalls and plunge pools lead down to huge rock reef bay with LT sandy strips and pools.

From A39 Clovelly follow signs through Hartland to Hartland Quay. Take coast path L (S), past St Catherine's Tor, 1.2km. Plunge in pools above waterfall cliff, on field edge (take care) or at bottom, by beach.

A Hartland Quay is popular for swimming in calm seas, as is the adjacent shingle rock beach with formations. Hotel 🍴 and museum (SS225249 01237 441218). △

B Welcombe Mouth beach 7km to S is popular local's beach down rough track with parking, rock pools and sand strips (SS213180, EX39 6HL). From Hartland return to A39 S and take second R at Welcombe Cross. L at Welcombe church (4km) then hard R at bottom of hill (200m). L after 1km then R.

30 Duckpool

Grid ref.	SS201116
Postcode	EX23 9JN (700m W)
Walk	1 min, easy
Train	Barnstaple, 38km

Dramatic rock and (LT) reef beach at lane end with stream and pool. △

Turn L 6km after Bude/Stratton (A39 N). Follow lane through Stibb to Coombe and turn first L down lane to Duckpool.

A Sandy Mouth NT, is 1.5km S of Duckpool (2km, SS202100). Parking and NT café 🍴. Lifeguards. L 700m after Stibb. △

B Stanbury Mouth, wild and remote. Rock and LT sand. As for Duckpool but take second L out of Coombe, up v steep lane, past radars then L at cross-roads (2km). Pass Stanbury Farm and park 500m at road end. Follow track W to cliffs (500m, W) then L down to stream and beach (SS199134, 1.5km W of EX23 9JQ). At crossroads you could continue 1km N to Morwenstow: pub 🍴 (Bush Inn, EX23 9SR, 01288 331242), church, vicarage (B&B 01288 331369) and Hawker's Hut on cliff.

31 Crackington Haven

Grid ref.	SX143969
Postcode	EX23 0JG
Walk	1 min, easy
Train	Bodmin Parkway, 53km

Popular cove with pub 🍴 (Coombe Barton Inn, 01840 230345). Lifeguards and surfing. Great sunsets. Off A39, R, 12km S of Bude. At LT follow rocks on R of bay 300m to deep inlets (Mermaid Pool) for jumping beneath Pencarrow Head. Walk 2km on L of bay, S to Strangles Beach – rips when rough. △

32 Shipload Bay

Grid ref.	SS248275
Postcode	EX39 6AU (500m NE)
Walk	15mins, diff
Train	Bideford, 25km

Wild, deserted N-facing NT shingle cove under steep cliffs. Broken steps mean rocky scramble at bottom. From Clovelly (A39), take B3248 through Hartland then lanes (5km) signed Hartland Point. At Titchberry park in lay-by on corner and follow track through farm to coast. Turn R and find descent on L after 500m.

North Devon: Clovelly to Woolacombe

North Devon's coastline was celebrated by the writer Henry Williamson, who settled in the village of Georgeham after the First World War. Here he wrote about the adventurous life of an otter, *Tarka*, who was in constant flight from danger.

It was in the sea caves of Baggy Point, just next to the now popular surfing beach of Croyde, that Tarka and his mate Greymuzzle hid their cubs when on the run from otter hounds. On a hot afternoon in July I set out to retrace their footsteps, following the path out along the edge of the headland, engulfed by the scent of tamarisk and rhododendron, with limestone ledges dipping to the sea and grasses wavering atop the knolls above. The route passed a tiny natural harbour with an old slipway hewn into the rock, a large mooring ring still attached. Here steps lead down into a natural lagoon and it was tempting to stop and swim but I had already spied caves set beneath a steep shoulder of rock where anglers gather to fish the deep waters off the point, about half a mile further on. Scrambling down I found the long cave tunnel and two smaller coves with caves as well.

Morte Point to the north, named after its many shipwrecked souls, also features in *Tarka*. There are several tiny coves here and Barricane is the most popular. It has a little island lookout, steep rocks from which children jump and gritty shell-sand washed in from the Caribbean. The whole scene is set aflame at sunset. After a day's swimming, buy

34

33 **Enjoy Sri Lankan curry on the beach**

34 **Low-tide route to Lee Bay**

a plate of delicious Sri Lankan curry from the beach shack here and imagine you are far away, staring out into tropical waters.

Grunta cove, a little further on, is less busy; it came by its curious name after a cargo of pigs was washed up here a hundred years ago. Further round you'll find remote Rockham Bay, with camping fields above and some of the best views in Devon. As you continue onwards the rock strata become ever more silvery, smoothed into perfect soapstone shapes at the secret beach near Lee Bay.

The southern part of Devon's coastline, between Hartland and Bideford, also has watery literary connections. Charles Kingsley, author of *The Waterbabies*, was brought up at Clovelly, and his fame and influence helped found the Bideford Railway and establish the pioneering seaside town of Westward Ho! Along this steep pebbly coast Clovelly is typical of many Elizabethan settlements that grew up around the herring industry. Incoming boats would bring 'culm' from Wales – a mixture of coal and lime that would be burned in kilns to fertilise or 'sweeten' the acid Devon soil. Outgoing boats would carry valuable cargoes of herring, but the eventual exhaustion of fish stocks brought poverty to the whole coast.

The tourist kitsch of perfectly preserved Clovelly is probably best avoided, but at Buck's Mills, two miles east, you get a sense of a once-bustling port. There is a ruined limekiln, a fallen quay and a sandy 'gut' blown out of the rock with gunpowder to help land boats. According to local legend, the devil began building a rock promontory here, the Gor, to help him to get to Lundy Island. He allegedly abandoned the project after some two hundred yards when his Devon-made shovel broke.

For a wilder experience, make the effort to reach the shingle beach at Peppercombe, another two miles east, with a delightful walk through wooded glades of bluebells and ramsons in spring; or search out the spectacular wild rocky beach at Blackchurch Rock two miles west of Clovelly. Follow the path along the stream down from medieval Brownsham Farm through thick forest to reach the old cottage in the woods. At high tide on a calm day you can swim under the massive angular rock arch, one of the most awe-inspiring sights on this coast.

North Devon: Clovelly to Woolacombe

33 Barricane Shell Beach

Grid ref.	SS454445
Postcode	EX34 7EB
Walk	2 mins, easy
Train	Barnstaple, 20km
Cycle	Route 27

Beautiful sand cove near Woolacombe surf beach. Good swimming and jumping. Bring your own wine and rug and eat Sri Lankan curry at sunset.

From Woolacombe beach turn L down the Esplanade. 300m, opp Devon Beach Court, see signs L. Café 🍴 opens in fine weather, summer, from 6pm. The next cove along (Grunta, 500m N, SS452449) is quieter and can be reached via coast path from further along road (L after hotel).

A Baggy Point sea caves (SS423403, EX33 1PA). Coming from Braunton pass through Croyde village and turn L up Moor Lane, past holiday park to NT car park at end of lane (1km). Continue through gate up track 1km. Pass houses, whalebone and old natural harbour with carved slipway and iron rings L (good swimming). 300m further, take faint path L to rock outcrop. Best at LT/MT, calm seas. ▲▲

34 Lee Bay

Grid ref.	SS476467
Postcode	EX34 8LP
Walk	15 mins, mod
Train	Barnstaple, 23km
Cycle	Route 27

Silver shingle cove with soapstone rocks and small caves. Rocks for jumping.

Exit Mortehoe (dir Ilfracombe) and turn L after 2km. Follow lane steeply for 2km to park by bay. Follow LT causeway L (W), across rocks 300m via carved steps to cove. If HT, walk back up hill 300m and take footpath, R on to NT cliffs. 250m across heath bear R to find steep wooden staircase to cove.

A Coast path continues 3km W via Bull Point to remote sand/shingle **Rockham Bay** (SS459461, EX34 7EG). The bay sits below North Morte Farm Caravan Park 🏕 in Mortehoe (01271 870381, turn by church, North Morte Road). Many static caravans but keep going through site to find quiet fields near sea. △

B Tunnels Beach and tidal pools in nearby Ilfracombe. Well signed. Lots of swimming history. Bath Place, EX34 8AN (SS513478).

35 Peppercombe

Grid ref.	SS384246
Postcode	EX39 5QD (500m N)
Walk	20 mins, easy
Train	Barnstaple, 10km

Remote shingle and sand NT beach with waterfall at bottom of cliffs and delightful woodland walk.

6km W of Bideford, at Horn's Corner, turn R and park by Coach and Horses (01237 451214). Continue down lane (N), bear R on private road into woods to reach Peppercombe beach and waterfall after 1km. Best LT sand to the R. The Hoops Inn 🍴 can be found 1km further along A39 (01237 451222). Next R after Hoops Inn (3km) leads to **Buck's Mills** (2km), a time-capsule village, stone beach, sandy 'gut', waterfall and limekiln (SS354238).

A 300m after Clovelly roundabout turn R on B3248 (dir Hartland). Take R after 2km and follow lanes 2km to park at Brownsham Farm (NT). Turn R through farm, down into woods for 1km, turn L keeping stream to R for 1km to **Blackchurch Rock** arch (SS99267) HT, calm seas. ▲▲

North Devon: The Exmoor Coast

The steep cliffs are cloaked in woodland and waterfalls tumble from moorland down to the sea. As you explore the Exmoor coast it's difficult to imagine an easy way to access the remote and dramatic foreshore lying far below, often invisible from the land.

The same thoughts were probably in the minds of German sailors over 60 years ago. It's now known that this coast was a favoured place for U-boat landings during the Second World War. According to one German veteran's account, his U-boat moored at Heddon Mouth one night to refill with much-needed fresh water. He rowed ashore with some of the crew, carrying pipes to collect water from the stream. After months cramped in the tiny living quarters it felt wonderful to be free in the night air for a few hours. They took a swim to get washed and played football on the shingle beach with a ball fashioned from rolled-up overalls. The scenery was so spectacular in the moonlight that the German sailor promised to return one day in peacetime.

Today, on the beautiful walk from the Hunter's Inn down to the stony beach, it feels that little has changed since the U-boat visits. Bilberries, gorse and heather grow on the hillside and sessile oak, rowan, holly and hazel flourish along the pretty stream. After a two-mile walk to the east, Woody Bay opens up dramatically beneath the trees. High moors give

37B

39

36

way to dizzying drops of 800 feet or more, and the cliffs are studded with deep, dark ravines. Far below, the boulder-strewn beach is almost unvisited, save for gulls and guillemots, but a few visitors do make the long descent. The bay has an ancient cobbled track winding down past a limekiln. There's also a quay that is only revealed at low tide. This is a very rocky beach but a waterfall and a serene rock pool – presumably built by hot, tired fishermen – is hidden on the far side, offering a welcome opportunity to bathe if the sea is too rough to swim. Float in the pool here, stare up into the steep wooded cliffs and you may hear the sounds of the woodpeckers, warblers or pied flycatchers that inhabit these wild shores.

To the west, at Combe Martin, Wild Pear Beach has long been used by naturists, but Broad Sands is the best-kept secret. It's a deep double cove set far beneath wooded cliffs with many caves, and a refuge from the busy campsites at Water Mouth harbour. Development of this area as a tourist destination began in the 1820s with the arrival of the railway and the decline in fishing. Indeed, the only obstacle to Ilfracombe becoming a leading seaside resort was its lack of sand so the 'Tunnels' were drilled by a local entrepreneur to provide access to a cove on the other side of the cliffs. Two separate tidal bathing pools were also built, one for men and one for women. Naked bathing was common in the early nineteenth century – its health benefits were deemed excellent – and guards were employed to ensure no peeping Toms caused trouble. Today the complex has been renovated and re-opened, and provides a fascinating insight to the history of sea bathing.

Heading in the other direction from Heddon's Mouth you pass a second Lee Bay (not to be confused with swim 34 near Ilfracombe) and the dramatic formations of the Valley of the Rocks, evidence that Devon was once glaciated. Nearby Lynton was also developing as a fashionable resort and proved popular with writers Coleridge and Wordsworth; Coleridge wrote his unfinished poem, *Kubla Khan*, at an isolated house between Lynton and Porlock. Lynton's wild beach is Sillery Sands while Porlock has Selworth Sands; both are steep walks to north-facing sand and shingle beaches. Despite being the only two significant stretches of sand along the entire coastline, you're likely to have them much to yourself, even on the hottest days of summer.

North Devon: The Exmoor Coast

36 Heddon Mouth

Grid ref.	SS655497
Postcode	EX31 4PY (1.5km N)
Walk	30 mins, easy
Train	Barnstaple, 26km
Cycle	Route 52

Stony beach at end of wooded valley and stream. U-boats landed here. △

Exit Combe Martin on main road up valley. After 4km turn L at crossroads, dir A399 Lynton. L after 500m and follow signs for Trentishoe/Hunters' Inn. Park at inn (01598 763230) and take track R down valley, 1.5km, crossing bridge half-way.

A Back to pub turn L up steep lane, then L at junction. Pass Martinhoe church and turn L after 1km. 500m down steep lane find car park lay-by R. Take next L to **Woody Bay** (SS678490, EX31 4QX). Continue on foot for 2km on steep private road. Disabled drivers and hotel users (01598 763264) can continue. Rock shingle beach with waterfall, old quay and limekiln. Bathing pool on far side. Continue E on lanes to Lee Bay (2km, easy-access shingle beach, SS694493), and Valley of the Rocks (1km) and Lynton.

37 Broad Sands

Grid ref.	SS563479
Postcode	EX34 9SR
Walk	15mins, mod
Train	Barnstaple, 17km
Cycle	Route 56

Quiet and dramatic double cove hidden in busy holiday area accessed via steep cliff and woods. Fine shingle beach and caves.

Take main coast road out of Combe Martin (A399 dir Ilfracombe) and turn sharp R just after brow of hill, signed Sandy Cove Hotel (01271 882243). Turn L at end (300m) and continue on foot, past hotel, along track through woods. After 500m, near picnic area, drop down through woods R to find steep stairway to cove.

A **Wild Pear Beach** is a naturist NT shingle beach beneath steep cliffs. Accessed via partly eroded steps, W side of Combe Martin, 700m along coast path (SS582477).

B **Water Mouth** is a scenic harbour. Park at Water Mouth Castle, follow path across harbour, on to headland to ruined folly and drop down to rocks on L at HT (SS552484). △

38 Sillery Sands

Grid ref.	SS740498
Postcode	EX35 6JN (2km E)
Walk	20mins, difficult
Train	Barnstaple, 26km
Cycle	Route 59

N-facing shingle and sand beach backed by steep cliffs. Leave Lynmouth on steep A39 coast road, dir Minehead. After 1km, halfway to Countisbury, park in small lay-by on R. Cross road and climb down to coast path 20m below. Follow lower path E (R) for 500m, dropping down difficult path L into steep wooded gorge.

39 Selworthy Sands

Grid ref.	SS907493
Postcode	TA24 8HJ (1.5km N)
Walk	30 mins, diff
Train	Tiverton Parkway, 48km

Exit Porlock, dir Minehead, turning L to Bossington immediately before hill. Park in village (1.5km), cross footbridge and follow coast path/bridleway along hill bottom to E end of Porlock Bay. Climb up and around Hurlstone Point. After 300m find path to beach – steep scree-scramble with rope.

South and East

Dorset is dominated by the remote fossil-filled bays of the Jurassic coastline and the grand sandstone arches, caves and rock pools of Lulworth and the Purbecks. Heading east, the lagoons and chalk cliffs of Sussex, the desolate shingle spits of Kent and Suffolk and finally the sweeping sandy coastline of north Norfolk combine to offer a rich and diverse array of wild-swimming gems, all of them well away from busy resorts and coastal development.

South and East Highlights

40–42 A string of remote south-facing beaches from Seatown to Sidmouth beneath the fossil-studded Jurassic coastline cliffs of Lyme Bay in west Dorset.

43 Dramatic limestone cliffs, caves and jumps are characteristic features of the Isle of Portland.

47–48 Swimming through Durdle Door archway is a classic wild swimmer's rite of passage, while Stair Hole lagoons and sea catacombs are a snorkeller's watery paradise.

49A Follow Britain's only snorkel trail at remote Kimmeridge Ledges where the shallow bay is teeming with amazing underwater wildlife.

51 Lounge on hot rocks and pretend you are in the Mediterranean at Dancing Ledge, a man-made rock pool under dramatic cliffs where Ian Fleming learned to swim.

55 You can reach tiny old-fashioned Steephill Cove on the Isle of Wight only by foot. Visit the beach shack selling crab sandwiches and walk to Orchard Bay.

57 & 58C Head for the superb shell-white sands at East Head spit and remote Pilsey Island, a short cycle ride from Chichester.

61 Wild Cuckmere Haven was where Virginia Woolf and the rest of the Bloomsbury Group bathed. There are iconic views to the Seven Sisters and access to a little-known walk beneath the cliffs to Beachy Head.

70 & 70A Eat the best and freshest seafood in Britain at the Company Shed, then swim from the oyster-shell beach at the Mersea Stone.

80–81 Scolt Head Island with its pristine white beaches is accessible only by wading at low tide.

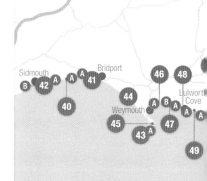

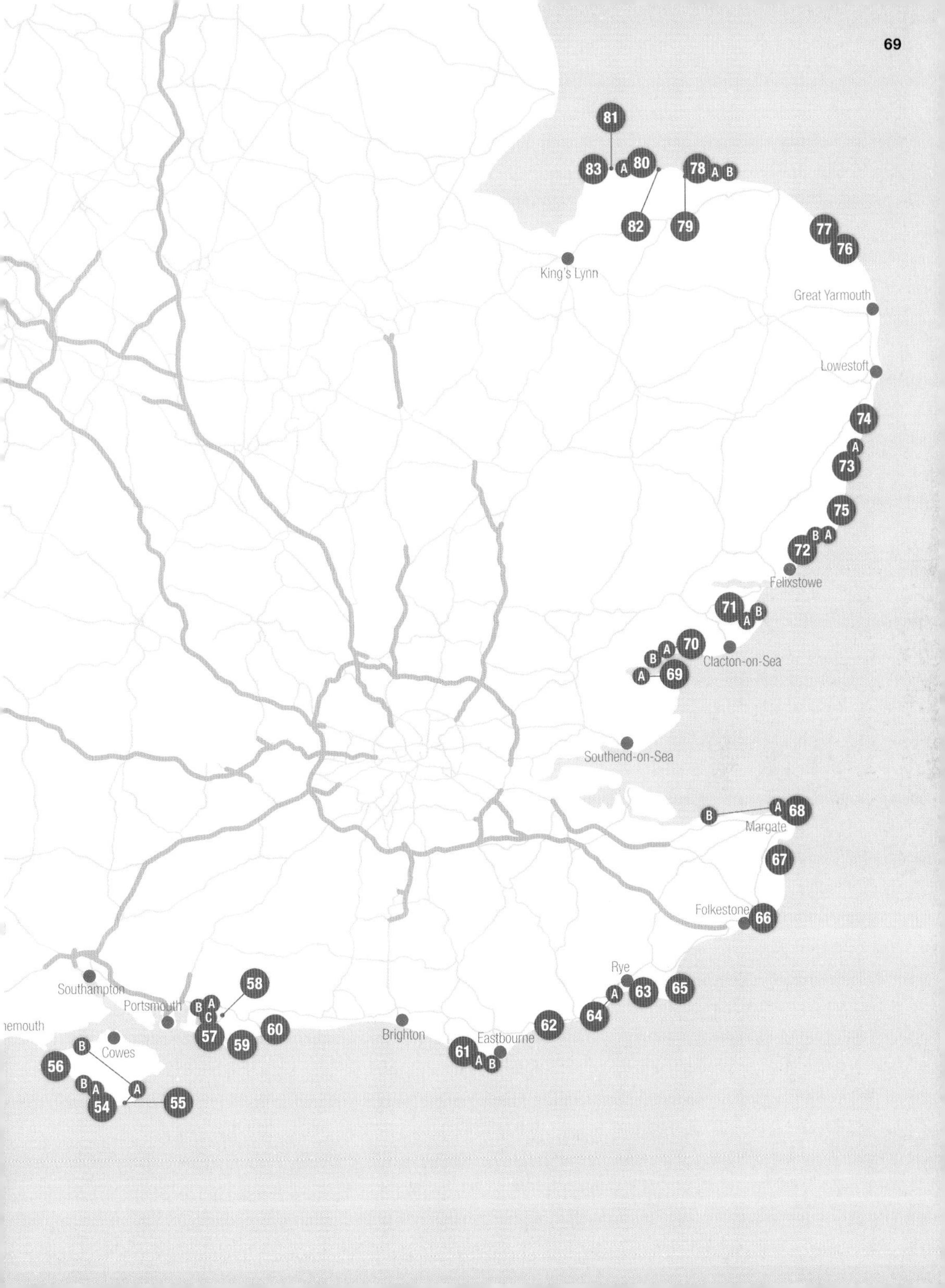
81
83
A
80
78
A
B
82
79
77
76
King's Lynn
Great Yarmouth
Lowestoft
74
A
73
75
B
A
72
Felixstowe
71
A
B
B
A
70
Clacton-on-Sea
A
69
Southend-on-Sea
B
A
68
Margate
67
Folkestone
66
Rye
65
A
63
64
62
Eastbourne
61
A
B
Brighton
60
59
58
B
A
C
57
Portsmouth
Southampton
Cowes
B
56
B
A
54
A
55

West Dorset and Lyme Bay

On Christmas Eve 1839 a massive 45-acre chunk of land came sliding down the cliff here after a few days of intense rain. A great chasm then appeared – more than 300 feet across, 160 feet deep and three-quarters of a mile long.

As the land hit the sea a huge reef was pushed up, yet the crops of wheat and turnip remained intact on the top of what became known as 'Goat Island'. This strange phenomenon attracted many visitors, even Queen Victoria, and the canny farmers charged sixpence for entrance and held a grand reaping party when the island wheat ripened.

The area of the avalanche is today known as the 'undercliff', a nature reserve and site of a unique ecology. Though Goat Island has long gone, an overgrown hillside jungle of great floral diversity remains, concealing one of the south coast's most hidden beaches. Residents and friends of the Rousdon Estate holiday cottages have exclusive access to this beach, via a short steep footpath. The track emerges into sunlight at the cliff-top and then you descend through wild rose bushes and rhododendron. The sandy strand has the air of a desert island, hidden away far below beneath such dense foliage. We spent the morning there undisturbed, feeling like castaways, and made a Robinson Crusoe-style swing with jetsam rope on a fallen tree bough that had been naturally polished by sand and sea.

Just a few miles to the east is Lyme Regis, once a major wool port. Like many coastal towns it reinvented itself in the nineteenth century by promoting the health benefits of sea bathing. Now it is most famous for its horseshoe Cobb, featured in two novels: John Fowles' *The French Lieutenant's Woman* and Jane Austen's *Persuasion*. The Austens were particularly keen swimmers and bathed here for a whole season in 1804. Today local youths jump from the Cobb at high tide and there is a newly 'restored' beach, complete with sand from France and rocks from Norway.

41 **Fossil hunting under Golden Cap**

40A

42

'The bathing was so delightful this morning and Molly so pressing with me to enjoy myself that I believe I staid in rather too long, as since the middle of the day I have felt unreasonably tired...'

Jane Austen writing in Lyme Regis, September 1804

The unstable green sandstone, limestone and watery clay of this coast are a perfect preserving medium for its abundant fossils. One of the most famous fossil-hunters of the area was 12-year-old Mary Annings, who sold her treasures on the beach and who was probably the inspiration for the tongue-twister 'she sells seashells on the seashore'. In her explorations, Mary discovered an almost complete 30-foot ichthyosaur skeleton that changed the course of palaeontology. Today some of the most popular ammonite hunting spots are the beaches beneath Golden Cap, three miles to the east of Lyme Regis. The auburn-tinged summit – the highest on the south coast – can be accessed from quaint Seatown with its convivial beach-side Anchor Inn. Alternatively, explore the remote west hillside via the evocative ruins of St Gabriel's chapel and beach.

More wild beaches below cliffs can be found at the west end of the bay. Beautiful, pastoral Weston Mouth, five miles west of Seaton, is reached after a walk of about a mile, down through woods and fields following a stream. Easier to access is the charming National Trust beach at Branscombe, where you'll find the oak-beamed village pub set right on the remote beach. West, beyond Sidmouth, the coastal geology changes abruptly, this time into towering red sandstone cliffs. These are spectacular, especially at Ladram Bay where they have formed into sea caves, stacks and giant rock pools.

The waters of Lyme Bay have incredible ecological diversity. Its offshore reefs are home to around 300 recorded species of plants and animals, including the pink sea-fan, the rare sunset coral, sponges and starfish. For many years this habitat was threatened by scallop dredging but recent campaigns and the growth of diving and angling have afforded the area a high degree of conservation. An increasing appreciation of the sea for its beauty, as well as its food, will surely safeguard its wildlife.

At Ladram Bay adventurers can escape the caravan park by swimming round the headlands and scrabbling into adjacent Sandy Cove or Chiselbury Bay. Be careful, though, for while there may not be landslips here, the stacks are in a constant process of erosion and one sailor told me how he had watched a one-tonne lump of red rock crash down near his boat sending a mini tidal wave crashing over his stern.

42B Ladram Bay stack

West Dorset and Lyme Bay

40 Charton Undercliff

Grid Ref.	SY298900
Postcode	DT7 3XY
Walk	30 mins, mod
Train	Axminster, 11km
Cycle	Route 52

Remote, isolated private beach in deep woodland. Access via coast path.

Leave Lyme Regis on A3052, W, dir Seaton. After 4km turn L at Charton Cross (1km before Rousdon), turn R at end and park beyond farm in dead end. Follow bridleway and after 500m, after gatehouse, turn L on track through woods, arriving after 800m at the coast path (connecting to Lyme Regis). Turn L past ruined (Allhallows) pump station and find gate on R indicating private path to beach. (As access is private you should be a guest, or friend of a guest, staying at Peek House Holiday Cottages on the Rousdon Estate, 01297 444734).

A Local kids jump from the famous **Lyme Regis Cobb** on calm days at HT. The cobb has a lip so make sure you know the depth. Lyme Regis also has a newly restored sand and shingle beach (SY340915). △

41 Seatown, Golden Cap

Grid Ref.	SY420917
Postcode	DT6 6JU
Walk	1 min, easy
Train	Crewkerne, 25km
Cycle	Route 2

Swim in the sea and then eat fish and chips. Head W to find fossils galore or climb Golden Cap.

Turn L at Chideock off A35, 4km W of Bridport, dir Lyme Regis. 1km via lanes. Shingle beach and cliffs with good pub, Anchor Inn 🍴 (01297 489215).

A Continue 1km past Chideock and turn L for NT Langdon Hill car park. Head S through wood to Golden Cap (1km), then descend R (W) via ruins of St Gabriel's church and hamlet, to **St Gabriel's Mouth beach** (1km) at bottom of stream valley, access via wooden steps (SY396922). Important fossil site. Long walk back!

B Popular **Hive Beach, Burton Bradstock** for honeycombed shaped cliffs and seafood café 🍴 (DT6 4RF, 01308 897 070). Popular for swimming. 4km E of Bridport, R off B3157 (SY491888). Steep pebble beach – watch for undertow in rough seas. △

42 Weston Mouth, Sidmouth

Grid Ref.	SY165879
Postcode	EX10 0NU
Walk	20 mins, mod
Train	Honiton, 13km
Cycle	Route 52

NT beach with shingle, sand and rock pools at bottom of secluded steep valley.

Leave Sidmouth on A3052 E and after 2km turn R for Weston (past Donkey Sanctuary). Park at NT car park on R. Cross gate and follow path down valley.

A **Branscombe** (signed off the A3052 E of Weston) is a delightful NT village leading to shingle beach via a deep valley. Masons Arms 🍴 has beamed rooms, wood-burning stoves to warm up by, real ale and good food (EX12 3DJ, 01297 680300).

B **Ladram Bay** is a cove with red cliffs and stacks. Adventure swims around S headland 200m to Chiselbury Bay or around N headland, past stacks, to Sandy Cove 400m. △△ Access only via huge caravan park complex, near Otterton (off B3178, W of Sidmouth on A3052) SY097852, EX9 7BX.

Chesil Beach with Moonfleet Manor lagoon in the distance

South Dorset: Chesil, Portland and Ringstead

Hard, bright Portland limestone was used to build St Paul's cathedral and to clad the UN headquarters in New York. This limestone isle offers some of the most spectacular clear-water snorkelling in Britain, and there are sea caves and stacks for swimming around with aquatic rock gardens to explore.

The Isle of Portland is also renowned for its great tidal currents, some of the fiercest in Britain. The peninsula and its long underwater ridge create swirling eddies and standing waves that have terrified sailors for centuries. Thankfully these currents don't operate near to the shore, but you should chose a neap (half-moon) tide for swimming or stay in close – within a hundred yards of the shore. And remember, the currents on the east side of Portland Bill always pull south, whatever the tide.

Start your exploration at Portland Bill lighthouse, then head north to explore the old hand-worked quarries with wooden cranes that dot this industrial coastline. The first derrick you come to is still used to haul fishing boats up and down the low white cliffs. This spot is popular for jumping and the water below is crystal clear, almost indigo blue when the sun shines and reflects off the bright stone. Carry on walking past further quarries and another crane. There's an old iron

43A

46

45

'Yet I love to see it best when it is lashed to madness in the autumn gale, and to hear the grinding roar and churn of the pebbles like a great organ playing all the night.'

Chesil Beach, described in J. Meade Faulkner's *Moonfleet* (1898)

ladder down to the sea here, small stacks to explore and several sea caves. Look out for shoals of orange wrasse and enjoy the colourful pink anemones and purple kelp.

For a more traditional beach swim try nearby Church Ope Cove, located down a steep path beneath the ruins of St Andrew's church and Rufus Castle. There is a white shingle beach here and a scattering of colourful, ramshackle gardening huts. The beach looks out over the south Dorset coast where the quiet beaches at Ringstead Bay and below Eweleaze Farm – with its superb seasonal campsite open during July and August – are also recommended.

On your way back to the mainland you can't help but notice amazing Chesil Beach stretched out beneath you. Over the years hundreds of ships have been wrecked here, beached by violent south-westerly storms. This 18-mile-long, 600-year-old 'tombolo' or isthmus is naturally graded. Pebbles at the west end are the size of a pea while the cobbles at the east end are more like potatoes. Smugglers landing on the beach at night knew which way to walk by the size of the pebbles. The steeply shelving gradient of the beach gives it a notorious undertow when the surf is up. When the sea is calm, of course, it is safe to swim and one of the easiest acess points is quaint Abbotsbury where there is parking, a swannery and the excellent Ilchester Arms.

An alternative is to test the shallow waters of West Fleet itself, subject of J. Meade Faulkner's classic tale of smuggling and child heroism, *Moonfleet*. You can visit the ruined church and crypt at East Fleet near Chickerell but the best pace to swim is Gore Cove by Moonfleet Manor Hotel or follow the track through the fields beneath Langton Herring. This last section is opposite the most central and remote part of Chesil Beach, a place frequented only by the occasional fisherman. The waters of the fleet – warm, shallow and brackish – are remarkable for their midnight phosphorescence. So why not make the journey to the cove on a clear night, ideally under a full moon. Everything around you will be glowing and when you reach the massive empty beach, it will be just you, the shimmering milky light, the stars above, and the souls of a thousand shipwrecked sailors in silent communion with the sea.

Jumping from Portland Bill crane

South Dorset: Chesil, Portland and Ringstead

43 Portland caves

Grid ref.	SY680684
Postcode	DT5 2JT
Walk	5 mins, easy
Train	Weymouth, 15km

Two amazing limestone-cliff swimming sites on Portland Bill with ladders, jumps, caves and wonderful deep, clear waters for snorkelling.

From Portland Bill lighthouse and car park turn L and head up the NE coast 200m, past café to first crane. To R is a popular inlet for jumping at high or low tide. Ladder has broken so exit from slanted rock slab on opposite (S) side.

Calm seas only and stay very close to land. Strong southerly tides flow 30m offshore. Be cautious and chose neap tides and slack water (2 hours either side of HT Weymouth). △△

A Continue 700m up coast, past cave hole, to **Red Crane**, below which you will find a complete iron ladder that allows easy entrance and exit to the sea. This more remote location has offshore limestone ledges and stacks for jumping, and caves for exploring (SY686690). △

44 Moonfleet Manor

Grid ref.	SY616805
Postcode	DT3 4ED (200m S)
Walk	5 mins, easy
Train	Dorchester, 16km

The shallow lagoon behind Chesil Beach is warm but weedy, with phosphorescence at night. Join coast path via track on L, 200m before the remote Moonfleet Manor hotel (01305 786948, via East Fleet. Turn L after Chickerell, B3157 4km W of Weymouth). Or walk/drive 2km down Coastguard Road to Langton Hive slipway, behind Langton Herring village (Elm Tree Inn 🍴 DT3 4HU, 01305 871257, B3157, 6km N Weymouth). Gives access to the most remote parts of the beach via 300m swim.

45 Church Ope Cove

Grid ref.	SY697710
Postcode	DT5 1HU
Walk	10 mins, moderate
Train	Weymouth, 12km

Pretty pebble cove with huts. Ruins of Rufus Castle and church. Pass through Easton and find car park near museum.

46 Ringstead

Grid ref.	SY750813
Postcode	DT2 8NG
Walk	3 mins, easy
Train	Moreton, 12km

Quiet, remote family beach with fine pebble sand and offshore rock reef for snorkelling and clambering. Good café with mackerel and chips in garden. 🍴

From Weymouth on A353 turn R for Upton 2km after Osmington Mills. Turn R again after 1km for toll road down to beach. Or continue up hill for free NT car park and long walk from Burning Cliff down to beach.

A **Eweleaze Farm** opens for camping July and August on several grassy fields above a quiet, shingly cove by **Redcliff Point** (SY714816), also accessible on coast path between Osmington Mills and Overcombe. The beach has rock pools and is good for snorkelling and swimming. Eweleaze Farm, ▲ Osmington Hill, Osmington, Dorset, 01305 833690, DT3 6ED (www.eweleaze.co.uk, booking required).

Jumping into the cave grotto at Stair Hole, Lulworth

South Dorset: Lulworth and Durdle Door

The Lulworth coast, from Kimmeridge to Bat Hole, is one of the most dramatic in Britain, featuring the famous cathedral-like rock arch of Durdle Door and a host of lesser-known caves and hidden bays.

On a hot sunny day, Stair Hole is one of my favourite snorkelling venues in the whole of Britain. This catacomb of collapsed sea caves and tunnels has created a shallow lagoon with three routes out to the ocean. The first is a great archway that you can climb and jump from. The second is a series of smaller holes including the 'Blue Door' – a deep, narrow lateral chasm that only becomes negotiable at low tide. In the middle is the cavern, open on both sides, with ledges for sitting, jumping or diving.

For many, however, the greatest draw on this Jurassic coast is nearby Durdle Door, gnarled and scaly like an old dinosaur. To swim through this ancient archway is a rite of passage. The distance is not great but the scale is awe-inspiring: when the watery chasm below you deepens into purple and indigo and the limestone columns above you veer skyward, you'll feel a sense of absolute wonder. The beach can become busy,

49

47A

48

despite the long walk from the car park, so for a more peaceful location visit nearby Man O'War beach on the opposite side of the Durdle Door headland. Its offshore rock ledges are excellent for jumping and snorkelling. Or escape the crowds altogether by heading west down the beach via Scratchy Bottom towards Bat Hole with its tiny keyhole arch. Should it rain there are several caves in the cliffs that will provide shelter on the way. The quietest beaches, however, are to the east of Lulworth Cove. A half-hour's walk from Lulworth past fossilised tree stumps and calcified dinosaur prints brings you to tranquil Mupe Bay, a wide white curve of shingle with a backdop of marram grass, high cliffs and the Mupe rock pinnacles.

A few miles on, via country lanes to the east, the ruined village of Tyneham has an eerie feel. In 1943 the unfortunate villagers were evicted from their idyllic location by the army who wanted to set up a temporary training ground for the war effort. They were never allowed to return. Now the woods and fields are havens for wildlife. Worbarrow Bay, below, is a great, perfect semicircular sweep of pale blue water and yellowish shingle. To the right is tiny Pondfield Cove with a chalk cave, clear water for snorkelling and masses of luminous yellow thongweed with spaghetti-like strands.

For the best chance of spotting underwater wonders, Kimmeridge Bay is the place to visit. Here, great ledges of slate are home to abundant rock pools and marine life. The area is under the protection of the Purbeck Marine Wildlife Reserve, the longest-established marine nature reserve in Britain. Owing to the unusual double low tide, Kimmeridge Bay is empty of water for much of the afternoon during spring tides and is great for rock-pooling. If you want to snorkel and swim, however, neap (half-moon) tides offer the best opportunities. A unique snorkelling trail was created here in August 2006 and the visitor centre will provide a waterproof guide-sheet and route map. If you don't fancy getting wet, then try your hand at fossil-rubbing, identify wildlife in the centre's aquarium or grab the joystick and go 'virtual snorkelling' using the remote-controlled sea-bed camera.

Durdle Door

47 Durdle Door

Grid ref.	SY805802
Postcode	BH20 5PU (800m S)
Walk	15 mins, mod
Train	Wool, 9km

Iconic sea arch on dramatic coastline. Often busy. Long steep shingle beach – undertow in surf conditions. △

From Wool (A352) turn by station for Lulworth Cove (B3071 then turns into B3070). After 6km turn R in West Lulworth and continue up hill 1.5km to Durdle Door Holiday Park. Enter and park in field on far side of trees. For Sailors Return 🍴 (East Chaldon, DT2 8DN, 01305 853847) and a pint of Durdle Door, go past holiday park and turn L after 4km.

A Man O'War beach on E side of Durdle Door (L set of steps) is more sheltered and less busy. Offshore reefs for snorkelling and jumping (SY808802).

B Continue W on coast path 500m to **Scratchy Bottom** (SY802804) to drop down to quieter section. Continue W on beach to Bat Hole sea arch (a bit sea-weedy though swimmable at HT). △

48 Stair Hole, Lulworth

Grid ref.	SY822798
Postcode	BH20 5RH (200m S)
Walk	5 mins, diff
Train	Wool, 8km

Superb inland lagoon with maze of sea caverns and arches leading to sea. Difficult scramble. Good jumps. Amazing rock formations.

Park in main car park at Lulworth Cove (B3071 then B3070 from Wool) then follow footpath signs behind Heritage Centre for Stair Hole (200m). Cross rope barrier and scramble carefully down scree slope. Go at HT, can empty in spring LT. Best in calm clear seas.

A A half-hour's walk E brings you to remote, beautiful sheltered chalk cliffs of **Mupe Bay** (SY843799). Walk around edge of Lulworth Cove (high route via path or low route via beach) and join coast path E. Pass Fossil Forest and old concrete lookout to find stairs after 1.5km down to bay. Snorkelling 300m to R, around Mupe rocks, in calm seas. Continue along coast path for another strenuous 3km to Worbarrow Bay.

49 Worbarrow Bay

Grid ref.	SY870797
Postcode	BH20 5NY (4km W)
Walk	20 mins, easy
Train	Wareham, 8km

A perfect crescent of light shingle at end of remote track through fields and woods, set below the ruined army village of Tyneham.

Heading N from Lulworth Cove to Wool (B3070) turn R to East Lulworth after 2km then R at pub after 300m and climb steep narrow lane 4km. Take hard R down to Tyneham and follow footpath signs to sea. White chalk Pondfield Cove on immediate L with sea cave. (Pronounced 'Worbrough'!)

A Ignore hard R above. Continue 1km and turn R into larger lane. Turn R after Steeple (2km) dir Kimmeridge village 2km (visit Clavell Farmshop, BH20 5PE, 01929 480701), then 2km to small shingle beach and rock pools of **Kimmeridge Ledges**. Small visitor centre and marked snorkelling trail at HT. Collect your waterproof route map from centre. (SY907791, BH20 5PF, 01929 481044).

South Dorset: The Purbecks and Poole

The Purbeck Hills form a stately upland sweep of land with sea on three sides. To the north is Poole, which has the second-largest natural harbour in the world, and to the east are the sandy expanses of Studland Bay. To the south is a series of rugged limestone sea caves, inlets and rock pools, including the famous Dancing Ledge.

The small-scale quarrying along these limestone cliffs calls to mind the workings on Portland Bill, and throughout the eighteenth century many of these supplied high-quality limestone for the rapidly expanding Georgian squares of London. From cliff-edge quarries, massive stones would be lowered down to waiting boats. In some places the entire profile of the coast was altered when new inlets, pools, ledges and lagoons were excavated. Some of these new features are ideal for wild swimming.

Winspit is one of the most spectacular examples, a natural cove at the end of rolling fields beneath pretty Worth Matravers. An old bridleway passes through wildflower meadows and medieval hillside ridges, then a small waterfall leads down to a large rocky ledge extending to the edge of the sea. There's a lagoon to the left, rock ledges for jumping, plus several impressive limestone pillars.

50A

51

50B

Remains of the old quarries stretch up and along the cliff edge, their slopes now overgrown with purple ragwort and their caverns filled with bats. The coast path heading west carries on to a similar set of quarries known as Seacombe Cliff. This cove and ledge also provide opportunities for jumping and diving, though the ocean drop-off is deeper. Another mile brings you to the most famous of the Purbeck quarries. Here at the bottom of rolling downs a great sea-level platform, as in an amphitheatre, has been hewn from the cliffs. Dancing Ledge is so called because it has the standard dimensions of a ballroom. On a hot day lie on the ammonite-encrusted rocks until you are well and truly baked, then tiptoe to the edge of this deep-blue abyss and dive straight down. Feel the sea soothe your hot, prickly skin, watch the sun's rays filter through layers of green and listen to the guttural groans of the heaving sea moving on the distant sea bed.

If the sea is too rough, then you can always take a dip in the natural rock pool, blasted from the rock ledge for use by pupils at nearby Spyway boys' prep school at the turn of the century. Ian Fleming, creator of James Bond, reminisced about the invigorating early morning swims here and film-maker Derek Jarman, also a former pupil, was so moved by his swims that he entitled his autobiography *Dancing Ledge*.

Around the next headland, in the waters of Poole Harbour, Lord Baden-Powell was keen to promote the health benefits of sea bathing for growing boys. The first Scout camp was held on Brownsea Island in August 1907. There were lessons in woodcraft, observation, life-saving, patriotism, chivalry and endurance with daily sea bathing at midday. The Scouts swam below the Baden-Powell memorial where the original camp was held but you'll find the beach is sandier a little to the east. The island is still an exciting destination for youngsters with stands of Scots pine, and red squirrels and peacocks roaming free. Jump in one of the yellow ferry boats from Poole Quay or Sandbanks and experience the traditional outdoor pursuits of yesteryear.

South Dorset: The Purbecks and Poole

50 Winspit, Worth Matravers

Grid ref.	SY977760
Postcode	BH19 3LF (1.5km S)
Walk	25 mins, mod
Train	Wareham, 13km

Rock lagoon under cliffs with caves and jumps. Old quarries. Timeless Square and Compass 🍴 (01929 439229) pub has ales, pies and quirky local museum. △

1km after Corfe Castle (A351, dir Swanage), turn R (B3069) up through Kingston, turning R after 3km to Worth Matravers. Park on R as entering village. Walk into village, past green, turn L (Winspit Rd, blue-painted cottages) and continue down valley to sea (1.5km), descending by waterfall to rock platform. Old quarries above R. Lagoon on L with jumps from rock table L.

A Continue on coast path E 1km to next valley bottom cove, **Seacombe Cliff** (SY 984766). Rock jumping from ledges L. △

B Drive through village 1km to park at Renscombe Farm for steep 1.5km walk across fields, down to **Chapman's Pool** (SY956771), a rounded grey-shingle bay.

51 Dancing Ledge

Grid ref.	SY998769
Postcode	BH19 3HN (2km S)
Walk	30 mins, diff (at end)
Train	Wareham, 13km

Man-made rectangular pool in rock ledge. Swims also possible off ledge into deep sea. Several sea caves 100m to R for exploring in calm sea. △ 2km W to Seacombe Cliff and Winspit.

From Swanage (A351, dir Corfe) turn L after 2km (B3069) to Langton Matravers. Turn L into Durnford Drove (signed Langton House) and park at road end. Follow footpath signed to Dancing Ledge. Descend into quarry. Tricky drop on to sea ledge at end but easier to L. Tom's Fields camping (next L after Durnford Drove) is popular (01929 427110) though Acton Field 🏕 next L, is often quieter and cheaper (01929 424184).

A Cliff and sea access at narrow inlet below and beyond **Tilly Whim Caves** at Durlston Country Park, signed 2km S of Swanage, 500m walk (SZ030770). Strong currents in spring tides. △△

52 Brownsea Island

Grid ref.	SZ100881
Postcode	BH13 7QN
Walk	30 mins, easy
Train	Poole, 8km

NT-owned island famous for connection with Scouting Association. Brownsea Island Ferries (01929 462383) leave from Poole Old Town quay (£8.50, BH15 1BQ) or Bournemouth's Sandbanks (£5, BH13 7QN). From Branksea Castle pier bear L towards S beach – a mixture of shingle, sand and seaweed with woods behind. Sandier at E end but deeper towards W. For deepest swimming bear L at memorial, along coastal path, to Pottery Pier and shingle beach. △

53 Studland Bay

Grid ref.	SZ038851
Postcode	BH19 3AH
Walk	10 mins, easy
Train	Poole, 12km, plus chain ferry

Massive NT beach with dunes at back. Café, visitor centre at Knoll Beach end. Sandiest at Shell Bay N end (BH19 3BA); wild and naturist in-between.

51 Returning home from Dancing Ledge, Purbecks

Isle of Wight

Officially the sunniest place in Britain, the Isle of Wight has been a popular holiday destination since the eighteenth century when the aristocracy flocked to its beaches and Queen Victoria eventually settled there. Today the isle is enjoying a resurgence in popularity and, thankfully, retains large stretches of undeveloped coast. There are white cliffs and landslip jungles as well as remote ravines or 'chines' and sleepy coves.

One of the best ways to get a sense of the isle's varied scenery is to join the annual round-island cycle tour along miles of spectacular coast roads. The south-west section is without doubt the most impressive. High cliffs protect around 12 miles of shingle and sand with access only possible by descending the sheer ravines or chines that streams and waterfalls have cut through the soft clay and chalk cliffs. Shepherd's Chine and Whale Chine are the most dramatic – perfect places to watch the sun set over the western Needles and swim in the bronze-hued twilight.

The most remote end of this long strand and the most southerly tip of the isle is Rocken End. It lies below dramatic Gore Cliffs, ancient sea cliffs that became landlocked when sea levels fell and landslips accumulated. There are several interesting coves on the east coast too. Luccombe Chine, with yellowed rocks and low-tide sand, is reached by a series of stairways down through tumbling foliage. Shanklin Chine, its better-known neighbour, is illuminated with fairy lights on warm summer nights.

Steephill Cove, just outside Ventnor, welcomed many royal visitors in its heyday but has reverted to a backwater with a handful of

55

54B

55 **Woody Bay**

deck chairs, beach huts and crab shacks serving freshly caught and dressed crab in sandwiches. A short walk west brings you to the coast path below Ventnor Botanic Garden and to Orchard and Woody bays. Lord Jellicoe, Admiral of the Fleet, swam almost daily in Steephill Cove, and Queen Victoria and Queen Mary were frequent visitors. Tennyson, Dickens, Keats, Swinburne and Alfred Noyes are among the literati who immortalised this romantic and rugged stretch of coastline in their writings.

The Needles are probably the most famous coastal landmark around the Isle, and the cold-war rocket-testing station behind them is its most unusual site. The best approach is the three-mile blustery walk along Tennyson's Down from Freshwater Bay. At neighbouring Watcombe Bay look out for the locked metal door – behind it is a tunnel leading down to the cove. Adventurous swimmers can access this cove, its tunnel and the adjacent sea caves by traversing the coast from Freshwater Bay's west side using a mixture of swimming and scrambling. Once on the beach, chalk caves at head height lead into the remains of the old tunnel. Towards the end of the beach you'll find more caves, and another short swim leads to further sea caves around on the west side. If scrambling and swimming along the coast doesn't appeal you can take a tour with Isle of Wight Sea Kayaking, located behind the beach car park at the Sandpipers Hotel. On a calm day you can be taken all the way to the Needles and even make a landing in Scratchell's Bay alongside the famous pinnacles.

The sleepy hamlet of Newtown, a remote tidal estuary on the north-west of the Isle, is a good place to end your explorations, and you might care to sample the New Inn's famous seafood platter. In the thirteenth century Newtown was the Isle's biggest town and harbour. Today only its crooked town hall remains, perched alone on the village green, a relic of a once-thriving port that slowly silted up. The old port, a mile's walk across the wetlands, has long since been submerged under marsh grass and mud but it still has a quay and now provides a peaceful and magical place to swim, to think, and to ponder the changing fortunes of this famous island.

Stream at Shepherd's Chine

54 Rocken End

Grid ref.	SZ490758
Postcode	PO38 2NG (1km W)
Walk	20 mins, diff
Train	Southampton, 51km
Cycle	Route 67

The isle's most remote beach, at the bitter end of Chale Bay with Blackgang undercliff and St Catherine's Point lighthouse. Undertow in rough seas. △

From Ventnor (A3055) turn L into Niton Undercliff Drive (still A3055), signed St Catherine's Point Lighthouse. Take Sandrock Road, not St Catherine's Lighthouse road. Park at end of lane (1km). Head down to sea bearing R to cross stream at bottom. Scramble across mud and rock slide to find beach end.

A Continue 6km W on A3055 to find lay-by on L (600m after turning for Pyle on R) and **Whale Chine** (SZ470784). Wooden steps but a final scramble required at end. △

B Shepherd's Chine (SZ451799) is 2km further on, opp Compton Fields, before Chine Farm campsite △ (good cliff-side pitches, PO38 2JH, 01983 740901). Park in lay-by. Path via N (R) side of stream. △

55 Steephill Cove

Grid ref.	SZ550768
Postcode	PO38 1UG
Walk	10 mins easy
Train	Southampton, 48km
Cycle	Route 67

Old-fashioned cove with crab shacks, some sand and deck chairs. No cars. Coast path to undeveloped Woody Bay.

1.2km from Ventnor, heading W to Niton (A3055), look for Love Lane on L, signed to Steephill Cove. Park on main road. Small path, signed 'crab shack' 🍴, leads off lane to cove. Continue on coast path 1km, passing Botanic Gardens on R, then Orchard Bay (with house) to **Woody Bay** (SZ542765). Or access all coves by parking and visiting Ventnor Botanic Gardens (01983 855397).

A A steep path to sand and stone **Luccombe Chine** (SZ583793). 2km E of Ventnor, turning R on Nansen Hill. △

B HT swim at remote **Newtown Quay** (SZ419912, PO30 4PA). Turn L out of New Inn 🍴, Shalfleet (01983 531314), first L, L again then L after the old town hall to road end and cross meadow (500m) to quay. △

56 Watcombe Bay, Freshwater

Grid ref.	SZ343855
Postcode	PO40 9QZ
Walk	2 mins, easy
Train	Southampton, 48km
Cycle	Route 67

From Freshwater Bay (family beach with pub) an adventurous swim leads to inaccessible Watcombe Bay with coarse sands, stacks and many caves. A secret tunnel connects to the cliff above. △△

Freshwater Bay is at W end of the island coast road (A3055). Scramble to far W end of the bay, past the timber staircase, then swim, wade or scramble over reef rock (depending on the tide) to headland, followed by 150m swim in deep water along cliff base to Watcombe cove. At near end of cove find hole that allegedly leads up into smugglers tunnel on cliff-top. From far (W) end of Watcombe find beach caves. A swim leads to a series of adjacent sea caves. Take wetsuit or 'wet bag' with clothes. Set off before LT to allow plenty of time. Isle of Wight Sea Kayaking behind Freshwater Bay (PO40 9QX, 01983 752043). Afterwards visit Red Lion 🍴 in Freshwater (PO40 9BP, 01983 754925).

57 Over the dunes at East Head to Chichester harbour

Chichester and West Sussex

Chichester Harbour's wide expanses and intricate creeks are major wildlife havens and here is the ancient site of King Canute's stand against the incoming tide. One of the least developed sites on the south coast, this is a paradise of muddy tidal creeks and perfect white sandbars.

Pilsey Island is perhaps the most remote of the harbour's beaches and Sussex's very own answer to a desert island. It's actually an acre of cockle beds, mud flats and shingle, fringed by white beaches on its east side and accessible only by boat or via a very long walk across military land. Pilsey Island borders the deep Thorney Channel and has a steeply shelving beach for a refreshing plunge at any state of the tide. Beachcombers will find little treasures such as pearl-lined limpet shells, razor clams and whelks. The bird life is also outstanding.

Easier to access but much busier on hot summer days are the famous West Wittering beaches, probably the most spectacular of any beaches within two hours of London. If you do come exploring here make for East Head, a long spit of white sands and dunes that, through a gradual process of erosion and deposition, is forming itself into an island within the harbour mouth. This is a paradise of silver sand dunes and green marram grass with burrows and hollows where you can stretch out and listen to skylarks twitter overhead. The extreme tip is a popular anchorage for dinghies and yachts on summer days and, owing to its depth, it's also great for swimming. To the left of the head, on the

60

58C

59

seaward side, the beach is shallow. As the tide flows out sparkling water flows in rivulets around your ankles, tugging you towards the sea.

To the right of the head there is a wonderfully squishy mud lagoon where children make ramps and mud slides. After a sunny day the water becomes exceptionally warm, almost tepid, and as the tide ebbs people wallow in the river channel, throwing mud pies, administering mud packs and swimming with summer abandon.

By far the best way to reach the Witterings is to take the train and then use the brilliant new 11-mile Salterns rural cycle route from Chichester train station (driving can mean long frustrating tailbacks). The route follows dedicated paths across wheatfields, passing flint-walled cottages and waterways covered in lily pads before it arrives at the dunes. On the way, stop off at some of the pretty villages that border the harbour, such as beautiful medieval Bosham where King Canute set down his throne and failed to hold back the tide. Bosham still has problems with the tide and its main road is inundated daily. There is a beautiful church here, a fantastic pub and an ancient quay from which the local children practise their leaps and jumps at high tide and when the harbour is not too busy.

Pagham is a much smaller natural harbour, but rich in wildlife and a place of solitude. It is best accessed from the south, via ancient Church Norton. The harbour itself is now too silted and shallow for swimming but the unspoilt shingle beach, with its colonies of sea kale and sea-lavender, feels wonderfully isolated.

On the far side of Bognor you can find Sussex's last 'rural' beach before the urban onslaught of the south coast begins in earnest. Climping is at the end of a lane with only a pub and a mobile café in the tiny car park for sustenance. Here, a dedicated group of sea-swimmers gathers every morning to dive from the groynes, swim the length of the beach and then huddle together in front of steaming mugs of tea. The fields and woodlands around are alive with birdsong and offer a small oasis to those seeking solitude. From here you can glimpse Littlehampton, yet this surprisingly rural place provides solace for those of us who yearn for land without buildings and a coast without concrete.

Jumping from dunes at East Head.

Chichester and West Sussex

57 East Head, West Wittering

Grid ref.	SZ768994
Postcode	PO20 8AU
Walk	20 mins, mod
Train	Chichester, 13km
Cycle	Salterns Way

A beautiful and undeveloped beach – sand bars, dunes, deep swimming from the tip of East Head spit. Very busy in summer. Popular with kids for crabbing and mud slides.

Head S from Chichester bypass on A286 following signs to Birdham, then West Wittering beach. Drive to far end of beach car park (1km) and walk N (1km), past crabbing pools and away from main beach, to explore East Head spit. To the L waters run fast over the 'Winner' sand flats on the harbour mouth – accessible at LT △ . At the spithead deeply shelving beach creates a popular anchorage for boats and the best swimming. To the R the lagoon can be warm and the ebb tide drains via a warm muddy channel, good for swimming and mud slides. An excellent new rural cycle route – the Salterns Way – links to Chichester station www.conservancy.co.uk/out/cycling.asp

58 Bosham Quay

Grid ref.	SU803039
Postcode	PO18 8LZ
Walk	5 mins, easy
Train	Bosham, 2km

Ancient harbour village (King Canute) with a quay that kids enjoy jumping from at HT. △ Good pub Anchor Bleu 🍴 (01243 573956).

5km W of Chichester on A259, dir Emsworth, turn L to Bosham. Head down Shore Road to far end of quay, by black building. Do not impede boats.

A On A259 continue 3km to Southbourne, turn R through **Prinsted** 800m to find HT bay (SU766051).

B Another 1km on A259, turn L and find **Emsworth** Yacht Harbour on R (PO10 8BP). Follow harbour wall S 500m for steps, good at HT (SU752048).

C Continue on road taking next L (300m) to Thornam Marina (PO10 8DD). Park and follow coast path 4km S. Cross sand flats to remote **Pilsey Island** to find E beach. Pilsey interior is a nature reserve. Strong currents as the tide flows. △

59 Church Norton, Pagham

Grid ref.	SZ875951
Postcode	PO20 9DT (700m E)
Walk	15 mins, mod
Train	Chichester, 12km

Remote shingle beach next to Pagham Harbour nature reserve. From A27 follow B2201 towards Selsey Bill. After 9km, just before Selsey, turn L at corner for Church Norton and park by church (1.5km). Follow path to R 500m, alongside natural harbour and mud flats to shingle beach by sea.

60 Climping

Grid ref.	TQ006007
Postcode	BN17 5RL (500m S)
Walk	1 min, easy
Train	Littlehampton, 4km

Also known as Atherington Beach, a quiet rural shingle and sand beach between urban sprawls of Bognor and Littlehampton. 3km from Littlehampton on A259, turn L down Climping Street, signed Climping Beach. Palm-decked former smuggler's pub, Black Horse Inn 🍴 (01903 715175). Also beautiful Baliffscourt Hotel 🍴 (01903 723511).

The Seven Sisters from Hope Gap, Cuckmere

East Sussex

The famous Seven Sisters chalk cliffs halt abruptly at Cuckmere Vale where the broad green meanders of the River Ouse roll out across the valley floor. A lone house sits on the hill and in the distance the shingle beach of Cuckmere Haven churns between the waves, sun and sea.

Arriving here brings a welcome sense of relief: open countryside prevails after 30 miles of south-coast conurbations. There is something quintessentially English about the Sussex Downs. Vanessa Bell, Duncan Grant, Virginia Woolf and the rest of the artists and writers who made up the Bloomsbury Group spent time at Charleston, the famous house two miles up the vale, and came to Cuckmere Haven to picnic and bathe on summer days.

There are four ways to reach the beach. It's possible to take the right bank of the river's new cut via the Golden Galley pub, but the classic route follows the left bank from Exceat past the oxbow lakes, now gleaming and disconnected from their stream. You can also camp in Foxhole Dale, where there is a medieval camping barn.

A less well-known but more dramatic route is via Seaford where a stairway brings you down to Hope Gap, a rocky ledge puckered with pools and caves carved out by wind, rain and sea. But the very wildest approach is from Birling Gap and along the foot of the Seven Sisters themselves – an inter-tidal no man's land of tiny coves and cliff tunnels. Here you'll find some of the most remote beaches in southern

61A

63

61 Hope Gap cave holes

England. Make sure you leave three hours before low tide to give yourself plenty of time for the slow three-mile return scramble to your starting point, or you'll risk being cut off.

Birling Gap itself is a good place to swim. At this remote spot a narrow gut of sand opens up among the rock pools at low tide and there is a single decaying hotel, perched high on the cliff, with a fusty bar featuring Victorian seaside memorabilia. A rather ugly stairway leads down to the beach next to a vertiginous boat-launching ramp with hoists and winches. Local people have swum here for decades and hardy types will enjoy the rugged rocky scene.

It's also possible to walk east from the gap to Beachy Head, Britain's tallest chalk sea-cliff. The name comes from *beau chef*, or beautiful headland. You can visit its beach by climbing down via Cow Gap to explore the small low-tide zone with its lighthouse. If you wish, wade out across milky bedrock and sticky sand into the shallows of the Channel and swim out towards France.

Past Eastbourne the chalk turns to shingle. Those in search of peaceful shingle beaches to swim from could do worse than Cooden, with its lone station and hotel, or Norman's Bay two miles west, the site of the famous 1066 Norman landings. But if you continue on to Fairlight Glen on the east side of Hastings, you'll find a magical rocky haven beneath a wooded glade. Situated at the bottom of a shadowy chine with a waterfall and pools, access down the final section of the path can be difficult, but this wild naturist beach has wonderful bronze-coloured sand at the lowest spring tides.

For the best sand in East Sussex, though, head to Camber on the border of Romney Marsh. Long considered a tacky resort, the west end of Camber is, however, undergoing a minor renaissance led by the newly opened bar, grill and hotel – The Place – offering good quality food and wine just minutes from the beach. Across the road there is an uninterrupted stretch of fine sand to the water's edge, with shallow swimming over the warm flats. And you can always escape among the dunes, bounded in late summer by sea buckthorn with golden berries.

East Sussex

61 Cuckmere Haven

Grid ref.	TV518975
Postcode	BN25 4AD (2km S)
Walk	30 mins, mod
Train	Seaford, 4km
Cycle	Route 2

Dramatic remote shingle and sand beach at base of the Seven Sisters cliffs.

Park at Exceat, 3km E of Seaford on A259. Follow valley past meanders to beach and find sandiest section at E end (L) under cliffs. Access W beach via Golden Galley pub on other side of bridge. Dumping surf in rough seas. Avoid river mouth. △ Also access via **Hope Gap** 1km W (TV510973). Follow signs for golf course from Seaford town centre, go to end of Chyngton Road, then R to South Hill Barn car park (BN25 4JE). Foxhole camping and barn ⌂ 01323 870280.

A Birling Gap (East Dean, A259, dir Eastbourne) beneath faded hotel 🍴 (BN20 0AB, 01323 423163).

B Unusual swim at chalky Falling Sands (TV592955) below **Beachy Head** and the Countryside Centre (BN20 7YA), accessed via Cow Gap 500m along coast to NE.

62 Cooden Beach

Grid ref.	TQ710064
Postcode	TN39 4TT
Walk	1 min, easy
Train	Cooden Beach

Shingle and sand beach W of Bexhill is remarkable for absence of buildings, except for train station (1.40 hr to London) and hotel with beach veranda (01424 842281). 2km up the line is desolate Norman's Bay (1066 landing site) with large seaside campsite ⌂ (01323 761190). A259 E of Eastbourne.

63 Camber Sands west

Grid ref.	TQ958178
Postcode	TN31 7RB (500m SW)
Walk	10 mins, mod
Train	Rye, 6km.
Cycle	Route 2

Chose the W car park (first if approaching from Rye) and park at far R (W) end to find a path through dunes. Don't swim too near the river mouth. △ Nearby, The Place 🍴 is a trendy bar and grill (01797 225057). Broomhill (4km E as Jury's Gap, as road turns inland to Lydd) is more desolate and only has sand at LT.

64 Fairlight Glen, Coverhurst

Grid ref.	TQ853105
Postcode	TN35 5DT (1km S)
Walk	20 mins, diff
Train	Ore, 3km
Cycle	Route 2

A hidden cove and beautiful woody stream glen in the limestone cliffs between Hastings and Winchelsea.

Best for swimming in calm LT conditions, or if you can locate sandy stretches and avoid rocks. △ Path is sometimes blocked at bottom due to landslips, but usually passable. Large boulders at HT, large patches of sand at LT. Popular with friendly naturists.

Follow A259, 3km E out of Hastings and turn R at church up Fairlight Rd. Park at the picnic site by transmitter after 1km (Fire Hills). Cross road, down track 800m and just before Place Farm, by green, bear R then L to find Fairlight Glen footpath sign leading down through woods with stream. Not to be confused with Fairlight Cove.

A Continue on road 6km, past Fairlight Cove, to groynes and shingle expanses of **Winchelsea Beach** (TQ911153).

Botany Bay, south cove.

Kent

The Royal Sea Bathing Infirmary – a grand Palladian palace built in 1791 – is one of the first buildings you see as you drive into Margate. Its size is testament to the huge popularity of sea bathing and the central role played by the Kent coast in developing this national pastime.

Established by a Quaker physician, the Infirmary originally opened to treat scrofula, a form of tuberculosis. Sufferers were not only given sea water to drink but were also immersed in it on a regular basis. It wasn't long before the healthy were also visiting Margate, many to escape the squalor of London and enjoy an invigorating summer dip.

Margate still thrives as a resort and has two impressively large tidal bathing pools but the real treasures are its chalky coves to the east. Botany Bay is an unlikely find, hidden behind residential streets on the way to Broadstairs. There are no facilities here except the delightful café that Alison, a local resident, sets up in her cliff-side garden every summer. Below, white sand stretches out beneath low chalk cliffs and, in the next bay to the right, which you can only access at low tide or by wading, you can try to climb into the cliff chambers where smugglers once hid their booty. Broadstairs is said to have grown prosperous on the proceeds of smuggling and was once so fashionable that luminaries such as Charles Dickens chose to live there. In Roman times, however, the area was a remote island – the Isle of Thanet – separated from the mainland by the Wantsum channel.

The island marshes of Kent and the Thames Estuary have long yielded delicious oysters. Once consumed only by the poor, oysters are now considered a luxury and this fashionable shellfish has been central to the resurgence of nearby Whitstable, which has beach huts for rent as well as hip, art-deco oyster bars as. The steep, shingle harbour beach is perfect for a refreshing morning plunge or a midnight dip.

65 **Prospect Cottage, Dungeness**

66 **To Lydden Spout from Samphire Hoe**

68 **Alison's tea garden**

Shingle predominates as the coast curves around to the south of Kent through the desolate open flats of Sandwich before reaching the famous white cliffs of Dover. Here you can explore one of Britain's newest landforms, Samphire Hoe. The cliff-hugging foreshore here was once a no man's land, home to those on the fringes of society, housed in ramshackle shelters and living on fish and chalky spring water. The construction of the Channel Tunnel brought radical change as the tailings removed from the tunnel were dumped on this shore. A new country park, Samphire Hoe, has been created and is accessible by a steep road tunnel off the A20. The area still manages to retain its air of wild, frontier territory and you can find several miles of the original beach under the steep cliffs at Lydden Spout, with one or two outback huts surviving. Smoke trails up from their chimneys and you come across the odd ancient digger, used to help shore up the huts with primitive sea defences.

There is a similar 'edge-of-the-world' air about Dungeness, a place frequented by gulls, terns and gadwells as well as artists and philosophers who established retreats in the old railway cabins and fishing huts on the bleak shingle spit. This is one of the largest and most important shingle beaches in Europe, a unique habitat that is incredibly sensitive to disturbance.

Prospect Cottage, once owned by film-maker Derek Jarman, has been lovingly preserved here, its famous driftwood garden imaginatively decorated with iron and wood *objets trouvés*. I follow the track opposite across the shingle and towards the sea. The landscape is littered with rusting railway machinery, old sheds and peeling wooden boats in pastel pinks and greens. As I scramble down the steep shingle bank to the beach, the sand is silver and wet and dark clouds are rolling in from the east. This is where I swim, among the quiet bleakness of a beautiful wasteland. On the far horizon Dungeness nuclear power station hums and glows, and the new lighthouse flashes intermittently through the dusk, warning wise sailors to stay away. Despite this the whole shingle mass is moving eastwards at two yards a year (or it would be if trucks were not constantly moving the shingle back to where it came from to ensure the nuclear power station does not fall into the sea).

68 Botany Bay, Broadstairs

Kent

65 Dungeness east

Grid ref.	TR093183
Postcode	TN29 9NE (300m E)
Walk	10 mins, mod
Train	Rye, 24km
Cycle	Route 11

Bleak but atmospheric shingle spit. Prospect Cottage, fishng huts, lighthouse and nuclear power station are a quirky mix.

LT sand and HT shingle on E side opp Prospect Cottage. Avoid spring tides and mid-flows. Don't swim at Dungeness Head – strong tidal currents and undertow. ΔΔ

At New Romney (A259) take beach road (Littlestone, Romney Sands) then turn R and follow beach 7km. Just after the Pilot Inn (built from shipwreck timber, 01797 320314) turn L, dir Dungeness. After 600m you'll see black-and-yellow-painted Prospect Cottage, R. Park beyond and cross shingle to L (E), through old boats and sheds 300m to reach the sea. Continue on to the Old Lighthouse and Britannia pub. Explore coastline to N via the Romney, Hythe and Dymchurch miniature railway (rhdr.org. uk, 01797 362353).

66 Lydden Spout, Dover

Grid ref.	TR283387
Postcode	CT17 9HH (2km W)
Walk	20 mins, mod
Train	Dover Priory, 4km
Cycle	Route 2 and 17

Remote undercliff beach. Leave Dover on A20. Samphire Hoe is signed to the L 1.5km up the hill after last roundabout. Continue down through tunnel to car park. Walk to W end of park (1km) to find beach extending 800m to Lydden Spout cabin and Abbot's Cliff. Shingle at HT, deep rock pools and sand at LT. Avoid sea wall area. On cliff above are tunnels of WW2 battery. Δ

67 Chequers, North Deal

Grid ref.	TR371558
Postcode	CT14 6RG
Walk	10 mins, mod
Train	Deal, 4km
Cycle	Route 1

From Deal follow sea front N, past Royal Cinque Ports Golf clubhouse and then Golf Road to reach Chequers restaurant and bar (01304 362288). Footpath to the shingle beach is just after bar on R, via golf course.

68 Botany Bay, Broadstairs

Grid ref.	TR391712
Postcode	CT10 3SD
Walk	2mins, easy
Train	Broadstairs, 4km
Cycle	Route 15

Remarkably undeveloped sandy bay with white cliffs and caves. Best at HT, some rocks at LT.

From Broadstairs follow B2052 coast road N (dir Margate), passing **Joss Bay** (2km, popular for surfing), **Kingsgate Bay** (500m further, beach with caves and Captain Digby pub), then bearing inland for 1km before turning R into Botany Road. Park at bottom of residential road with fantastic tea room in Alison's front garden 🍴 (open 12–6, Thur–Mon, when sunny, 01843 867662). Bear R (at LT) to find second bay and smugglers' caves.

A Margate's **tidal pool** (TR369716) is beneath Bethesda Medical Centre and Bowls Centre on Palm Bay Ave (CT9 3NR).

B Trendy **Whitstable** has shingle beach (TR112673) and oysters at Hotel Continental 🍴 (Beach Walk, CT5 2BP, 01227 280280).

Beaumont Quay at high tide

Essex

St Peter-on-the-Wall, one of the most ancient churches in England, stands on the edge of the remote Essex marshes looking out to sea. St Cedd, who was ordained at the monastery on Holy Island, landed here by boat in 653 on a mission to convert the heathen East Angles.

The great saint began to build his great church from the remains of an old Roman fort and it continued to be a place of worship for over 600 years. But eventually the church fell into neglect, probably owing to its remote location. Its original purpose forgotten, it became variously a grain store, cattle shed and smugglers' hideaway until the building was rediscovered in the 1920s by a passing rambler. In 1946 the Othona Community was established here and it became a sacred place again.

Today you can stay within the community and there are regular swimming sessions from the sandy strip by the sea wall. The beach closest to the church borders the Dengie Flat, but the water is shallow and the only satisfactory swimming is at high tide. Look out for markers that show where old stakes protrude from the mud. It's better to continue a mile up to Sales Point where there is a beach with shells and sand that shelves deeply into the estuary mouth.

Despite the nuclear power station at nearby Bradwell, the Blackwater and Colne rivers have some of the cleanest waters in the South East; Mersea Island, between the two rivers, has been famous for its oysters since Roman times when they were supplied to the garrisons at Colchester. Today the Company Shed is one of

69 **St Peter's-on-the-Wall**

70 **Oyster shells at Mersea Stone**

69 **Sales Point from Mersea**

the finest and yet most unpretentious eateries in the region. Bring your own wine and bread, sit down at one of the plastic-topped tables and enjoy freshly prepared, unadulterated seafood. Start with a dozen flat oysters and lashings of tabasco sauce, some succulent local cockles or maybe a superb lobster washed down with cheap, ice-cold wine. Almost everything on the menu has been caught within an area of a few miles.

Mersea's best beach is at the Mersea Stone at the end of the island's only road, across an area of ponds and marsh grass. The beach here is made up of thousands of oyster shells with pearly linings that give the place an ethereal white glow. As at other estuary mouths the beach is deep at the spit head, perfect for swimming but with more gently shelving sections to the sides. Remember that currents will be strong here at mid-tide, between low and high tide, especially on spring tides.

From Mersea Stone you can take the ferry over to Brightlingsea and its beaches. Off Mersea Island you can also swim in the tidal harbour pool at Tollesbury – a lovely setting among old boathouses. But for an adventure straight out of *Swallows and Amazons*, make for Hamford Water and Horsey Island, an Essex archipelago of tiny creeks and islands and the setting for Ransome's delightful book *Secret Water* published in 1939. In this, his eighth book, the Swallows and Amazons sail their new boat, *Goblin*, to one of the islands. Once there they fend for themselves, chart the many creeks, fight a local band of sailor-children and nearly drown on the Wade, a tidal causeway to Horsey Island.

You can still get across to Horsey by road via the Wade, or swim from the pontoon at high tide, but the best places for summer dipping are Beaumont or Kirby tidal quays. At Kirby-le-Soken a walk across two fields leads to a pontoon and beach. Even better is Beaumont Quay near Thorpe, built in 1831 using the twelfth-century stones of the old, dismantled London Bridge. From here, brown topsails drifting out across the flat marsh skyline, flat-bottomed barges would set sail loaded with haystacks for London's horses, and return with manure for the Essex fields: 'Hay out, muck in', as the saying went. Now, at high tide, this is an idyllic swimming spot.

Pontoon near Kirby-le-Soken at mid-tide

69 St Peter's, Sales Point

Grid ref.	TM031089
Postcode	CM0 7PN (2km NE)
Walk	30 mins, easy
Train	Southminster, 13km

Remote cockle-shell beach near one of England's oldest churches, St Peter's, though close to Bradwell nuclear power station.

From Burnham-on-Crouch follow B1021 N via Southminster. After 10km turn R for Bradwell then R again in village by church, before Cricketers' pub (01621 776013). Follow Eastend Rd, past second pub, 2km. Park and continue on foot to church, and then 800m on to sea (Othona community buildings on L). Watch out for old submerged stakes here; an area free of them has been marked. △ Or continue 1km N along sea wall to Sales Point on estuary mouth (by channel buoy) to cockle beach with deeper water and fewer mud flats.

A Shingle beach in front of **Osea Island** at Marconi Sailing Club (TL932059, CM0 7NU), 3km up Stansgate Road, 7km E of Latchingdon/Maylandsea. Or try nearby Ramsey Island (2km).

70 East Mersea Stone

Grid ref.	TM073155
Postcode	CO5 8US (1km E)
Walk	20 mins, mod
Train	Colchester, 19km

Famous oyster island. Remote oyster-shell beach with deep swimming. △

Mersea Island is 12km S of Colchester. Immediately after crossing on to island turn L dir East Mersea. Continue 5km to road end and find parking (by Ivy House). Walk 500m to sea wall, turn R then cross to beach L. Follow beach around to tip at mouth of estuary to find steep oyster-shell beach. Watch the currents at mid-tide. Also reached by ferry from Brightlingsea (01206 302200).

A No visit to Mersea Island is complete with eating at the **Company Shed** 🍴 West Mersea (CO5 8LT, 01206 382700). Bring your own white wine and bread.

B **Tollesbury**, 15km S of Colchester on B1023. Tidal swimming pool in old harbour (Woodrolfe Rd, CM9 8TB) or walk out to Shinglehead Point (TL991105). △

71 Beaumont Quay

Grid ref.	TM190240
Postcode	CO16 0BB (300m S)
Walk	2 mins, easy
Train	Thorpe-le-Soken, 4km

Setting for Ransome's *Secret Water* with several excellent HT swimming holes.

From Colchester follow A120, A133, B1033 dir Walton-on-the-Naze. At Thorpe-le-Soken turn L (B1414) and turn into farm track R after 2km. Pass through yard 200m to find Beaumont Quay written on wall R. Walk R 50m to quay and old barn. Two hours either side of high tide.

A Continue from Thorpe 4km to **Kirby-le-Soken** on B1034 (TM224227). Park in village and turn L near post office down Quay Lane (CO13 0DS) and walk 500m to Kirby Quay, past cottages. Cross bridge to L 50m before quay, cross two fields, 300m, to reach jetty and small beach. HT only. Take next L after 500m for Island Lane/Road to The Wade, 1km, leads to original Ransome 'Secret Island' of **Horsey** (TM232244).

B Continue into **Walton-on-the-Naze**, L at church and 3km N for Naze Country Park, remote beach beneath cliffs (CO14 8LG).

Dunwich, Minsmere

Suffolk

Suffolk's sand and shingle coastline is one of the least developed in England. Its villages and resorts, set among woods and marshland rich in wildlife, have an unspoilt charm as well as a slightly eccentric air.

One of the prettiest places is Orford, complete with ancient castle, medieval pub and shop selling home-made baskets. From here several walks radiate out along the tidal creeks, my favourite being the westerly path to Butley Creek. At the old ferry crossing a telephone number allows you to summon the rowing boat from the west bank, but when I arrived the ferryman had vanished so I decided to swim between the two wooden pontoons. Easing myself into the deep water, just able to touch the creamy silt with one toe, I glided around among the moorhens and admired the bucolic scene.

The main attraction at Orford, however, is its Ness, the largest shingle spit in Europe. In the Middle Ages the spit choked and closed Orford's port and it is still growing, extending its long tentacles southwards. A top-secret military base in the Second World War, it is now a precious ecosystem where sea-lavender and sea kale flourish. The National Trust runs ferry trips to the spit from Orford and from here an extensive network of paths unfolds. For a similar shingle experience but with a shorter walk to the sea, visit the settlement of Shingle Street at the southern tip of the Ness. This remote beach community has a handful of flint-fronted coastguards' cottages and several Napoleonic Martello towers, but little else.

72A

72B

75

Heading up the coast you'll pass through classical-music-lover's paradise, Aldeburgh, funky 1920s Thorpeness and come to the nuclear reactor at bleak Sizewell, where the power station actually heats up the sea water via two cooling towers. Some say this is the best wild beach on the Suffolk coast because no one goes there. The next treat is Minsmere, near Dunwich – two miles of sand and dunes backing on to heathland. In summer you can watch avocets and marsh harriers or hear booming bitterns; in autumn and winter you will see many wading birds and waterfowl. Listen for nightingales singing in the scrub from mid-April, and for great spotted woodpeckers drumming. Little terns nest in a designated, fenced area on the beach and water voles swim in the adjoining ponds. Under an evening sky at low tide, with the surf rushing over the sand, the sea fades into a soup of pink and mauve, making this a mesmerising place to swim.

Of Dunwich village itself only a few cottages, a ruined abbey and a pub remain. It's amazing to think that 900 years ago, before the waters closed over it, this village was a city boasting 12 churches and extending a mile out to sea. Longshore drift is still eroding the coast at over three feet per year and depositing the debris downstream on spits such as Blakeney or Orford. It's the same story at many places along this coast: the road ends abruptly and runs straight over the cliff at remote Covehithe, which has a dramatic ruined church, a beautiful beach and a lagoon.

At nearby Walberswick the proceeds of the British Open Crabbing Championship are donated to the Sea Wall Defence Fund. Fortunately for the fund the championship attracts over a thousand participants each year and is the largest crabbing competition in the world. Everyone pays a pound and has 30 minutes to catch the largest possible crab. You're only allowed to use a simple line and bait and the casting techniques and bait recipes are closely guarded secrets. This is an addictive sport that children, in particular, will love, so get here early in the season and start practising!

79A Walberswick beach at sundown

Suffolk

72 Shingle Street

Grid ref.	TM367425
Postcode	IP12 3BE (500m S)
Walk	15 mins, mod
Train	Woodbridge, 15km
Cycle	Route 1

A remote shingle beach. Strong undertow in surf conditions. △

From Woodbridge (A12) take A1152 2km, then B1083 dir Sutton 1km before turning L across Sutton Common to reach Hollesley, 6km. Go over crossroads and follow narrow lanes 3km to Shingle Street. Initial beach, before the cottages, has river currents so continue on and park closer to the Martello tower (700m).

A Beautiful **Orford** (B1084 from Woodbridge, 12km, IP12 2LL) has NT ferry access to the mysterious military ness. Long path leads to the black tower and steep shingle beach but only swim in calm seas (undertow) and when tide is on the turn (strong tidal currents off headland). △

B 3km down Gedgrave Road follow cycle path R to **Butley River** (500m) and bear L to ferry pontoons for a swim (TM392482).

73 Dunwich, Minsmere

Grid ref.	TM478675
Postcode	IP17 3DJ
Walk	10 mins, mod
Train	Darsham, 9km

Beautiful sand and shingle beach bordered by lagoons, heath, heather and birdlife.

1km N of Yoxford (A12) follow signs R to Westleton (4km) then Dunwich. After 3km turn R to Dunwich Heath (Minsmere Rd). Continue 2.5km to NT car park with tea room, 01728 648501). Drop down to beach on path. Go L towards Dunwich on shingle beach, to fishing boats, café and the Ship Inn 🍴 (IP17 3DT, 01728 648219).

A Arty **Walberswick** 4km N has a sand beach with dunes, beach huts and footpaths S across open marshland. The **crabbing championships** take place in the shallow channels behind the beach. The Anchor 🍴 is the best pub with excellent beer and food (IP18 6UA, 01502 722112). Swim in the Blyth anywhere upriver from the row-boat ferry jetty, or near the windmill on Tinker's Marshes (2km).

74 Covehithe

Grid ref.	TM524809
Postcode	NR34 7JW (800m S)
Walk	20 mins, mod
Train	Halesworth, 18km

From Wrentham (A12) turn R down lanes for Covehithe (2km) with its massive ruined church and eroded cliff road. Park at the junction, 300m before church, taking care not to block the road. Continue 50m and take the footpath R, before Church Farm, to follow the field edge 1km down to the beach and dunes next to Covehithe Broad.

75 Aldeburgh and 'scallop'

Grid ref.	TM468582
Postcode	IP15 5BH (1.5km N)
Walk	3 mins, easy
Train	Saxmundham, 12km

Medieval Aldeburgh's shingle beach offers great seafood and fish-and-chips (try 226 High Street 🍴) and is never too crowded. Head 1.5km N by road to the scallop-shell sculpture or 2km S by road to the Martello tower, which are less popular. Funky Thorpeness is 3km north.

Blakeney Point pool at low tide

East Norfolk: Blakeney and Stiffkey

North-east Norfolk has miles of coast shaped and funnelled into creek-filled harbours, shingle spits and towering dunes. Here you can swim with seals, ride the tides, wade out to uninhabited islands and return home with cockles and samphire for supper.

I began my explorations late one night at Horsey Corner, a remote lane that leads down through scrub to a car park among sand hills. The sea was thrashing about in the keen wind as I set up my billowing tent. That short summer night brought whistling rain, but as dawn broke the sky was blue, the sun was shining and the surf was up, peaked with silver caps.

These north-eastern beaches take the full brunt of the prevailing winds and tides from the North Sea. This is where longshore drift hits full on, turning left to drag south to the Thames or right to run into the Wash. Feeling hot in the tent and with the sun beating down, I ran to the beach, silky sand underfoot, but swell still crashing on the groynes. The sideways tow was instant, dragging me along the beach at about three knots. As I struggled with the waves a seal popped up almost within reach and swam with me and around me, appearing and disappearing. For about five minutes it watched me wide-eyed as it ducked in and out of the waves.

Two miles up the beach at remote Waxham – just a medieval barn, church and farm shop – I warmed up with tea and creamy

79

79

79B

scrambled eggs and heard stories of the North Sea flood of 1953. A freak combination of tides and winds came together to create the worst peacetime disaster in British history. Over 500 people died and 1,000 miles of coastline were devastated as a huge wall of water surged down. Here at Waxham and Sea Palling the dunes were breached and a church entirely washed away. Today a concrete sea wall extends along the entire Norfolk coast; its huge iron sea gates can be clamped shut at a moment's notice. From here all the way to Blakeney along the winding B1159 coast road you'll find evidence of the sea's gradual onslaught. This is a battered, conquered coastline with whole villages relentlessly eroded, cliffs crumbling and tree-stumps floating – a place of shipwrecks and lighthouses but not one single safe harbour.

A sense of relief returns for the sailor, and swimmer, from Cley beach onwards. The coast turns west and a succession of creeks offers refuge. Harbours since medieval times, these inland quays or 'staithes' are reached via tortuous winding inland tidal channels that empty and fill with the ebb and flow. At Blakeney, one of the finest and richest villages in Norfolk, local boys make good use of these flows, swimming and floating up the channel as the tide comes in. At Morston, now the main harbour for boat trips to see the seals, you can make the long walk out across the harbour's low-tide marsh and cockle beds to swim in the channel off Blakeney Point. Here, among the shingle and sand and against a backdrop of elegant old lifeboat houses, you will be closely observed by basking seals.

A simpler route to Blakeney Point is via Stiffkey, below the popular campsite. This walk borders Patch Pit Creek with its six wooden footbridges, and then heads out for a mile across the low-tide sands. The sea is so far away and so shallow that the best places to swim here are the creeks. At high tide you can swim anywhere but at low tide head for Stiffkey pool, which is always reliably deep. Watch children jump and slide in this endless flat land, muddy samphire marshes on one side, sand flats stretching out on the other – a true interface between land, sky and sea.

Stiffkey, Freshes Creek pool at low tide

East Norfolk: Blakeney and Stiffkey

76 Horsey Corner

Grid ref.	TG465242
Postcode	NR29 4EQ (800m NE)
Walk	5 mins, easy
Train	Acle, 18km

Remote NT beach, with 6km of dunes and heath between Winterton and Waxham. Seals regularly swim here. From Winterton (10km N of Great Yarmouth) follow road 5km N via Somerton and Horsey (Nelson Head pub, NR29 4AD, 01493 393378), turning R down track at sharp L corner 1km beyond Horsey. Camping at Walnut Farm ▲ 01692 598217 beyond on R.

77 Waxham

Grid ref.	TG442264
Postcode	NR12 0EA (500m N)
Walk	3 mins, easy
Train	Worstead, 19km

4km beyond Horsey, a tiny village centred on historic Old Barn 🍴 with excellent tea room and cakes. Sandy lane leads through dunes to beach. Adjacent Sea Palling (1km N) is much busier (jet-skis) with offshore rock reefs and artificial coves for swimming.

78 Blakeney Point pool

Grid ref.	TF984455
Postcode	NR25 7AA (2km NW)
Walk	40 mins, diff
Train	Sheringham, 16km
	(or Kings Lynn, 40km)

Dramatic low-tide walk across the cockle beds and salt marshes to the deep sand banks and pool at Blakeney Point. Many seals. Know your tides. △△

Set off 1–2 hrs before LT. From Morston harbour (A149) follow the path along the creek N, past the boats, crossing two tributary footbridges (500m), then curving L to skirt the edge of Morston salt marshes, W. With the mud flats of Blakeney Channel on your R continue for 1km. Once you're well past the old lifeboat station on the opposite (N) bank, bear off path R towards Blakeney Point, across cockles, mud and sands, crossing Freshes Creek in your bare feet. After 500m you'll hit the main channel; shallow, flowing water over sand. Splash across to reach the steep sand banks of the point and continue on to find a place to swim in the deep pool as the channel turns N out to sea. Never approach seals on foot, allow them to come to you in the water.

79 Stiffkey, Freshes Creek

Grid ref.	TF973448
Postcode	NR23 1QF
Walk	20 mins, easy
Train	Sheringham, 21km
	(or Kings Lynn, 40km)

Popular LT swimming hole in the tidal creeks of Stiffkey marshes and flats.

Leave Stiffkey dir Wells, and turn R after the Red Lion (01328 830552) into The Greenway. Pass Stiffkey campsite ▲ (01328 830235) and park at bottom of track (700m). Bear R (E) along woods 700m, joining Garborough Patch Pit Creek, then follow path to L, crossing six mini footbridges, to arrive at sand flats. Follow creek (L) 200m to find sharp bend to the R. 20m before this corner is deepest part of the creek (2m), mud on L side, sand on R.

A Back in **Blakeney** walk out along the channel then catch a ride on the flood tide back in (NR25 7NQ, TG027449). △

B **Cley** beach 2km E is steeply shelving shingle, great for serious swimming (TG048454). Summer phosphorescence. Reach Blakeney Point via long walk.

West Norfolk and Scolt Head Island

Scolt Head is Britain's very own desert island. A whale back of white sand and dune hills, decked with green marram grass, it is accessible only by small sailing boat or by swimming.

To the north of the island is the sea but the south side is a network of snaking sandy channels and pools which, with the help of a little local knowledge, you can navigate. The best routes out are from Burnham Overy Staithe, one of the prettiest harbours on this coast and also where Nelson, whose father was a rector at nearby Burnham Thorpe, learned to swim and sail. The raised path follows the right-hand side of the creek up to Burnham beach, a dazzling stretch of sand with panoramic views from the dunes atop Gun Hill. A channel empties across the beach to make a warm paddling and swimming pool at low tide, but head west up the beach to arrive at the deep pool that separates you from Scolt Head Island. Brightly coloured dinghies are stored safe on the Island's sands opposite: this is a favourite local swimming hole and a sheltered spot for learning to canoe and sail. It makes a great swimming pool on a turning or rising tide but watch out for seaward currents on a spring falling tide.

The Island is also accessible from Burnham Overy Staithe at low tide via the old cockle path used by cockle pickers on the creek's left bank. The journey consists of a shallow wade, then a very muddy path – great fun in bare feet – with several mud slides made

80 **The Cockle Path**

80 **Burnham Overy Staithe**

80 **Burnham Overy Staithe**

by children along the way. The flows up and down the creek here are relatively gentle and safe, so if you have never ridden a tide, this is a a great place to learn. In one spot the creek almost meets one of its upper tributaries, in a tight meander. Hop out of the water, cross the grass, and jump back in its upper reaches for another tidally assisted circuit. You can keep going round until the tide turns.

The west side of Scolt Head Island is more remote and the channel deeper and larger compared to that at Burnham Overy Staithe, owing to the much larger body of water that rushes in and out. From Brancaster you can see the iconic shipwreck of the 1894 SS *Vina* steamship, sitting like a beacon on the western edge of the island. Originally used for trade with Baltic ports, SS *Vina* was sunk on the sand flats by the military in 1944 for use as a target for bombing practice. Every day the waters reveal and then submerge the wreck as they ebb and flow across the sand flats. Her mast is, in fact, a beacon and the great limpet-fringed holes in her midriff and broken, rusting hull are a stark reminder of the power of the sea,

Visiting the ship from Brancaster beach is a great adventure, but one that requires planning and caution. As with many of the channel swims in this chapter, understanding the flow of the tides will create a deeper connection to the wild Norfolk world between land and sea. The channel that crosses Brancaster beach is deep (and fun to swim in at low tide) but there is also a ford where it becomes shallow at low tide and from there it's just a short splash and 300 yards to the wreck.

When I first made this crossing my guide taught me three golden rules about channels. First, always set off two hours before low tide and ensure the channel is still flowing to the sea as you cross. Second, mark your crossing point in the sand using a stick well above the water level, in case the rising tide makes finding your fording point difficult on the return. Third, if you miscalculate the tide times and are forced to swim, don't panic and don't fight the current. The rising tide will be taking you into harbour not out to sea, and you will still be able to swim across the channel and reach the safety of the landward side upstream.

Wreck of SS *Vina* on Scolt Head Island west

West Norfolk and Scolt Head Island

80 Burnham beach

Grid ref.	TF854459
Postcode	PE31 8JE (2km NE)
Walk	35 mins, mod
Train	King's Lynn, 37km
Cycle	Route 1

Superb beach with white dunes and access to Scolt Head Island east beach and various swimming holes and mud slides. △

Park in Burnham Overy Staithe harbour, 7km E of Wells. Bear R on path along E edge (R bank) of Overy Creek passing various swimming holes. Continue 2km to high white sand dunes and beach below. Swim in the channel or at sea edge. Take care at HT ebb as the emptying channel can create a strong L to R seaward current.

A Bear L (300m) along channel to reach pool opposite white beaches of **Scolt Head Island E**, a classic swimming and sailing spot (TF848457). Swim across or reach this beach from the harbour at LT/MT via the 'cockle path': wade across harbour, follow muddy path 1km N, crossing bridge, reaching flats. Turn L for 'creek riding' or straight on for deep wade to Scolt Head beach. △

81 Brancaster beach

Grid ref.	TF771452
Postcode	PE31 8AX
Walk	10 mins, easy
Train	King's Lynn, 35km
Cycle	Route 1

White beach with views to Scolt Head west and wreck of SS *Vina*. Deep (2–3m) channel on R makes a great swimming pool at LT and MT. △

Brancaster is 6km W of Burnham Overy on A149. Turn R at church and park at golf club (1km). Crossing to SS *Vina*/**Scolt Head Island West** (2km) is possible with extreme care. △△ Depart 1–2 hours before LT and ford the channel while water is still flowing seaward. Beach to L (W) is channel-free. △

Shallowest ford is at far E end of beach, beyond wreck, on cockle beds and between transmitter and church tower landmarks. Mark the best crossing point in sand to assist your return. Unwind afterwards at the White Horse 🍴 gastro-pub, Brancaster Staithe (just off A149, PE31 8BY, 01485 210262) – great views from the wooden deck.

82 Holkam Bay

Grid ref.	TF890452
Postcode	NR23 1RL (1km E)
Walk	10 mins, mod
Train	King's Lynn, 43km
Cycle	Route 1

A huge wild well-known beach, but good swimming only at HT. Turn R 2km W of Wells (A149) and park in Lady Ann's Road. Cross dunes through forest. Turn L for naturist stretch and on to Burnham Overy (3km), turn R for 2km forested stretch to Wells. Informal Victoria 🍴 (01328 711008) is excellent gastro-pub, with rooms.

83 Thornham beach

Grid ref.	TF719451
Postcode	PE36 6LT (2km N)
Walk	20 mins, mod
Train	King's Lynn, 20km.
Cycle	Route 1

Beautiful beach with lake and forest. 6km E of Hunstanton (A149) turn L into Staithe Lane and continue 1.5km to end and park. Bear L then R along marshes. Good swimming at all tides. Turn R 1km to swim in Harbour Channel. △ Lifeboat Inn 🍴 in village, with rooms (01485 512236).

Wales

The Gower Peninsula and the Pembrokeshire Coast National Park offer some of the most spectacular coastal scenery, caves, islands and secret beaches in Britain. Cardiganshire is equally impressive but lesser known. In north Wales the beaches of Snowdonia, the Lleyn Peninsula and Anglesey – as dramatic as their high mountain backdrops – are punctuated by coves, rock arches and dunes.

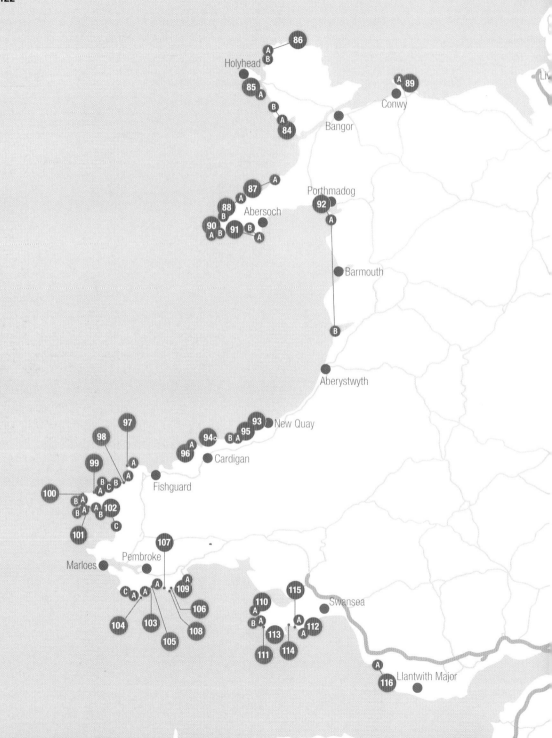

Holyhead

86
A
B

85
A
B
A
84

Bangor

A
89
Conwy

Liv

Porthmadog
92
A

A
87
88
B
Abersoch
90
A B
91
B
A

B

Barmouth

Aberystwyth

97
98
93
New Quay
95
94 A
B A
96
A
99
Cardigan
B
A C B
A
Fishguard
100
B A
B A
A B
102
101
C

107
Pembroke
Marloes
C A A
A
109
A
106
104 103
108
105

115
110
Swansea
B A
A
112
113
A
111 114

A
116
Llantwith Major

Wales Highlights

86 Unmarked roads and tracks lead to the old ruined harbour, brick works and rock arch of Porth Wen on Anglesey.

90 Bardsey Island was considered one of the most sacred places in Britain. Visit the holy well at the old embarkation point.

92A Harlech Beach, with its backdrop of mountains and a ruined castle, is probably the wildest and most beautiful stretch of sand and dunes in Wales.

94 Historic, remote and beautiful, Mwnt is one of Wales' most perfect coves, sited beneath a tiny church with opportunities for snorkelling nearby.

96 The Witch's Cauldron is a dramatic inland lagoon with a beach, formed when a massive sea cavern collapsed. You can swim in through various cave and waterfall entrances.

99 Abereiddi Blue Lagoon is a drowned slate quarry, now breached by the sea, with a series of jumps from the old engine house.

98B & 99C Two islands on this stretch both have caves that pass through their centres. Close to the famous Sloop Inn.

101 Saint David was said to have been born at the holy well above St Non's Bay, where the modern sport of coasteering evolved.

102C Druidstone is a magnificent, remote stretch of long sand. A hotel with an excellent bar is perched above.

103–105 One of the most spectacular stretches of coast in Britain. St Govan's Chapel is hidden in the cliffs, plus many more caves and sea caverns, and the beautiful beach of Barafundle.

106 A secret tunnel leads to the white sands of Skrinkle Haven.

110 Bluepool Bay on the Gower has rock arches, sand and a very deep rock pool into which you can jump from ledges.

111 The little-known beaches of Mewslade and Fall on Gower lead to Worm's Head tidal island where Dylan Thomas was once stranded overnight.

Porth Wen abandoned brickworks and harbour

Anglesey

Ancient Anglesey, a land of burial cairns and neolithic sites, contains some of the finest sand coves on the north Wales coast, and some of its most dramatic coastal features, from caves and arches to volcanic lava flows.

About 570 million years ago during the Cambrian era much of Wales lay beneath the ancient Iapetus Ocean. Volcanic islands were common, with lava spilling out of vents on the sea floor. Some of this pillow lava, the oldest rock on earth, is still visible around the neck of Llanddwyn Island, a narrow isthmus studded with sandy inlets that is set against the vast tracts of Newborough Warren and forest.

The forests and dunes of the warren lie on much newer land, but were almost obliterated during the thirteenth century by sand storms. Three centuries later Elizabeth I forbade the cutting of the marram grass in order to protect the area and this ensured its long-term survival. The magic of the beach at Llanddwyn is due not only to its its eight miles of deserted shore but also to the spectacular backdrop of Snowdonia. Rising up from across the Menai Strait this mountainous region resembles an enchanted land with ever-changing cloud and light patterns played out on the sea.

The best swimming is among the tiny coves of Llanddywn Island. A whole community of pilots who helped to guide the ships in and over the notorious shifting sand bars of the Menai Strait once lived on this stunning outcrop. Go right to the end of the island where you will find coves by the

86B

84

85 Bwa Gwyn, the White Arch

lighthouse and beneath the old pilots' cottages. These have the best views and are fantastic for swimming.

Looking north from here you might be able to spy further coves up the coast to Aberffraw. There's no public access: the farmers are fiercely territorial and have refused all requests for a coast path. To reach these untouched gems you will need to walk for several miles along the shoreline, south from Aberffraw. Bring a picnic and make a day of it. The only other people who know about these coves are those with boats.

Two miles north of Aberffraw the popular surfing and swimming cove of Porth Trecastell (Cable Bay) has easier access direct from the roadside. The rock ledges along the right are good for jumping and there is a chambered cairn on the headland that you can explore with a torch if you collect the key from the local shop in nearby Llanfaelog.

Rhoscolyn and Borthwen (White Bay), another 10 miles north, are on the Holy Island separated from the rest of Anglesey at Four Mile Bridge. There's a gastro-pub here, the White Eagle, and, as you would expect, a white sandy bay with several little islets, one with an iron bridge over a gulley. A dramatic walk from Rhoscolyn leads up to St Gwenfaen's Well, one of Wales' best-preserved holy wells where the water is said to cure mental illness, though you'll need to throw in a white quartz pebble first. From here you can descend past caves, chasms and blowholes to Bwa Gwyn and Bwa Du – the White and Black Arches – and after a steep scramble down to the water you can swim through them on calm days.

To the east of Holyhead Porth Trwyn and Porth Swtan (Church Bay) are idyllic sweeps of white sand with flower meadows behind. Set well back on the lane behind Church Bay, The Lobster Pot, a tiny local seafood restaurant, is worth a visit. Finally Porth Wen, near Amlwch up on the north coast, is one of the most interesting but spookiest of Anglesey's many coves. Down an unsigned, little-used path you come upon a ruined harbour and old brick works with a honeycomb of furnaces and chimney stacks to explore. Enjoy the perfect white shingle beach and rock arch as you think about the people who once lived and worked here and rejoice that nature has reclaimed this quiet place for herself.

Anglesey

84 Llanddwyn Island

Grid ref.	SH387625
Postcode	LL61 6SG (3km NE)
Walk	20 mins, easy
Train	Bodorgan, 7km
Cycle	Route 8

Tiny sandy coves on Llanddwyn Island peninsula. Many miles of beach with stunning backdrop of Snowdonia.

From Menai Bridge (A4080) enter Newborough, take L at post office (signed Llys Rhosyr). Follow road 1km to toll (£2) and then 2km to car park. Follow beach or forest track R up shore 2km to 'island' then head to island tip, cottages and lighthouse.

A From Newborough continue on A4080 7km to **Aberffraw** (LL63 5BX). Walk 1km S to Traeth Mawr. Explore the remote sandy coves SE (SH360665 to SH368652) only accessible via 3km seashore scramble from beach end. △

B Continue on A4080 3km to **Porth Trecastell** (Cable Bay/SH333707) by roadside lay-by. Popular for swimming and surfing with rock jumps on R side. Chambered cairn on headland, door key from shop at Llanfaelog.

85 Rhoscolyn Arches

Grid ref.	SH259762
Postcode	LL65 2NJ (1km W)
Walk	40 mins, diff
Train	Valley, 5km
Cycle	Route 8

Dramatic coastal walk leads to cliff-top holy well, then two rock arches for adventure swim. △△

From Valley (A55, J3) take B4545 dir Trearddur. At Four Mile Bridge (2km) turn L. After 2.5km turn L before church to White Eagle gastro-pub 🔟 (01407 860267) and continue on to beach. Turn R, via beach and cottages to coast path, then up through fields (W) to St Gwenfaen's Well (1km, SH260754). Continue down 1km past pink cove and on to find **Bwa Gwyn** (White Arch/SH259762). Use steep bank on opposite slope for difficult scramble down to water. Swim only in calm sea at HT. **Bwa Du** (Black Arch/SH260763) is 300m beyond.

A The beach at **Rhoscolyn** (Borthwen, SH271351) has parking, good sands, safe swimming and various interesting islets and inlets to explore.

86 Porth Wen

Grid ref.	SH402946
Postcode	LL67 0LN (2km E)
Walk	10 mins, mod
Train	Valley, 18km

Cove-studded NE coast leads to eerie secret bay with old ruined harbour, brickworks, rock arch and beach.

From Valley (A55, J3) follow A5025 coast road N 19km to Cemaes. Continue 2.5km and turn L into unsigned lane. After 800m by bend find 2 footpath signs on R, take L footpath (metal kissing gate) and descend to bay (500m). Arch to R beyond beehive kilns, beach beyond main brick building.

A Porth Swtan (Church Bay/SH301894, LL65 4EU) is a beautiful white sand cove with Lobster Pot restaurant 🔟(01407 730241). Heading N on A5025 turn L 1km after Llanfaethlu (Chapel Street, signed Rhydwyn), then 2km.

B Porth Trwyn (SH296877, LL65 4HD) turn L off A5025 in Llanfaethlu, then continue 2km to sea and turn R. Or continue 2km S of Church Bay above.

Porth Iago

North Lleyn and Llandudno

A tiny rocky headland looks out across two sweeping bays and the looming mountains of Yr Eifl. Picture-perfect seashore cottages huddle by the beach around the red-roofed inn.

Porth Dinllaen is a remote north Wales village set on the tip of the Lleyn Peninsula and has no road access. It was the site of one of the fiercest of Welsh contests: the battle to establish the official crossing-point for the proposed London to Dublin railway. Porth Dinllaen, a perfect natural harbour, had the backing of Isambard Kingdom Brunel, and the Porth Dinllaen Harbour Company was formed in 1808 to advance its cause. In 1810, however, Parliament rejected its plans and voted for Thomas Telford's more accessible road developments to Holyhead via the north Wales coast.

Anglesey's gain preserved the Lleyn Peninsula and it remains largely untouched by development. Porth Dinllaen, still a car-free hamlet, is now owned by the National Trust and can be reached only on foot. Ty Coch (the Red House) the old-established inn, is popular on summer evenings. Further round the harbour by the lifeboat ramp are two tiny sandy coves that are good for swimming, and you'll see seals basking on the rocks.

Across the bay to the north is the towering peak of Yr Eifl, with a beachside settlement of old quarrymen's cottages below it. This is now home to the National Welsh language Centre (Nant Gwrtheyrn) and is reached by one of the most dramatic mountain roads in Wales that snakes down through alpine forest with stunning views out to sea. It's worth calling in just for the drive alone. There's an excellent café here too, and the long shingle foreshore is almost always deserted.

87A **Nant Gwrtheyrn from Porth Dinllaen**

89

88A **Porth Towyn, second cove**

*'The Walrus and the Carpenter
Were walking close at hand;
They wept like anything to see
Such quantities of sand.'*

Lewis Carroll, *Alice in Wonderland*
(writing in Llandudno)

Along the peninsula's north-western coast mountain gives way to moorland and a string of pearly coves. Porth Oer (Whistling Sands) is perhaps the best known of these coves and the grains really do squeak underfoot, piping shrill notes when the wind blows in from the west. A small National Trust café provides sustenance after a morning of body surfing and swimming, and the cliff walk immediately south leads to the small island headlands of Dinas Bach and Dinas Fawr with sea caves for exploring.

Near Porth Oer, Traeth Penllech has a long stretch of sand reached across open fields and a small stream, while Porth Towyn further up the coast has two small coves with good rocks for scrambling. You can camp at nearby Towyn and Ysgaden farms and explore the tiny shingle inlets of Yslaig and Ysgaden where Irish sea salt and Welsh language almanacs were once smuggled in. Do make time to visit Porth Iago, my favourite among all these coves for wild swimming. The thick slice of white sand occupies a deep cleft between the cliffs and there are perfect rocks for diving, jumping and snorkelling – the archetypal swimmer's cove.

This rich scenery contrasts dramatically with the drab lines of caravan resorts along most of the north Wales coast, from Bangor to Chester. The notable exception is Llandudno. Named after sixth-century St Tudno and once a rich copper-mining town, Llandudno took full advantage of the Victorian sea-bathing craze and was one of Britain's most upmarket resorts with some of the finest shops outside London. It was here that Lewis Carroll wrote parts of *Alice in Wonderland* and created the Walrus and Carpenter characters.

The great carboniferous limestone hulk of the Orme – meaning 'worm' or 'serpent' – affords truly magnificent views of Snowdonia, Anglesey and the coast. Daredevils jump into the sea from some of the low cliffs to the right of the road and swim into Porth Helyg (Pigeon's Cave), but the best swimming is on Little Orme's Head at Porth Dyniewaid (Angel Bay), which is also popular with climbers. It's a short walk across gorse-covered headland to this tiny sand and pebble beach. There are good rocks for jumping and a sense of seclusion and ruggedness – a striking contrast to the faded grandeur of genteel Llandudno.

North Lleyn and Llandudno

87 Porth Dinllaen

Grid ref.	SH276416
Postcode	LL53 6DB
Walk	10 mins, easy
Train	Pwllheli, 11km

From Caernarfon follow A499, B4417 coast roads to Morfa Nefyn and park next to Fairway Country Hotel. Follow beach to Ty Coch Inn 🍺 01758 720498 (1km) or take gated track across golf course. Below L (300m) is shingle cove of Borth Wen (SH274411). Beyond pub 500m, through cottages, find lifeboat station, tiny coves and rocks with seals. Also long Nefyn beach 2km to E.

A Just before Morfa Nefyn on B4417 turn R at Llithfaen for spectacular drive down to **Nant Gwrtheyrn** (SH350448, LL53 6PA), the Welsh Language Centre, with shingle beach under mountains. Café, restaurant 🍴, heritage centre, cottages for rent (01758 750334).

88 Porth Iago

Grid ref.	SH168317
Postcode	LL53 8LP (1km NW)
Walk	1 min, easy
Train	Pwllheli, 20km

Series of lovely sandy coves along N coast of the Lleyn peninsula: Towyn, Oer and Iago.

Porth Iago, SH168317: 1km before Porth Oer, turn R at small 3-way junction with old barn on L. After 1km turn L (signed). After 400m turn L into Ty Mawr farm. Continue through farm (£2) to parking area above beach. Steep rocky sides for jumping, with care.

A **Porth Towyn**, SH232374, LL53 8PD: From Morfa Nefyn (*see* swim 87) take B4417 5km SW to Tudweiliog turning R into lane just before village. Continue 1km to farm to find double cove (explore R) with camping ⛺ and very small café.

B **Porth Oer** (Whistling Sands) SH167295, LL53 8LH: From Tudweiliog follow B4417 6km to Pen-y-groeslon then R on B4413 (dir Aberdaron). After 0.5km turn R (signed Porth Oer). Car park after 4km on R. Local favourite, with NT café 🍴.

89 Porth Dyniewaid/Angel Bay

Grid ref.	SH818827
Postcode	LL30 3RN
Walk	10 mins, mod
Train	Llandudno, 5km

Shingle cove on the lesser-known Little Orme's Head set under cliffs and popular with climbers. Daredevil kids jump from Fisherman's Rock.

Walk 1km around headland from far E end of Llandudno Bay. Or driving from Llandudno follow seafront Parade E on B5115 (dir Penrhyn and A55 J21) heading inland up hill. After 1km take first exit at roundabout (Glan Y Mor Rd), then L on to Penrhyn Beach Rd and quickly R on to Penrhyn Beach East. Continue 1km until road ends in cul-de-sac. Walk up hill and bear R to end of headland (300m) and drop down to cove. Fisherman's Rock on R of cove. Don't swim out far as there are currents at headland. △

A Rock platforms at old quarry at **Ogof Colomennod** (Pigeon's Cave/ SH779839) on Pen Trwyn headland of Great Orme. Popular with anglers, climbers and daredevil high-divers. 1km N of Llandudno pier. △△

South Lleyn and the Rhinog Coast

Bardsey Island sits at the distant tip of the Lleyn Peninsula and glimmers in the waters of Bardsey Sound. From here Cardigan Bay stretches out in a great arc to the remote and dramatic Rhinog mountains of Snowdonia.

There's been a church on this 'island in the tides' for 1,700 years and it was once considered as sacred as Iona in Scotland or Holy Island (Lindisfarne) in Northumberland. Devout Catholics considered three pilgrimages to Bardsey were worth one to Rome and to die here guaranteed a place in heaven. Many travelled here to spend their last days praying in the sea caves and holding vigils on the cliffs. It became known as 'the island of 20,000 saints'.

The journey across to the island has always been treacherous: on full spring tides currents flow like rivers. Pilgrims would embark from a narrow inlet near Aberdaron beneath the church of St Mary, now a ruin. A path still runs down to the embarkation point and here you'll come across St Mary's Well, a small natural trough near the low tide line. On a calm, bright day the water in this deep harbour cleft radiates light and rock ledges provide tempting places for jumping and snorkelling. However, you should only consider such antics on neap, turning tides when there is little tidal stream, and you should never venture out of the inlet into the main passage. Porth Felen further around the headland was also used as a harbour in stormy weather and offers a safer swimming option.

92A

90

92 **Morfa Bychan, east end**

Exploring the lanes east, beyond Aberdaron and its 'Two Doors' cave, we came across a leafy path along a stream glade down to the hidden cove of Porth Ysgo. Here there are old mine workings and tunnels overgrown with ragwort and bindweed, and on the grassy cliff-tops we found ruined engine houses and rusted turning wheels. Once at the beach I swam out to the old mooring rock that still has its iron ring. Larger boats would once have waited here for the smaller craft ferrying manganese ore from the shore, but today this podium makes an excellent place to jump and dive. It's also a great vantage point for admiring the bay's serpentine and gabbro rocks. Black, rough and crystalline, these started life in the heart of the Earth, where they were fiercely cooked and then slowly cooled.

Further up the coast Abersoch is the main resort. Photographer Martin Turtle, who runs the Turtle Gallery, took me from here to explore Porth Ceiriad, a remote beach with powerful surf that refracts off the golden sandstone, and where there is also a cliff-top campsite. On calmer days it's good for snorkelling and you might see thornback rays, skate, mackerel, flounders and whiting. A rare Kemp's Ridley turtle was washed up on this beach not so long ago.

East from here, the coast passes the castle towns of Pwllheli and Criccieth before reaching Porthmadog, from where Prince Madog is said to have set sail to discover America almost 300 years before Christopher Columbus. The town stands at the head of the great Glaslyn Estuary, a dramatic plain that drains the Snowdon massif. One of the best views is from Borth-y-Gest where there are deep sandy pools and lagoons at low tide. It's also possible to bathe in the river in front of the village of Portmeirion – which has an eccentric mix of architectural styles – on the adjacent Dwyryd Estuary, but take great care when the tide is flowing seaward.

Cross on the toll bridge and continue seven miles to the foreboding ruins of fourteenth-century Harlech Castle, built when the sea still lapped at its massive crag. The stunning beach below is one of the few dune systems in the country that is accreting, extending ever further into Cardigan Bay. You might also catch a glimpse of dolphins offshore. In the distance the Rhinog summits rise up, their slopes studded with Bronze-Age tracks and stone circles. This is ancient Wales, a land of mountains, islands and sea.

River Glaslyn at Borth-y-Gest sands, low tide

South Lleyn and the Rhinog Coast

90 St Mary's Well, Gwyddel

Grid ref.	SH140252
Postcode	LL53 8BY (1km SW)
Walk	10 mins, mod
Train	Pwllheli, 25km

A steep, deep rocky inlet where pilgrims embarked for Bardsey Island. St Mary's Well appears as a pool at low tide by the water's edge.

From B4413 entering Aberdaron turn R before bridge (dir Uwchmynydd). Continue 2km to second chapel then bear R, past Penbryn Bach Seafood Restaurant 🍴 500m (01758 760216) and Mynydd Mawr campsite △ 500m (01758 760223). As road bends up to R park and follow path downhill via stream to rocky inlet. Well is 30m to R. Jumping and snorkelling but only in a flat calm sea on turning, neap tides. Strong currents in Sound. △△

A **Porth Felen** (SH144250) is a safer rocky bay. Bear L (SW) around Gwyddel headland 1km. Stay inside cove. △

B Aberdaron **Ogof Ddeuddrws** ('Two Doors' cave/SH186256), near far E end of Aberdaron shingle beach. △

91 Porth Ysgo

Grid ref.	SH208265
Postcode	LL53 8AN (100m S)
Walk	15 mins, easy
Train	Pwllheli, 18km

A remote NT sand and shingle cove beneath old mine ruins in secret valley.

From Aberdaron take coast road E (dir Rhiw, Mynytho). After 4.2km turn R at cross roads (dir Llanfaelrhys) and park at junction (800m). Follow path/track down stream 600m (tunnels on L worth exploring) to cliff. Bear R through gate and down stairs.

A **Porth Ceiriad** is a quiet beach with strong surf (SH311248, LL53 7DB 1km SE) From Abersoch take Sarn Bach road (SW). After 2km continue over cross-roads, bear R after 300m, turn L after 1km (signed Nant-y-big Park, not Corn Farm). Continue down lane, through farm, 1km, to car park above beach. Nant-y-big campsite △ (01758 712686) has (exposed) pitches on cliff. N

B **Hell's Mouth** is classic wild bay, four miles long, undeveloped, good for surfing (SH286266). Llanengan Rd from Abersoch.

92 Borth-y-Gest

Grid ref.	SH562370
Postcode	LL49 9TY (300m W)
Walk	15 mins, easy
Train	Porthmadog, 2km
Cycle	Route 2

Long stretch of sand and pools at mouth of estuary. Superb views of mountains. Strong currents but safe on a low-to-incoming tide. △

Cross cob into Porthmadog and turn L after 300m up Bank Place then turn L after 500m down Borth Rd 1km to village. Park and continue round to road end by church and drop down to follow beach for up to 1km. Connects to **Morfa Bychan**.

A Beautiful 6km **Harlech Beach** (SH569316, LL46 2UG, 500m W) backdrop of dunes, mountains and Harlech Castle. Dolphins in bay. Take A496 S to Harlech and turn R by shop, after station, to beach. Huge beach campsite △ 4km S at Shell Island (Llanbedr, 01341 241453).

B Popular beach with dunes at **Ynyslas Estuary** 40km S between Machynlleth and Aberystwyth, 6km N of Borth (SN610941, SY24 5JZ), off B4353, off A487. Jet-skis E side, quieter W side. Visitor centre.

Cardiganshire

It was early evening as I followed the lanes down through twisted woodland and along a stream glade to emerge at the cove of Cwmtydu, its walls lined with caves.

The sun was sinking rapidly in a cloudy pink haze and I rushed to set up camp on the headland. It was a warm night and after a deep sleep I woke early, already too hot in my sleeping bag, and scrambled down to the beach to plunge into a clear sea. After a few lengths I clambered out on to some black rock ledges near a cave and explored tentatively inside, keeping an eye on a seal that bobbed about in the middle distance watching me.

A short walk on the coast path north from Cwmtydu, just before the faint hillside remains of Castell Bach, brings you to another cove and you can swim from one side around a mini-island to the other. Flower meadows bloom here and cliffs drop dramatically to the sea. When I arrived a couple from a seal-watch charity were already in residence, warning walkers to stay away. Down below a tiny white seal pup was flopping about on the beach and the couple were concerned it would be disturbed (walkers' dogs can be particularly worrying) and that the mother might then abandon it.

Cwmtydu is a pleasant, low-key place with a little shop, a campsite and a stream leading down to the shingle beach. Even more picturesque is Llangranog, a few miles down the coast, with excellent sea-facing pubs and a jumble of cottages clustered on the steep

95B

94

94 **East of Mwnt**

lanes above. This is the kind of village that I imagine Dylan Thomas had in mind when he wrote *Under Milk Wood* in nearby New Quay.

There are caves here, too, and rock stacks known as the Giant's Teeth. At low tide you can follow the sands along to Cilborth Cove or gain access via wooden steps from the cliff path above. The sandy inlets continue all the way along the cliff base to the dramatic pointed finger of Ynys-Lochtyn headland. Here a precarious cliff promontory leads to an island with ledges, a rock arch, a hidden beach and a low-tide causeway.

Two miles south you'll find longer beaches at Penbryn and Tresaith but I continued 10 miles west to Mwnt and arrived at the most perfect sandy cove sheltered by sandstone cliffs, which is great for snorkelling and exploring and is watched over by an ancient church. As you approach the coast through empty countryside and down miles of tiny lanes it's difficult to imagine that this area was the scene of a major twelfth-century battle. Whole skeletons are still unearthed periodically from the fields around.

Mwnt, though remote, is far from secret and popular with families, so if you're yearning for a wilder adventure, explore a few hundred yards along the coast path to the east. Here you'll find great slabs of rock that shelve into perfect pellucid seas, ideal for sea-caving and snorkelling. If you want a *really* big cave adventure though, head for the extraordinary landscape of Ceibwr Bay and the Witch's Cauldron. Twisted, contorted layers of black rock make up this remote and forbidding coastline. Deep caves and sea tunnels punctuate the headlands and 20 minutes from the main bay you'll find an open lagoon with a beach in a chasm behind the cliffs. On hot days the water is clear, green and iridescent. According to local legend the Cauldron was a sea-witch's lair and she would consume anyone who ventured in alone. Indeed, it's remarkably easy to imagine mythical creatures floating out from the catacombs and shimmering in the air. The Witch's Cauldron has three separate entrance tunnels leading you in from a rocky cove: one is a scramble down a waterfall and underground stream bed; the other two are sea caves that meet in an underground cavern. If you plan to explore, bring waterproof torches and plenty of courage.

Cardiganshire

93 Castell Bach, Cwmtydu

Grid ref.	SN360580
Postcode	SA44 6LQ (300m N)
Walk	15 min, easy
Train	Fishguard, 55km or Aberystwyth, 33km

Popular Cwmtydu beach with car park (SN356576). Shingle cove with caves. Walk NW 500m on coast path to next cove with tiny island (Castell Bach) or 1km to second cove at bottom of stream (SN 362583). Excellent Crown Inn 🍴 nearby (Llwyndafydd, SA44 6BU, 01545 560396).

94 Mwnt

Grid ref.	SN193519
Postcode	SA43 1QH (200m W)
Walk	5 mins, easy
Train	Fishguard, 27km

Remote but popular NT sandy cove beneath ancient church and rocky dome. Jumping from steep rock walls. Take B4548 from Cardigan and follow signs. Camping 🏕 (with caravans) at Ty Gwyn (01239 614518). Follow path beyond church E, 500m, to find large slab rocks descending to sea with stacks and caves.

95 Ynys Lochtyn, Llangranog

Grid ref.	SN315551
Postcode	SA44 6SP
Walk	15 mins, mod
Train	Fishguard, 50km or Carmarthen, 36km

Stunning headland with island and several secret beaches near charming Llangranog with its seafront pubs.

From Ship Inn 🍴 climb steps to follow coastal path NE. Note steps to 'secret' **Cilborth Cove** L (300m) or continue on to headland and Ynys-Lochtyn (1km). Drop down on R of headland to find steps to Traeth-yr-Yynys beach, in shadow of cliffs. Explore sea ledges and rock arches around headland if sea is calm. (Pentre Arms 01239 654345, Ship Inn 01239 654423.)

A Carreg-y-Ty (SN301535) is 1.5km SW from Llangrannog, a very remote sandy sheltered cove with a tiny island pierced by a long sea cave. At footbridge drop down R to follow stream through woods then rock scramble. Also faint path on far (SW) slope.

B Long, wild **Penbryn Sands** 1.5km further SW (SN293525).

96 Witch's Cauldron, Ceibwr

Grid ref.	SN102451
Postcode	SA43 3BU (1km NW)
Walk	20 mins, mod
Train	Fishguard, 17km

Dramatic, highly folded, cave and arch-ridden coastline. Witch's Cauldron is an inland blue lagoon accessible by land and via sea cave in calm seas. △

From Moylegrove (7km W of Cardigan) follow lane 1km to Ceibwr Bay and park on grass by sea (SN108457). Follow coast path W 1km to find lagoon (collapsed cave 'Cauldron'). At footbridge and sunken stream descend into passage by waterfall (only if you think you can climb back out again!) to reach lagoon beach. Or at LT use sea cave on R – 100m swim leads in. Or at MT, in calm seas, swim out of cove 30m and back in via inlet and arch, far R.

A From grass ledge at Ceibwr bay itself a 200m swim SW leads to the giant **Careg Wylan** (Gull Rock, SN105457) with sea cave through connected headland. A very long (100m) cave tunnel pierces next headland too at SN104456 – bring torch and wetsuit! △△

97 Diving from the old fishing platform, Pwll Deri

North Pembrokeshire: Abereiddi to Strumble Head

After a bumpy ride along twisting lanes through a landscape of scattered Neolithic remains, catching glimpses of sea through the hedgerows, we arrived at remote Pwll Deri Youth Hostel on Strumble Head. A great silvery lagoon glimmered below in the afternoon sun and we imagined Jason and the Argonauts setting sail across the Ionian Sea.

There are dramatic steps leading diagonally down the cliff-face at Porth Maenmelyn, half a mile up the coast path, but the rusty railings hang off at right angles and many of the steps have crumbled away. So we spent much of the afternoon searching for a safer way down to the water's edge. Scrambling to the top of the grassy headland lookout of Ynys Melyn, the hot afternoon sun beating down, we saw seals bobbing and kittiwakes squawking around their cliff nests. Melyn was an Iron Age fort and the remains of earthworks survive at the narrow neck leading to the summit. From there a rough goat path descends through gorse to a rocky spur and an old fishermen's ladder. The deep, silky water shifted slowly in lazy ripples and kelps in shades of purple and indigo waved below the surface. There was only the gentlest of splashes as we dived in and began exploring the caves. Once we were alongside, water gurgled through fissures along the rock base and the cliffs rose vertically from the sea.

98B

98

98A

The grandeur and remoteness of the cliffs along Strumble Head make this stretch feel like a final frontier. By complete chance this is indeed the site of the last invasion of Britain: in 1797 a motley band of French revolutionaries, intent on taking England at Bristol, were blown off course by a storm and landed at this headland some days later. Jubilant, they looted the first farm they found and couldn't believe their luck when they came upon several hundred gallons of wine stored there in readiness for a wedding party. The soldiers quickly became exceptionally drunk and incoherent and were all too easily rounded up by a group of angry farmers' wives with pitchforks.

From Strumble Head 20 miles of perfect coastline unfold to the south. The first stop is Pwllcrochan, a wonderfully remote and dramatic cove with low-tide sands, rock formations and a difficult climb down via a rope and waterfall. Aber Bach, the next inlet, at the bottom of bumpy lanes and woods filled with bluebells in spring, gives access to a set of large sea caves with walls of pink and purple rock and dark pebble coves inside. At the tiny fishing village of Abercastle we waded over to an island with a cave that runs right through its centre and makes a fantastic swim or scramble. The village is overlooked by the ancient Careg Sampson 'cromlech' or burial chamber.

West of Porthgain – a pretty harbour village with a restaurant, gallery and pub – there are more treats, including a swim through a giant arch at Porth Dwfn, the wide sands of Traeth Llyfn and finally Abereiddi's famous 'Blue Lagoon', a disused quarry long since breached by the sea to become an inland lake. The quarry's old wheelhouse provides three platforms for leaping into the deep blue abyss below – a famous rite of passage for local swimmers and visitors alike. But after a few leaps and lunch at the Sloop Inn at Porthgain, we decided to set out to explore Ynys-fach, a small islet just a mile to the north-east. From the coast path we climbed over a fence and down a steep overgrown path to a double shingle cove. A swim led round to a deep cave that extended all the way through the islet, as at Abercastle, and a path with ropes led up to the island's flat top, which was carpeted in sea thrift. Here we found the remains of a campfire and decided to sleep wild, high above the sea, the sparks from our fire flying into the dark night as we watched the stars moving gently across the sky.

North Pembrokeshire: Abereiddi to Strumble Head

97 Pwll Deri, Strumble Head

Grid ref.	SM888386
Postcode	SA64 0LR
Walk	10 mins, diff
Train	Fishguard, 6km

Rock ledge below ancient headland fort in beautiful bay surrounded by high cliffs. Caves and seals. Very 'Argonauts'. △

Follow signs for Pwll Deri from Goodwick/Fishguard, turning R at Trefasser (5km). At Pwll Deri Youth Hostel (white building, 0845 371 9536) take coast path N down hill 500m. Continue on to view Porth Maenmelyn (SM888392), with hazardous ancient stairway, or bear off L on faint path to headland (Ynys Melyn) and after 400m, at neck of headland (Dinas Mawr), bear L down gorse path, dropping to sea and iron ladder (50m). Swim 100m L to explore small caves.

A Bay S of **Strumble Head** lighthouse (Carreg Onnen, SM893421) is popular for swimming/scrambling. Work round caves and ledges 500m to S. Swim at site of last invasion of Britain at SM931405, W side of bay, 1km N of Llanwnda. △△

98 Aber Bach caves

Grid ref.	SM882353
Postcode	SA62 5UU (700m W)
Walk	20 mins, diff
Train	Fishguard, 8km

Pretty shingle cove with caves to N. △

From Goodwick A487 (dir St David's), turn R after 7km, dir Melin Tregwynt Woollen Mill. After 1.5km, at bottom of hill, turn L down dead-end wooded lane to Aber Mawr beach. Walk up coast path N 500m to Aber Bach Cove (with stream), then 300m on, past adjacent cove (Porth Dwgan), and immediately scramble down into gulley to find caves and swim around 20m N to find next larger cave with good jumps. Preseli Venture (01348 837709) run coasteering courses here.

A Pwllcrochan (SM885364) is 1.5km further N up coast path. Difficult descent to LT sands via path and rope. Waterfall. △

B Abercastle, another 4km W along coast (or via Mathry, A487) has island (Ynys y Castell) with cave that passes through middle (SM851339, SA62 5HJ). Careg Sampson on hill above R. △

99 Abereiddi Blue Lagoon

Grid ref.	SM795314
Postcode	SA62 6DT
Walk	5 mins, easy
Train	Fishguard, 17 km

Popular inland lagoon with wheel-house ruins for jumping.

From St David's follow Porthgain/Trefin road 5km, then turn L to Abereiddi beach and car park. Follow coast path 300m to N to find lagoon. Do not jump from top tower at LT. Bottom platform safe at all tides.

A Continue 1km N on coast path to large **Traeth Llyfn** beach (SM802319). Rips can develop in surf conditions – take care. △

B Another 400m NE leads to Porth Dwfn and **Penclegyr headland**. Excellent circumnavigation possible via S arch and N chasm (SM805328). △

C Continue to **Porthgain** and historic Sloop Inn 🍴 (SA62 5BN, 01348 831449). Continue 1km to view our secret island (Ynys-fach) with **cave tunnel** and camp (SM822327). No path. △

Cave arch at east end of St Non's Bay, St David's

Mid-Pembrokeshire: St David's to Druidston

The coast of St David's is home to Wales' patron saint and the location of some of its most savagely beautiful scenery. The combination of sandy coves and dramatic coastal formations is perfect for wild swimming.

David or Dewi was originally the name of a Welsh sea god. His totem, a great red serpent, was transformed over time into the Welsh national symbol, the red dragon. Up on the bare wind-blown moor of St David's Head, where fallen rocks and burial cairns lie among heather and gorse, it's easy to imagine that huge serpents may once have roamed the sea.

Below cliffs cloaked in buttercups and sea-lavender, Porthmelgan cove lies tucked into the rocks. There are sea caves in the left-hand wall but big swells here can generate rip tides along the cove edges so leave any explorations for a calm day. Neighbouring Whitesands Bay is a long sweep and a popular surfing beach. It leads down to Porthselau in the south, an excellent swimming cove with a campsite on the fields above.

The rocky promontory at the north end of Whitesands is called Trwynhwrddyn (Ram's Nose) and has a cave that passes through from one side of the nose to the other that's fun to swim through at mid-tide. It's also a good introduction to 'coasteering', a term coined back in the 1990s by TYF Adventures, a centre in St David's that runs such courses.

101A

100B

102

This outdoor pursuit is becoming increasingly popular all around Britain and is not dissimilar to coastal wild swimming. Put simply, it's a combination of scrambling along the foreshore and swimming the bits in between, but with plenty of jumps thrown in. Decked out in wetsuits, trainers, helmets and buoyancy aids, groups can go further, jump from higher up and enjoy heavier swells in locations such as the famous 'toilet bowl' at St Non's Bay, a classic coasteering venue, where large waves flush you out from between the rocks.

St Non's Bay is immediately south of St David's. I first explored this coastline in early May when primroses were growing in clumps around the delightful remains of St Non's chapel and holy well. The well water was considered particularly beneficial for women in childbirth and Saint Non, the royal princess, was said to have given birth to Saint David beside this bay in AD 500. To the far east of the bay is a sea cave with a towering, vaulted roof and a sandy floor. There are several entrances and a great skylight casts sunbeams down through the water. To the west you'll find Chanters' Seat, a series of stratified ledges dropping steeply to the sea with a deep inlet for swimming and diving. If you try, you can almost imagine a whole choir singing in praise of the ocean.

Further east at Porth Ffynnon, the purple and black triangular stacks were formed from red sandstone strata set on end. These are popular for jumping and climbing and can be accessed from below the campsite at Porth Clais. On the eastern side of Porth Clais harbour, you'll find another popular rocky swimming spot at Ogof Golchfa, a deep inlet with large shallow rock pools on either side, perfect for warming up afterwards.

The characteristic red and purple rocks of this coastline are most intense at Caer Bwdy Cove where the stone for St David's magnificent cathedral was quarried. Continue on to Porth-y-Rhaw, another remote shingle cove with islands for snorkelling, a waterfall and cave, a freshwater quarry lake, and scope for even more coasteering. There's an eight-foot-deep plunge pool here at low tide, but watch out for the keen claws of spider crabs lurking in the bottom when you jump in. If you survive all this then make for the Druidston Hotel, 10 miles to the south. Set high above the beach facing west, it's the perfect location to watch the sun go down.

Mid-Pembrokeshire: St David's to Druidston

100 Porthmelgan

Grid ref.	SM728279
Postcode	SA62 6PS (1km NW)
Walk	10 mins, mod
Train	Haverfordwest, 30km or
	Fishguard 24km

Sandy cove near popular Whitesands Bay with Ram's Nose through cave on way. In strong SW swell, rip currents can develop on cove edges. △

From St David's follow A487 (dir Fishguard) and turn L after 500m on to B4583, signed Whitesands Bay (2km). Park at beach car park and follow coast path N 1km, past Ram's Nose rocky promontory and cove to reach sandy Porthmelgan. Path continues to burial chambers of St David's Head.

A Trwynhwrddyn (Ram's Nose/ SM731273) has through cave at far end, swimmable at mid-tide but only in calm seas. △

B Porthselau is a good sheltered swimming cove at far S end of Whitesands Bay (SM727260) 1.5km by coast path or below Pencarnan campsite ⛺ (SA62 6PY, 01437 720580) off St Justinian's road.

101 St Non's Bay

Grid ref.	SM752242
Postcode	SA62 6BN (500m S)
Walk	5 mins, hard
Train	Haverfordwest, 23km

Dramatic bay, birthplace of St David and coasteering, with spectacular sea cave/ arch to E end. Many other features, but for advanced swimmers – with wetsuits and in calm seas only. △△

Leave St David's on Goat St (dir Porth Clais) and turn immediately L, signed St Non's. Park at end and walk R across field to St Non's chapel and well, then to coast path. Turn L (E), through gate and after 150m, by stream, climb down steeply to rocky inlet. Swim 250m E to cave arch (SM753242). Cliff-side Porth Clais campsite ⛺ (SA62 6RR, 01437 720256).

A Continue 400m W on coast path and, just before headland, climb down L to steep striated rock ledges and inlet of beautiful Chanter's Seat (SM748239). △

B Park at Porth Clais and 800m W on coast path, 150m beyond harbour mouth, find large LT rock pools and deep inlet of Ogof Golchfa (SM741236), popular for jumps. △

102 Porth-y-Rhaw

Grid ref.	SM786242
Postcode	SA62 6UH
Walk	15 mins, mod
Train	Haverfordwest, 19km

Rocky cove with cave, waterfall and plunge pools.

From St David's follow Solva road (A487) and turn R after 3km at Nine Wells Caravan Park. Tiny NT car park. Follow signs to cove, past lake (access to bank on far side) and find deep LT plunge pools on L side of cove, 200m steep scramble around far side of waterfall. Continue on coast path E 300m to 'Tank Bay' with steep slab and wreck remains. △

A Caerfai Bay, popular sandy cove. From St David's to Solva (A487) turn R by Visitor Centre (SA62 6QT, SM760243).

B Continue on coast path E 2km for Caer Bwdy Bay, stony bay with dramatic colours and source of cathedral stone. Check out coloured inlet of Barrel Zawn (SM769242) 300m E, popular with climbers. △

C 15km down the coast via Newgale find superb sands of Druidston Haven with pub/hotel 🍴 (SA62 3NE, 01437 781221).

South Pembrokeshire: Stackpole and Lydstep

Volcanic black basalts and rich red marls give way to silver and gold limestone as you enter south Pembrokeshire. This rock is the remains of reefs, corals and plankton that once flourished in a shallow tropical sea. Clefts and cracks in the rock make this coastline rich in caves, great arches and white sandy coves.

One such cleft on St Govan's Head hides the tiny chapel of St Govan (Gawain), a place of contemplation and pilgrimage for many centuries. A flight of worn stone steps – allegedly uncountable by mortals – leads down through the rocks to a small doorway. According to Arthurian legend Sir Gawain was being chased by pirates when a chasm in the cliffs suddenly opened up to give him an escape route. Once Gawain was safely inside, the rock face sealed itself, concealing the knight until his pursuers had given up and departed. Gawain is said to have established a hermitage here. The dim stone cell has a view of the ocean and its sixth-century altar is hewn from the cliff-face. Below, more steps lead down to the foot of the cliffs where giant boulders have fallen into the sea and sit draped in bladderwrack among jade rock pools. A holy spring reputed to cure leprosy once bubbled up from beneath the chapel.

Continuing up the coast to the east is New Quay, a deep snaking inlet that was once a narrow harbour and smuggling cove. From here it's possible to swim out to the left and around to impressive caves. A little further

109 **Draught sands**

107 **Swanlake Bay**

104B **Broad Haven sands**

along is Broad Haven, a popular and beautiful National Trust beach with Church and Star rocks out in the bay. Fields stretch right down to a couple of tiny coves just to the south of the beach and the farmer is happy for tents to be pitched here if you don't mind fairly basic facilities.

The tide ran a quarter of a mile inland from Broad Haven until the first Baron Cawdor dammed the tidal creeks during the eighteenth century and created a large freshwater lake system, the Bosherston Lily Ponds, which are covered in white lilies in early summer. Keep still and silent and you may catch sight of an otter in the pools along the banks.

If you are feeling adventurous, there are several dramatic swims between Broad Haven and Barafundle Bay. One of the best is at Confucius Hole, a huge crater that fills up into a great blue lagoon with each tide. In calm seas you can enter via a sea cave in the sea cliffs, though this is only accessible at low tide. Just to the left is the narrow chimney cave of Confucius Hole – a name bestowed on it by 'deep-water solo' climbers who love to scale its interior without ropes, knowing that if they fall there is deep water below them. It makes an exciting swim, too.

Further along is Sandy Cove, a totally inaccessible beach with caves and sand but no route down. Behind it is Sandy Pit, another great crater, filled with sand not water, which was once connected to the beach. The passageway is now blocked so we swam into Sandy Cove from a rock ledge on the inside of the south headland. It was a tricky scramble down followed by a 150-yard swim through beautiful crystal waters. Landing on this fabulous deserted beach and wading ashore in the bright sun was like being Robinson Crusoe for a day, washed up on a desert island.

Continue walking and beautiful Barafundle Bay comes into view, with its lovely dunes and woodland. Clamber down to the end of the headland to find three fantastic natural arches with Gaudi-esque spires supporting them. Rutted and puckered, the extraordinary formations continue underwater and the effect is like a sunken gargoyle-covered cathedral. Barafundle was once voted the most beautiful beach in Britain and from here the intrepid might like to try coasteering around to the north and east to Stackpole Quay, checking out the massive Lorts Cave on the way. If you've managed all this, a well-earned cup of tea awaits at the National Trust café, or you may be in need of something stronger at the recommended Stackpole Inn.

Just a few miles to the east, at deserted Swanlake beach, we enter red sandstone country. Thousands of foxgloves cover the headland in June, creating a sheet of purple that moves in the warm breeze. There are deep crimson grooves in the rock here and a remote, basic campsite in the field above the bay. It's only a mile to medieval Manorbier, where you'll find a Norman castle with a warren of corridors and cells, a church and an ancient dovecote. You might even agree with Gerald of Wales – whose famous twelfth-century book *The Journey Through Wales* is still in print – who describes this village as 'the pleasantist place in Wales'.

Follow the coast path on past King's Quoit, a Neolithic burial chamber dating from around 3,000 BC, to Presipe Bay. Steep steps lead down to this dramatic tidal beach, with shallow sandy pools in the hollows beneath the chine. Further on, the scenery reverts to rocky limestone at the adjacent coves of Skrinkle Haven and Church Doors, where striated pillars have created an abbey-sized archway. The steps to Skrinkle collapsed in 2008 but you can still access this superb beach via a tunnel from Church Doors at low tide. You can also swim around the dividing rock buttress, though it's further than it seems as Skrinkle's beach is lower and the waterline is further back.

More dramatic scenery awaits you at the last beach on this stretch: the multiple coves and caves of 'Draught'. At low tide a wide sweep of sand allows you to paddle around immediately to the right into various arched caverns with dramatic ceilings and rutted floor formations. Immediately to the left is a narrow cave with a long chamber leading to a skylight opening at the end. If the tide is up and the sea is calm, these make wonderful snorkel routes. But take care if there is any swell because the beach is very rocky. At low tide there's a chance to explore on foot or swim from the pure shore sands, laid out like fresh snow with a dramatic backdrop of caves.

103A **Broad Haven crater**

105 **Barafundle Beach**

104 **New Quay**

105 Barafundle Beach rock arch

South Pembrokeshire: Stackpole and Lydstep

103 Sandy Bay, Broad Haven

Grid ref.	SR983942
Postcode	SA71 5DR (2km E)
Walk	15 mins, diff
Train	Pembroke, 8km

Excellent family beach with stacks and freshwater pool. Coast path leads to inaccessible Sandy Bay with secret tunnels and deep lagoon formed from collapsed cave. △△

From Pembroke follow B4319 (dir Castlemartin, Bosherston). After 4km turn R and through Bosherston, then L to Broad Haven NT car park (£3). Cross beach (E) then 300m E on coast path to Sandy Bay. Tunnels from bottom of Sandy Pit behind are blocked. Instead swim in from small promontory (SR984941) – a tricky descent on R face of bay between the cove and Saddle Point headland.

A Massive **lagoon crater** (collapsed cave) on cliff edge 100m E from Broad Haven (SR982940). Feasible to swim/scramble in via cave below at LT, by swimming off steep rocks below L. Or swim 50m L to find Confucius cave with chimney. △△

104 New Quay, St Govan's

Grid ref.	SR975931
Postcode	SA71 5DR (2km S)
Walk	15 mins, mod
Train	Pembroke, 8km

Narrow sandy inlet with caves close to famous St Govan's chapel in cliffs.

From Broad Haven car park follow coast path 1km SW to the sandy snaking inlet. Caves 50m to N (L) , swimmable. △

A Continue 700m across headland to **St Govan's Chapel**. Possible to descend to rocks and swim (SR967929) in calm seas. △

B At S end of **Broad Haven** beach (SR977936) find tiny sand coves. Fields above are open for basic camping in summer (Trevallen Farm ⛺ use toilets at car park). St Govan's Country Inn 🍽 in Bosherston is an excellent pub with hearty food and real ales (01646 661311).

C Continue on Castlemartin Road (B4319) and turn L across ranges to view Elegug Stacks and Green Bridge of Wales. Also Flimstone and **Bullslaughter** bays, 1km E, connecting to St Govan's (5 km).

105 Barafundle Beach arches

Grid ref.	SR993948
Postcode	SA71 5LS (700m S)
Walk	20 mins, diff
Train	Pembroke, 7km

Beautiful undeveloped Barafundle Beach, one of the best beaches in Wales, backdrop of woods and dunes. Good for families. Leads to Lorts Cave or to triple rock arch. △

Approach from W via Broad Haven (2km walk). Or park to N at diminutive Stackpole Quay (1km walk) by turning off B4319 from Pembroke before Bosherston and passing through Stackpole village. From beach scramble/swim N to explore massive **Lorts Cave**. Or walk to S end of beach, up through woods and 300m along cliff, past Griffith Lorts Hole to find triple rock arch. Drop down via steep rock scramble on beach (N) side of arches and swim off rocks – calm seas only.

A Stackpole Quay is popular for jumping at HT (SR994957). Overlooked by NT café Boathouse Tearoom 🍽 (01646 672672) or walk up to excellent Stackpole Inn 🍽 (01646 672324) in Stackpole village. △

108 Presipe Bay

106 Church Doors

Grid ref.	SS081974
Postcode	SA70 7TT (500m E)
Walk	5 mins, easy
Train	Manorbier, 2km

Small cove with dramatic Church Doors arch and secret cave tunnel through to spectacular Skrinkle Haven beach with further impressive caverns. △

From Tenby A4139 turn L for Manorbier B4585 after 6km. After 800m turn L (dir Skrinkle Haven Hostel/Royal Artillery Range) and proceed to army gates (700m). Turn L and continue 1km on concrete road, past Manorbier Youth Hostel (modern building, 0845 371 9031) to curve round on to large concrete hard standing/picnic area. Walk back (W) along coast path 400m to find metal staircase down to Church Doors cove. At LT small cave tunnel on R allows access to Skrinkle Haven, via gulley scramble. At HT access via 150m swim is possible, even in swell, though it's further than it seems. At near (E) end of Skrinkle find large vaulted cavern with skylight to explore. Old stairs at W end of Skrinkle are now impassable.

107 Swanlake Bay

Grid ref.	SS046980
Postcode	SA70 8QP (200m SE)
Walk	20 mins, mod
Train	Manorbier, 3km

Remote sandy bay, 2km walk W of **Manorbier** on coast path or via West Moor Farm. Take steep lane out of Manorbier by beach, L at crossroads, L into farm after 1.5km, park then bear L (E) to bay. Farm has a tea room. East Moor Farm △ also does basic camping in field above bay (turn L before West Moor).

108 Presipe Bay

Grid ref.	SS069970
Postcode	SA70 7TT (700m W)
Walk	15 mins, mod
Train	Manorbier, 2km

Tidal beach with interesting rock and sand pools. Park at artillery range gates (see swim 106, for directions). Bear R across fields, following camp perimeter, bearing L down hill and R along top of bay to descend via steep steps at far (W) end. Shallow sand pools at far end of beach.

109 Draught sands and caves

Grid ref.	SS087976
Postcode	SA70 7TT (1km E)
Walk	10 mins, mod
Train	Manorbier, 2km

Part-sandy tidal beach with spectacular rock arches and hidden cavern. △

From Church Doors car park (see swim 106) head E on coast path for 500m, dropping down into steep valley leading to narrow rock and sand cove on R (Draught or Church Cove). To immediate L is narrow but long tidal cave with skylight at far end. To R are two large rock arches with caverns. At HT in calm seas it is possible to swim from rocks to explore both, but beware submerged boulders. At LT sand is revealed and it's possible to explore caves on foot and swim from beach, even in swell.

A Continue 2km along coast, to far N end of Lydstep Haven beach, to find interesting cave with skylight on coast path N of Lydstep Haven, 500m E of beach end and 400m before **Proud Giltar** (SS099986). Difficult scramble down. △△

Bluepool Corner giant rock pool, low tide

Gower and Glamorgan

We reached Gower's Bluepool late that afternoon, the cliffs bronze-tinted in the summer sun and a glinting sea pulling at the sand as the tide began its ebb. The great rock pool stood like a perfect tub beneath us while the Three Chimneys cave arches marked the furthest reach of the bay.

This is one of the best plunge pools in Britain, scoured out of the rocks by wave-driven eddies that tumbled giant cobbles in its depths. Myself and a friend had been given a tip-off about its location. We arrived on mountain bikes, threw them into the long grass and scampered down the rocky path to join a group of teenagers who were practising somersaults into the dark purple waters. I eased myself in and swam around for a while, 'plumb lining' to try to calculate the depth. But I couldn't touch the bottom so I joined the others and they showed me how to do a back flip.

If you make it to this lesser-known beach, tucked away at the top end of Rhossili Bay, you can also enjoy a swim in the surf and explore the Three Chimneys rock arch and caves, in which gold moidores and doubloons – Portuguese and Brazilian gold coins from an eighteenth-century shipwreck – can still be found. Adjacent is one of Gower's two ancient Culver Holes; when this one was excavated the remains of 30 bodies dating from the middle of the Bronze Age were found inside.

You soon realise that Gower is an ancient region, riddled with sacred monuments, standing stones and caves. It even boasts King Arthur's

112 **Brandy Cove**

110 **Bluepool Bay**

stone, a 6,000-year-old dolmen sited above a holy well. This limestone peninsula, extending out into the sea from the valleys of Wales, has remained a world apart and is steeped in its own legends and curses. Indeed Rhossili Bay is the site of what many consider to be the most haunted house in Britain, the Old Rectory, built in a desolate spot equidistant between the two churches it served, and surrounded by the sea and dunes. Even respected broadcaster Wynford Vaughan Thomas remarked that inthe depths of winter, 'something very unpleasant comes out of the sea and into the house'.

The day was drawing to a close as we left Bluepool with our bikes. We needed to find somewhere to wild camp for the night, so we headed south down the bay, pausing at the Old Rectory but moving rapidly on. We had considered Burry Holms, a tidal island with the ruins of a medieval monastic settlement where Gower's patron saint, St Cenydd, came to pray, but the tide hadn't been low enough to cross. So we pushed on to the famous Worm's Head, a giant serpent-shaped tidal promontory that marks the most westerly tip of Gower. Its name is derived from *wurm*, the Norse word for dragon.

By the time we arrived the tide was low enough to cross and we made the half-mile clamber through seaweed and jagged rocks to reach the steep grass slopes of the Inner Head, just before Devil's Bridge rock arch and blowhole. This was a favourite retreat of Dylan Thomas who came here to write poetry and explore. On one occasion he fell asleep, became stranded by the tides and spent a night alone on the Worm, consumed with fear, his imagination conjuring up all sorts of terrors. We, at least, were not alone, but sleep was fitful and we spent a rather uncomfortable night propped up against boulders to stop us rolling down the hill and into the sea. I woke periodically to listen to the waves in the blowholes and watch the gossamer-like Milky Way pass across the clear sky of a midsummer night.

By seven o'clock the sun was up and we roused ourselves with a dip before clambering back to the mainland to retrieve our bikes. The day was heating up nicely so we headed for Fall and Mewslade Bays, perfect sands beneath craggy golden cliffs encrusted with pinnacles

'I stayed on that Worm from dusk to midnight, sitting on that top grass, frightened to go further in because of the rats and because of things I am ashamed to be frightened of. Then the tips of the reef began to poke out of the water and, perilously, I climbed along them to the shore.'

Dylan Thomas

and tiny tors. The approach to these little-known beaches is via a
hidden valley near Pitton. From here the south coast unfolds: miles of
great rock slabs appear to be piled on top of each other and thrusting
upwards at an angle of forty degrees. The rock crevices are pitted with
neolithic caves, forts and chambers; in Paviland Cave the body of a
24,000-year-old Stone-Age hunter was discovered in 1823. South of
Port Eynon you'll find another Culver Hole, a smuggler's retreat fortified
with walls, windows, floors and staircases. At one stage it was owned
by the notorious John Lucas, head of the local smuggling dynasty.
These remote coves – and others nearby such as Pwlldu Bay and
Brandy Cove – were used to store contraband destined for the markets
of Swansea. Salt House was another old smugglers' retreat. Salt was
indeed produced there but it served principally as an armoury and
lookout to warn against approaching customs officers.

116 Traeth Mawr

113 Culver Hole

Pennard Castle, a legitimate military defence, is now a spectacular
ruin above the famously scenic Three Cliffs Bay. A small settlement
with a church grew up around the castle but was abandoned in 1532
when the inhabitants were overwhelmed by sandstorms. The Pill
meanders below, a beautiful river that opens out in a wide arc through
the sand before running into the sea. The headland has three peaks
above a natural sea arch. To the left is Pobbles Beach and to the right
Tor Bay, both good swimming beaches.

114 Three Cliffs, Tor Bay

Gower is without doubt the jewel in the crown of the south Wales coast
but there are many other places worth exploring too, especially during
the summer holiday period when the lanes and approaches to Gower
can become heavily congested. If you have enough time, make a detour
to visit the majestic Glamorgan heritage coastline south of Bridgend,
where the cliffs are composed of stacked limestone strata and flat
limestone pavements stretch into the sea. Monknash makes a perfect
base: from here a stream with a ruined mill leads to the vast beach of
Traeth Mawr, while back in the village the atmospheric Plough and
Harrow Inn, built from the ruins of the adjacent monastery, specialises
in real ales and ciders from the West Country. With a fire roaring in the
inglenook, this is the ideal spot to dry wet socks and towels and warm up
after a very long day of swimming.

Gower and Glamorgan

110 Bluepool Corner

Grid ref.	SS409931
Postcode	SA3 1JP (1km W)
Walk	20 mins, diff
Train	Swansea, 27km

Deep rock pool in corner of sandy tidal bay. Popular for jumping but difficult descent. Rock arch and nearby island.

From Swansea take A4118, then R on B4271 to Llanrhidian, then L on lanes to Llangennith (25km). Pass King's Head pub, over mini roundabout, on to Burrows Lane to reach Broughton Farm Caravan Park (2km). Park before gate and walk into and through park, bearing L and on to coast path. After 1km Bluepool Corner bay is directly below with pool at near (E) end about 3m deep for jumping. Tricky scramble down. LT only.

A Continue on path to **Burry Holms** tidal island with ruined hermitage. Swim from N facing beach (SS402927). **Llangennith** beach (N end of Rhossili Bay) stretches to L, good for surfing. Culver Hole and Three Chimneys rock arch/caves accessible to R (W) at LT, connecting to Bluepool Bay.

111 Mewslade Bay

Grid ref.	SS421871
Postcode	SA3 1PL (1km S)
Walk	15 mins, easy
Train	Swansea, 30km

Pretty valley walk to remote sandy LT cove. Dramatic cliff path on Fall Bay.

From Swansea take A4118, then R on B4247 at Scurlage, dir Rhossili village after 25km. After 4km turn L in Pitton and then immediately R on track to park in field (L) by farm. Walk 800m along stream valley to Mewslade Bay with LT sand.

A Continue on 1km hike W along coast path, up and down, to **Fall Bay**, sandy at LT. Drop down slightly early (300m E of Fall Bay) to inspect the Giant's Cave (SS415872), a favourite with climbers. It's possible to swim from the rocks on a calm day. △

B Further adventures to be had on the tidal island of **Worm's Head** (take great care when crossing). Devil's Bridge is a dramatic rock arch (SS389877). Strong N–S tidal currents at headland. Outer Head is a bird reserve so keep to rock edges. △△

112 Brandy Cove

Grid ref.	SS586874
Postcode	SA3 3BU (300m SW)
Walk	10 mins, easy
Train	Swansea, 11km

A remote, tiny smuggler's cove close to busy Caswell Beach. Rocks for jumping at HT. Sand at LT. Spectacular path leads on to remote shingle Pwlldu at bottom of delightful woodland walk with stream.

From Swansea and The Mumbles take the B4593 to and through Caswell. Leaving the beach the road bends sharply R at top of steep hill (1km). Park here (difficult) and follow footpath to Brandy Cove (on L) or continue 800m, bear sharp L, then after 300m, as road bears sharp R, turn L down cul-de-sac. Park at end and follow track/footpath down to cove.

A Pwlldu (Black Pool, SS576871) is a sand and shingle cove 1km walk W from Brandy Cove. Or access via Widegate (turn R down narrow lane by church at Pennard, on B4436 before Southgate, 4km W of Mumbles). Walk down L through woods, to follow stream 1.5km to beach.

113 Culver Hole

Grid ref.	SS465846
Postcode	SA3 1NN (500m SW)
Walk	30 mins, diff
Train	Swansea, 27 km

Fortified cave in cliff, accessible at LT. Limited swimming. Park at beach car park in Port Enyon (terminus of A4118 from Swansea). Take coast path (S) past campsite 700m to reach Salt House ruins. Bear R and climb headland over to stony Overton Mere Bay (700m), passing top of Culver Hole halfway. Drop down into bay and trace route back along rocky foreshore. Rope climb leads to entrance. Inside slippery stairs lead to cave levels. △

114 Three Cliffs – Tor Bay

Grid ref.	SS528878
Postcode	SA3 2HJ (800m S)
Walk	10 mins, mod
Train	Swansea, 16 km

Park by road in Penmaen (A4118). Take field track SE 1km across cliffs to Three Cliffs, or bear R halfway, dropping down to Tor Bay and Nicholaston Burrows.

115 Three Cliffs – Pobbles

Grid ref.	SS539877
Postcode	SA3 2DH (1.5km W)
Walk	20 mins, easy
Train	Swansea, 15 km

Beautiful bay with three-peaked cliff and tidal sea arch. River and stepping stones. Popular but never feels too crowded. Rip currents develop by river channel in rough conditions so take care. △

From Black Pill in Swansea turn R at Woodman Pub and follow B4436 (6km) to Pennard, then to Southgate (2.5km). Park by Three Cliffs Coffee Shop 🍴 (food menu, 01792 233230). If LT drop down steep path to find Fox Hole cove (SS553871) or follow main path W 2km to Three Cliffs, dropping down on broad walk through dunes to Pobbles Beach in front of cliffs to find arch.

A Alternative scenic route from Parkmill (A4118, near Penmaen) along top of **Pennard Castle** and valley. Park by shop (Shepherds), cross road and stream, bear R then climb up through wood. Excellent views from campsite (Three Cliffs Bay, Penmaen, SA3 2HB, 01792 371218 ⛺).

116 Traeth Mawr, Monknash

Grid ref.	SS901709
Postcode	CF71 7QQ (1.5km W)
Walk	25 mins, mod
Train	Llantwit Major, 7km

Woodland walk leads to tidal sands beneath remote cliffs with limestone pavements. Part naturist. Also good cliff walks to nearby St Donat's and Marcross.

From M4 J35 follow A473/A48 (dir Bridgend) 6km, at 4th roundabout bear L B4265 (dir Llantwit Major). After 6km Monknash is signed R. Continue 4km to find Plough and Harrow 🍴, ancient pub in village and once part of medieval monastery. Huge fireplaces. Excellent ales and cider (01656 890209). Turn R and park at end of lane by farm. Continue to end of lane, bear L over stile and follow woodland path 1km to beach. Bear R (N) 1km to find best LT sands.

A Merthyr Mawr's massive sand dunes lead 2km to beach. Park at Candleston Castle car park (SS872772, CF32 0LS). Take lane S off A48, Bridgend). Or via stepping stones at Ogmore Castle (B4524).

North

The famous Northumberland coast has some of the grandest, wildest beaches in Britain, bordered by ancient castles and holy islands. To the south the extensive dunes and skyscapes of Lincolnshire and Cumbria contrast with the dramatic caves at Flamborough Head and the high cliffs of the Yorkshire Moors. Here you will find secluded wykes, goblin holes and stories of *Count Dracula*.

North Highlights

123–4 The dramatic chalk cliffs of Flamborough Head are puckered with caves and tunnels, including huge sea caverns you can explore on foot.

126 Deep in the woods beneath the old railway station you will find waterfalls running down to Hayburn Wyke, a remote rocky bay clad with jungle-like foliage.

127 Boggle Hole and Stoupe Beck Sands are quiet coves near Robin Hood's Bay with its quaint red fishing village built up the hillside.

128 At Runswick Bay the long stretch of sand has a backdrop of high cliffs with 'Hob Hole' caves – old hobgoblin lairs.

129 Literary Whitby was home to Captain Cook and Bram Stoker's *Count Dracula*.

130 Skinningrove is a run-down old mine village. It attracts few visitors but has a stunning beach and an amazing old pier.

132 Visit the King of Piel with his pub and ruined castle on Piel Island.

133 This remote sand beach on the north coast of Walney Island has a deep tidal pool overlooked by Black Combe in the Lake District.

136 Cross the tidal causeway and visit Holy Island (Lindisfarne), birthplace of Christianity in England.

137 Take a refreshing dip in one of the many beautiful rock pools near dramatic Bamburgh Castle's beach.

140 Football Hole cove is set between two of the most beautiful bays in Northumberland. The nearby Ship Inn serves excellent crab sandwiches.

141 Dunstanburgh Castle is one of the most haunting ruins on the coast and is close to Craster village, famous for its seafood.

136 Holy Island
138
A
Bamburgh Castle
A
Craster
B
Alnwick
B
Warkworth A
142
C
Newcastle Upon Tyne

137
139
140
141

129
A 130
A
Middlesbrough

128
A
Whitby
127
A
126
125
Scarborough

122
123
A
Bridlington 121 A 124

120
Grimsby

119
A
118

Skegness
117

Lincolnshire and Humber

Lincolnshire, famous for its vast skies and endless beaches, is the site of Britain's first official cloud-spotting station, complete with parabolic mirrors, roof-top loungers and 'cloud-bar' menu. There are also dunes and wildflower meadows galore at Gibraltar Point and Theddlethorpe.

When the Cloud Appreciation Society was established in 2005 few thought it would develop such a cult following. With a manifesto pledging to fight the banality of 'blue-sky thinking' it aims to rekindle an appreciation of Britain's clouds and skyscapes. What better place than Lincolnshire – where endless fens merge with marine horizons inspiring painters and stargazers alike – to take a disused beach hut and construct a rooftop observatory. Anderby Creek is one of five beach access points along the surprisingly empty stretch from Skegness to Mablethorpe. Here, at this rather jaded and low-key coastal spot, you'll find a larch Cloud Bar. Instead of stools there are sky loungers, instead of a cocktail menu there's a cloud menu. Choose a cloud you'd like to see, grab yourself one of the parabolic mirrors on hinges then lie back and search the sky until your chosen cloud floats into view above you.

This isn't the only wacky venture to take root on this coast. In 1936 ex-showman Billy Butlin established Britain's first seaside holiday camp here, and it's still going strong. More recently, in Mablethorpe, the Bathing Beauties' Festival was established: not a pageant for

117 **Path to Gibraltar Point**

118 **Remote Wolla Bank**

117

beautiful bodies but a line-up of beach huts, with cabins and shacks of all kinds celebrated here every year.

For simpler pleasures Gibraltar Point Nature Reserve offers rare seasonal flowers such as yellow lady's bedstraw, cowslip and the tiny white, meadow saxifrage. Flocks of migrating birds also gather here: up to 10,000 dunlins at a time may break from their migration, descend from the clouds and come to feed upon the shore. The sea here is shallow but when you run out through the breakers – the huge expanse of the Wash to the south, dunes and meadows behind – you're reminded of the immensity of nature and the vast tracts of open space still left in Britain.

To the north at Theddlethorpe St Helen there are more dunes and an undulating beach with deep, wide furrows, so the depth can vary quite suddenly and rips can develop in rough conditions. It's best to swim here at low tide when large sandy bathing channels emerge, or on a rising tide as the channels fill from the sea. The dunes extend for five miles and are prettiest in midsummer when the sea buckthorn bushes bear golden berries and the sea pea forms violet carpets. In spring, whitethroats and linnets breed in the hawthorn scrub and skylarks nest on the saltmarshes. And at night the rare natterjack toads begin to search for each other with loud booming calls.

Looking north towards the Humber Estuary, it's almost possible to make out the southern tip of Yorkshire – Spurn Head, a low, narrow three-mile spit of beach and shingle growing inexorably south-westwards into the sea. Gaining several yards per year by 'recycling' material eroded from further up the coast, it represents a perfect balance between destruction and deposition. A toll road snakes through the dunes and marsh flats, there is a beach with groynes on the east-facing side, and at the very tip of the spit are two abandoned lighthouses. This location, right out at sea, is a windy place on most days and once in the water you can feel the pull of the swell tugging you southwards. But when the sun is shining and the surface of the sea lies flat and reflective, the huge expanse of water and sky all around you is humbling.

Lincolnshire and Humber

117 Gibraltar Point

Grid ref.	TF568583
Postcode	PE24 4SU (1.5km E)
Walk	20 mins, easy
Train	Skegness, 5km

4km of fine, wild sandy beach with gently shelving sea close to Skegness. Accessed via a long walk over nature reserve with dunes and ponds.

Enter Skegness from Boston, A52, and at train station gyratory take exit for sea front, then turn R after church (700m) into Drummond Rd. Continue straight (S) out of town for 4km, via Gibraltar Rd, to end of golf course. Park in the beach car park (L), 1km before visitor centre. Follow path past mere and lagoons, over Mill Hill, and down to sands. Some L–R cross-shore current in surf conditions. **Δ**

Home to huge numbers of breeding, wintering and migratory bird species often in vast flocks; also natterjack toads and pyramid orchids. The visitor centre includes the Wild Coast exhibition, Nature Discovery Centre, gift shop and the Point Café **⑪**, open every day 11–4 (Tel 01507 526667).

118 Anderby Creek

Grid ref.	TF552761
Postcode	PE24 5XT
Walk	2 mins, easy
Train	Skegness, 16km

An 8km stretch of undeveloped coastline accessed via breaks in the sea wall. Fine sands, some dunes and good swimming. Wolla Bank is the most remote.

Continue N of Skegness (A52 coast road) past Butlins and Ingoldmells, and turn R into and through Chapel St Leonards after 7km. Follow Skegness Rd, Church Lane, St Leonard's Drive to Chapel Point, 2km, with its greasy-spoon Point Café by beach (01754 871670, PE24 5UZ). Continue N on coast road 2km to remote **Wolla Bank** beach (TF557750). Continue 1.5km for Anderby Creek and cloud bar for sky-gazing (parabolic mirrors and loungers on top of a larch-clad hut).

A Sutton-on-Sea and Mablethorpe host the annual September **Bathing Beauties' Festival** dedicated to beach huts and sea bathing (www.bathingbeautiesfestival.org).

119 Theddlethorpe

Grid ref.	TF490884
Postcode	LN12 1NW (1km E)
Walk	10 mins, easy
Train	Skegness, 16km

Sands with wood, heath and dunes behind, popular with horse-riders. Some channels cross the beach to create warm tidal pools but depth is uneven. Seaward currents on the outgoing tide, and rips in surf conditions. **Δ** Safest on rising tide. Take A1031 N from Mablethorpe. After 4km reach Theddlethorpe and turn R (Sea Lane) then R again (Crook Bank) to remote parking, 1km.

120 Spurn Head

Grid ref.	TA408117
Postcode	HU12 0UG (1.5km N)
Walk	2 mins, mod
Train	Hull, 45km

Extraordinary, wild 8km-long sand and shingle spit growing into mouth of Humber. Strong currents run S down shore in surf conditions so don't swim from S end. From Hull take A1033 to Patrington, then B1445 to Easington. Toll road to lighthouse. **Δ**

Inside the Cathedral Cave, North Landing

Flamborough Head and Filey Brigg

Protected by high cliffs, deep caves and steep coves Flamborough Head – literally the 'dart-shaped headland' – has long been a place of defence and retreat.

An ancient earth wall and ditch still leads down through woody glades to the sheltered, chalk-pebbled beach at Danes Dyke – a relic of King Ida's Viking invasion of the seventh century. Today the area is a popular holiday destination with caravan sites and beach car parks, but don't be put off. If you persevere you will soon discover its celebrated wild caves and archways.

It was an early summer evening when I first visited. The cliff walls of Thornwick Bay are riddled with numerous dark caves and I decided to reach one by swimming across the bay. Through the calm ripples, the chalky reef beneath me was casting a blue light amid the turquoise haze. As I swam nearer, seaweed forests floated in the water below and the cave walls loomed up, displayinmg pastel-pink and white hues, streaked with green algae. I began to explore, half in the water and half out of it, like some primordial wading creature. I counted eight caves along this cliff wall and, peering into their dim recesses, partly illuminated by shafts of light, I realised the caves were all interconnected and formed a labyrinth of deep passages that was, sadly, too dark and cold to explore.

123A

124

121

Flamborough Head has more cave habitats than any other place in Britain and some extend underground for more than 50 yards. It also has some of the largest populations of nesting birds: gannets, guillemots, kittiwakes, puffins, razorbills, fulmars, herring gulls and shags gather on the sides of the sheer cliffs around Bempton and Scale Nab rock arch, a few miles to the north. From Thornwick Bay an eroded coastal footpath leads out on to adjacent Thornwick Nab, a headland of rock platforms and ledges now pitted with thousands of glinting rock pools. The chalky rock here, laid down millions of years ago, is composed of the corpses of trillions of tiny white-shelled sea creatures that lived in much warmer seas.

At North Landing, the next cove towards the head, a steep slipway leads from the café and car park to a pebble beach. More than 80 fishing boats – known locally as 'cobbles' – used to operate from this cove, though today's boats are mainly used for pleasure trips. The bay boasts around 20 interconnected caves and many, unlike those at Thornwick Bay, are accessible on foot at low tide. The most impressive among them is Cathedral Cave, a short scramble of about 100 yards along the right-hand edge of the bay. The entrance leads into the back of a massive cavern, which then shelves down to a large, arched opening facing out to sea.

Selwicks Bay, another mile down the coast path, is a popular bathing spot with a lighthouse and various cafés. To the right of the bay a scramble and swim leads to a cavern with a blowhole, formed when the roof of the sea cave collapsed. Further to the south, a few hundred yards along the footpath, is High Stacks, an isolated headland with a sea arch that is almost a stack.

The tidal currents can be ferocious in the open sea around Flamborough – the headland serves to 'funnel' the tidal flows. If you aren't a strong, experienced swimmer stay within the relative safety of the bays and coves since these are protected from the currents. If you choose to venture out under the cliffs chose a neap tide and go when the tide is on the turn. Remember that the tide flows from the north as it is rising (the flood), and from the south as it is lowering (the ebb). Do take care.

122 Arch on Filey Brigg, accessible by boat

Flamborough Head and Filey Brigg

121 Danes Dyke

Grid ref.	TA216691
Postcode	YO15 1DW (500m S)
Walk	15 mins, mod
Train	Bridlington, 5km
Cycle	Route 1

Walk through woods along ancient defensive dyke to sand beach with large white cobbles. 3km E of Bridlington on Flamborough Rd (B1255), signed on R. Or 3km walk from Bridlington N sands. Adjacent **South Landing** (TA231693, YO15 1AG, South Sea Rd) is signed on R from Flamborough village. Lifeboat-station shop. Sand and chalk cobbles.

122 Filey Brigg

Grid ref.	TA132815
Postcode	YO14 9ET (1km NE)
Walk	25 mins, diff
Train	Filey, 1km

A dramatic, narrow headland descends to many rock ledges and pools. Δ Follow signs for North Cliff Country Pk from Beach Rd. Very difficult LT scramble along base of N cliffs leads to 'Black Hole' and rock arch. Strong tides so boat support advised. ΔΔ

123 North Landing

Grid ref.	TA239721
Postcode	YO15 1BJ
Walk	4 mins, mod
Train	Bempton, 6km
Cycle	Route 1

A popular white chalk cove with HT sand, LT pebbles. Giant Cathedral Cave on R of bay to explore on foot.

Return to Flamborough village and follow signs to North Landing (2km) and park by café. There are plenty of rock pools and caves to explore on L but largest cave is on R, after first inlet (50m) beyond arch. The smallish cave entrance leads through to a major cavern with access out to sea. Strong tidal races operate along this shore, only 30m out to sea, so be careful if you decide to swim from here back to the bay. ΔΔ

A Thornwick Bay, 700m walk to the NW (TA233724), is also riddled with caves, particularly on E side. Walk around to Thornwick Nab, the eroded headland of pyramids to L, to find rock arch plus many ledges and inlets for swimming. Adjacent Little Thornwick cove also has a tunnel.

124 Selwicks Bay

Grid ref.	TA255708
Postcode	YO15 1AR
Walk	5 mins, mod
Train	Bempton, 8km
Cycle	Route 1

Pronounced 'Selix', this bay has rock pools galore plus several secret coves, tunnels and caves. Very strong tidal races, particularly at the headland. Δ

From Bridlington follow signs to Flamborough (B1255, 5km) and Flamborough Head (3km, B1259) and park by lighthouse. On the foreshore head L to far (N) end of beach and scramble round into deep inlet cove with further tunnel out to sea. Further swims/scrambles around the headland and many more coves. Watch out for tidal currents and take care. ΔΔ At the near (S) end of beach a LT scramble (HT swim) leads to a cave with skylight (100m) and further on to a series of ledges with deep water below.

A Return to coast path and explore 500m to the S to find **High Stacks** (TA259705) with arch. Descend via path and steps on S side. Beware tidal races here, choose slack water, neap tides only. ΔΔ

North Yorkshire: Scarborough and Robin Hood's Bay

Scarborough, the great Yorkshire resort that introduced sea bathing and the bathing machine, is the gateway to a dramatic coastline of high cliffs, goblin coves, rocky bays known as 'wykes', and the perfectly picturesque old smuggling village of Robin Hood's Bay.

Cloughton Wyke is one of the area's most secret and verdant coves and can be found just a few miles north of Scarborough down a narrow, dead-end lane. A short walk leads to a stream, and then a steep path descends into a rocky bay with a backdrop of steep cliffs and vegetation. Water drips from the deeply layered, fern-covered rock face and huge green boulders mark the site of past cliff falls. On a calm day the water is clear and it's a quiet place to snorkel among the ledges or look for the fossils of ammonites, sea-lilies and fish-lizards, for which this Jurassic coast is well known.

About two miles to the north, Hayburn Wyke, a wider bay, is hidden beneath a wooded valley and a double waterfall. Bracken and mistletoe run rampant on the slopes above and when the sea is calm this is a magical place to swim and admire strata upon strata of sandstone, mudstone and ironstone laid down through Yorkshire's various geological incarnations – desert, river basin, forest and ice sheet. The old railway station above the Hayburn Wyke Hotel was a minor stop on the Scarborough to Whitby railway line, now a stunning cycle route.

127A

126

126 Robin Hood's Bay

Old rolling stock in the sidings was turned into self-catering 'camping coaches' for holidaymakers with fresh eggs supplied by the local farmer. The coaches proved so popular with families that camping continued until well after the railway line eventually closed.

This whole area attained its peak of popularity in Victorian times, but Scarborough first attracted tourists in the early seventeenth century when a local naturalist discovered mineral springs, which then featured in Dr Wittie's 1660 book on British spas. Soon health-conscious bathers were venturing on to the sands and into the sea as well. Over the next 200 years doctors continued to promote the health benefits of sea bathing, which they recommended was performed naked so the skin could more readily absorb the water's beneficial qualities. An entire industry grew up around bathing machines, attendants and operators. Bathing was considered particularly good for chest infections and the young Anne Brontë took the waters on numerous occasions to improve her deteriorating health. During the Victorian era the resort flourished. Bathing for leisure replaced bathing for health, bathing suits replaced bathing machines and, when Scarborough was finally connected to York by railway and the Grand Spa Hotel opened (at that time one of the biggest hotels in the world), Scarborough became the undisputed queen of British watering holes, even surpassing its celebrated southern rival, Brighton.

Such was Scarborough's success that developers were keen to open hotels and create new settlements along the shore. To the north at the vertiginous Ravenscar Cliff, the highest point on the Yorkshire coastline, a plan was laid out for an entire resort with views over Robin Hood's Bay and its tightly packed smuggling village. (This Robin Hood wasn't the legendary hero from Sherwood Forest but a local name given to forest spirits and elves who were said to inhabit the wooded cliffs, coasts and coves.) The investors, however, pulled out, fearful of potential cliff erosion and ground instability, and the secluded woody beaches of Stoupe Beck Sands and Boggle or 'Goblins' Hole still remain likely places to meet the tree sprites. Walk a mile or two beneath the cliffs at low water from Robin Hood's Bay village or drop down on country lanes from Ravenscar to Stoupe Beck Sands. You can swim from the sand or snorkel around the rocky ledges, with the pretty red-tiled village making a perfect backdrop.

Remote Cloughton Wyke, near Scarborough

North Yorkshire: Scarborough and Robin Hood's Bay

125 Cloughton Wyke

Grid ref.	TA020950
Postcode	YO13 0AT (1km SE)
Walk	15 mins, diff
Train	Scarborough 8km
Cycle	Route 1

Remote bay with cobbles and rock ledges, set among foliage-covered cliffs on beautiful coastline. Swimming only in calm water owing to rocks. Tricky path down to bay with rope. △

7km N of Scarborough on A171 reach Cloughton village. Take small turning to R (Newlands Lane leading to Salt Pans Road) by Cober Hill Education Centre, at the junction with Ravenscar Rd. Follow this road over bike path down to small parking area (1km). Descend on foot to coast path (200m). Faint remains of salt pans on the rock ledges are on L. Turn R and follow coast path 500m to find stream flowing down to Cloughton Wyke. Follow path down stream, using chains to help you down slippery ledges. Rocks in water make getting in tricky. Explore far R of bay to find ledges good for snorkelling and diving. Cycle Route 1 follows the old railway along coast from Scarborough to Whitby.

126 Hayburn Wyke

Grid ref.	TA012971
Postcode	YO13 0AU (700m E)
Walk	20 mins, mod
Train	Scarborough, 11km
Cycle	Route 1

Stony bay set beneath jungle-like foliage with double waterfall – good for a splash. Beautiful walk down from hotel through glens. Swimming only in calm seas owing to rocky beach. △

7km N of Scarborough on A171 reach Cloughton village. Turn R by Cober Hill Centre on to Trattles Hill. After 2km turn R down steep lanes to the Hayburn Wyke Hotel 🍽 (01723 870202). From car park turn L to rear of hotel, through yard with old barn, and down track to gate to pick up footpath, bearing R through field and over a style into NT woodland (200m), and path down to sea (500m). Continue on Ravenscar Rd 6km to Raven Hall Hotel ≈(YO13 0ET, 01723 870353) where you can have an expensive drink with great views of **Robin Hood's Bay**, its historic and touristy village namesake at the far end, 15km back via the A171, B1447, or 5km walk via **Stoupe Beck Sands**.

127 Boggle Hole

Grid ref.	NZ955041
Postcode	YO22 4UQ
Walk	10 mins, mod
Train	Whitby, 13km
Cycle	Route 1

Small, sheltered sandy cove at the bottom of a wooded valley. Wave-cut platform for snorkelling and swimming. △

From Cloughton follow A171 N for 7km, then turn R at crossroads 1km past Flask Inn. Descend lane for 4km and park. Continue on foot to Boggle Hole Youth Hostel (0845 3719504) and cove. Walk L under cliffs at LT to reach perfectly preserved **Robin Hood's Bay** (1km) including delightful Laurel Pub 🍽 (01947 880400). Turn R to reach **Stoupe Beck Sands** (1km). Mill Beck Farm △ (where you parked) does very basic camping (no shower or toilet) in their field down the track.

A Stoupe Beck Sands can also be reached by steep, narrow lane from Raven Hall Hotel. Leave hotel and take second R down lane at windmill. Continue 3km to farm car park, then 300m down path.

130 Skinningrove jetty, with Cattersty Sands behind

North Yorkshire: Whitby, Runswick and Skinningrove

A night-time cliff-top walk among the graves and ruins of Whitby Abbey may well have inspired Bram Stoker to write the celebrated story of *Count Dracula*, who survives a shipwreck and is washed up on the sands below.

In the book, the mystery ship *Demeter* is later recovered but the log shows that members of its crew have been gradually disappearing since the ship left Varna in Russia. Further examination of the ship's hold gives the reader an insight into the shipwrecked Count's dark passions: it is full of coffins. Is it a coincidence that a few years before Stoker wrote the book a ship, *The Demetrius*, ran on to the rocks near Whitby harbour and its cargo of coffins tumbled into the sea?

Other writers have also been inspired by Whitby. Melville's *Moby Dick* is set during the town's whaling boom in the late eighteenth century and you still pass through a whalebone arch when you enter it. The famous seafarer, Captain Cook, also lived and sailed from here. Today Whitby's sands are enjoyed by thousands of tourists, but leave the crowds behind as you head out to the wide, wild sweep of Runswick Bay. The village of the same name has a delightful and popular family beach with a fine café, but fewer people visit Kettleness at the southern end of the bay, reached by walking down winding narrow lanes past a remote chapel and farm. Here, the slippery mudstone and silvery-blue shale cliffs shimmer in the evening light, feathers of

Whitby Abbey ruins

129

129A **Staithes**

rock extend in an arc out to sea, a steep path leads down to the sands and a network of rough trails fans out across a lunar plateau bearing the scars of old alum mine workings.

Between the seventeenth and nineteenth centuries alum was one of the most important industrial chemicals in Britain, and was used to tan leather, make paper and dye fabric. One hundred tons of cliff shale had to be mined to extract a single ton of alum powder and the unpleasant process involved relentless kiln firing and then further treatment with pungent-smelling human urine. Local inhabitants supplied urine by means of a night-time jar system and stocks were supplemented by public urinals in Hull and London.

From Kettleness you can walk north towards Runswick Bay and pass the 'Hob Holes'. Said to be inhabited by hobgoblins, these are the remnants of tunnels from ancient mine workings for jet, a semi-precious stone that became popular when Queen Victoria wore it in mourning. More mine holes can be found beneath the high cliffs of Boulby via the sand and reef beach at Hummersea, beyond Staithes. The finest swimming, however, is at decaying Skinningrove, another struggling mining community. Apparently, the village sits on top of more than 200 miles of old iron mines, many of them sites of catastrophic mining accidents. You can still explore some tunnels with the help of a guide, but beware, they are considered the most haunted mines in Britain.

More heartening is the superb and little-known bay at the bottom of the village – Cattersty Sands – with clear water and an old jetty built by the Skinningrove Iron Company in 1886 for loading ore on to steamers bound for Middlesbrough. Long since abandoned, the jetty is in good repair and adventurous swimmers can dive off it and swim in the deep water. There are plans to re-open the jetty as a visitor attraction, but funds have not yet been found. There's an air of decay about the whole of Skinningrove, but if you swim on a calm hot day you can see rippled sand beneath shimmering clear water that is as blue as the Mediterranean. On such days when local boys sail through the air as they practise their swallow dives, the place is vibrant again, its raw beauty a reminder of an industrial past long gone.

128 Kettleness Sands beneath old alum workings

128 Kettleness

Grid ref.	NZ830158
Postcode	YO21 3RY
Walk	15 mins, diff
Train	Whitby, 10km

Sand beach and rock scars beneath remote cliffs. Superb views of Runswick Bay.

Leave Whitby W on the A174 through Sandsend and up hill. Turn R into lane just after the village of Lythe (6km). Pass through Goldsborough (quirky bistro-pub Fox and Hounds 🍴, 01947 893372) and bear R for the tiny village of Kettleness (1km). Park at bottom near Kettleness Farm. By bench bear L on path through long grass (not the coast path) down on to headland with landslips and mine workings. After 300m find v steep path L down landslip to beach. Rope provided for final descent.

A Back on main road (A174) continue on to **Runswick Bay** village, a charming old-fashioned beach resort (TS13 5HT). Walk 500m S on sand, beyond sailing hut, to explore **Hob Holes**, the old mine tunnels and caves (NZ815155).

129 Hummersea

Grid ref.	NZ727201
Postcode	TS13 4JH (500m NE)
Walk	15 mins, diff
Train	Saltburn, 9km
Cycle	Route 1

Sandy stretches among rocky ledges and scars. Dramatic, remote location under Boulby cliffs. △

Continue on A174 past Runswick Bay, past historic Staithes (3km), and turn R after 2km at Boulby, up hill dir Upton. After 4km turn R at the T-junction. Pass through Hummersea Farm and park by gate on L (200m). Follow track to coast path and steep NT steps to beach. A new 'gut' was blown through the rocks here to allow a sandy passage to the sea for boats. Explore R 1km beneath cliffs to find old gut. Both provide access to the sea for a swim. There are old alum mine tunnels along the cliff base further along.

A On road between Staithes and Runswick Bay, **Port Mulgrave** is a ruined harbour. Turn R at Rosedale Lane behind church at the N end of Hinderwell. Park by telephone box (NZ799177, TS13 5LH).

130 Skinningrove jetty and sands

Grid ref.	NZ713206
Postcode	TS13 4BJ (300m NW)
Walk	10 mins, easy
Train	Saltburn, 7km
Cycle	Route 1

Beautiful sands hidden behind one of Yorkshire's most run-down villages. Big ruined jetty – excellent jumping. △

Leave Loftus, dir Brotton A174, and turn R for Skinningrove. Pass the Cleveland/Tom Leonard Mining Museum on R (haunted tunnel tours TS13 4AP, 01287 642877). Pass through village to reach beach car park with tractors, 1km. The jetty (300m) has deep, clear water over sand. Go to far end to find rusty steps down to water in R corner – difficult but not impossible. Eerie but exciting venue, though watch out for old metalwork and uncovered hatches. Jetty good for fishing. (NB Access directly from Hummersea beach by turning R down hill when leaving Hummersea farm).

A Cross to far side of jetty to find **Cattersty Sands**, an immaculate stretch of little-known beach (NZ710205).

Looking to Sandscale Haws and Black Combe from Scarth Channel

Cumbria and Lancashire

Cumbria may be celebrated for its mountainous interior but its vast coastline is well worth visiting. Moody and expansive, its beaches look out to the west and are truly glorious when sunsets fill the sky, outlining the dramatic peaks to the east.

Many love the silver, stone beaches and oak-clad shores of quaint Arnside on the estuary of the River Kent, a resort seemingly ignored by tourists heading lemming-like to the Lakes. The beach here is a mixture of sand and silt, and you'll see local people by the quay 'tickling' for flatfish with their bare feet or wallowing in the warm pools left by the outgoing tide. The peninsulas here border the sand and marsh flats of Morecambe Bay, so you need to beware of strong currents and shifting mud, especially if you venture far out on to the sands. The tide sweeps in so fast at Arnside that its arrival is heralded by a siren. The best place for a dip, however, is just below Grubbins Wood at high tide, or just under the trees at New Barns.

Heading north why not stop at Cartmel for some celebrated sticky-toffee pudding and a brief visit to the ancient priory before making for Walney Island. This 20-mile-long beach reef protects the port of Barrow-in-Furness. At the south end you'll find Piel

131

135 From Ravenglass to Drigg dunes

132

Island, empty save for a pub and a ruined castle. The publican is known as the 'King of Piel' and runs a small campsite and ferry service. I decided to swim across from the lighthouse and nature reserve at Walney's south end by crossing Bass Pool on a rising tide. It was a rather miserable day and the pub wasn't open when I arrived so I'd be inclined to recommend the north end of the island, North End Haws. There's no bar or local monarch but it is a truly remote isthmus of dune hills, freshwater ponds and smooth sands. The waters of the Scarth Channel snake in and around it, offering opportunities for a remote dip whatever the tide, and there are grand views out over the Duddon estuary to the whale-backed Black Combe mountain beyond.

Opposite is Sandscale Haws, another great swath of estuarine dunes. The best route to the wide estuary is via Roanhead. You can swim in the Duddon Channel with care – preferably at low and incoming tides – but if you'd prefer to swim in the open sea then make for Silecroft, on the opposite shore, which is considered to be one of the region's very best beaches.

Seven miles up the coast you'll come to the attractive estuary of the Esk at Ravenglass. This is the terminus for a steam railway that will take you up to Eskdale, one of the best wild swimming rivers in Britain, with its legendary Tongue Pot pool beneath Scafell Pike. Take your bike on the train, explore, cycle back down, then enjoy a pint in the upmarket lounge bar at the Pennington Hotel as you watch the sun go down over the estuary. Or, if you are adventurous, wade across the channel at low tide and make for Drigg Point, where a thousand acres of untouched dune unfold and a white desert-island shoreline extends four miles up to the village of Drigg. This area is a nature reserve and an important breeding site for the rare natterjack toad, so the dunes are out of bounds. Otherwise, this is a perfect, wild-camping beach, a place to lie awake by the moonlit dunes, snug in your sleeping bag, waves lapping on the sands and toads croaking in the dunes. This is a place to contemplate the enormity and magnificence of the universe, the bright gossamer of its galaxies above you stretching out to infinity over the endless sea.

Cumbria and Lancashire

131 Arnside

Grid ref.	SD442779
Postcode	LA5 0BN
Walk	2 mins, easy
Train	Arnside, 3km
Cycle	Routes 6 and 90

HT swim on the shingle mud banks of the Kent estuary, Morecambe Bay. Follow B5282 into and through Arnside, bearing L up hill and turning R into Red Hills Rd, becoming New Barns Rd. Continue until you reach caravan site and find shingle beach under oak trees to swim at HT. △

132 Piel Island, Walney

Grid ref.	SD230627
Postcode	LA13 0QN
Walk	15 mins, mod
Train	Barrow-in-Furness, 10km

The Ship Inn 🍴 (07516 453784), a castle, some camping and the 'King of Piel' are all you'll find here. Ferry from Roa Island peninsula (A5087 6km S of Barrow) or swim 200m across muddy tidal Bass Pool, 1km E of South Walney Reserve Visitor Centre (via South End caravan park, 3km S of Biggar, LA14 3YQ). LT on flood only. △△

133 Walney Island, north

Grid ref.	SD182737
Postcode	LA14 3YR
Walk	60 mins, mod
Train	Barrow-in-Furness, 5km

Remote north end of island. Just dunes, pools and the dramatic backdrop of Black Combe. △

Cross on to Walney Island and turn R after bridge on to the Promenade. Turn L in North Scale, 1.5km, into Cows Tarn Lane and park at beach at Earnse Point (1km). Walk N up beach 4km to reach North End Haws and tidal Scarth Channel for swim.

A On opposite bank are huts and shingle on Lowsy Point, and **Sandscale Haws** Nature Reserve. Access off A590 4km N of Barrow; turn L opposite Steeles Removals or, 1km further, turn L into Oak Lee Rd, then L again to car park. Swim only on rising tides owing to seaward channels on ebb. △

B Continue straight on after Walney bridge for **central beach** running 2km S. Turn L at beach to Biggar (3km), South End (3km), through caravan park to lighthouse and eventually the visitor centre for **Piel Island**.

134 Silecroft

Grid ref.	SD121810
Postcode	LA18 4NY
Walk	2 mins, easy
Train	Silecroft, 1km

Long stretch of sand under Black Combe. 12km SW of Broughton-in-Furness on A595. Turn L to Millom (A5093) then immediately R to Silecroft. Miners Arms 🍴 with accommodation (01229 772325).

135 Drigg

Grid ref.	SD065956
Postcode	CA19 1XR (2km W)
Walk	30 mins, diff
Train	Drigg, 1km
Cycle	Route 72

10km v wild remote beach 5km S of Sellafield. 20km N of Millom (A595) turn L for Drigg B5344, then L for beach (2km). Walk L 2–5km for huge dune system. Or adventurers can wade the LT river Esk from pretty Ravenglass (Pennington Hotel 🍴 CA18 1SD, 01229 717222) to reach the wildest S end dunes of Drigg directly. Also terminus of Ravenglass and Eskdale Mountain Railway, (01229 717171). △

Ross Bank Sands

North Northumberland: Holy Island

Our first experience of Northumberland was from the magnificent cycle route that snakes along much of this wild north coast. Equipped with just a lightweight tarpaulin we planned to bivouac in the dunes, gather driftwood and then cook our supper on the beach.

We were three lads – old school friends from way back – and were accompanied by Ciaran's little dog, travelling in a cycle trailer. Our first destination was Holy Island (Lindisfarne) and after hours of cycling across bog in an impenetrable wet mist, we only just managed to make it across the water before the tide enveloped the Island's causeway. The rising waters were lashing greedily at the road edge as we pedalled on, wet seaweed lay jettisoned on the tarmac and great barnacled waymarks loomed through the cloud. The sky was clearing to the west, though, and after a recuperative pint of ale at the Island's only pub we struck out across the hillocks of the interior to find little-known Coves Haven, a remote north-facing beach with red sandstone caves at its back, where we hoped to find shelter.

The rain had eased when we set up the bivouac on the bluff. Low rays of twilight started to break through the mauve-grey clouds

136

136

139

casting an auburn glow on to the beach below. Hot and tired, we dropped the bikes and tumbled down the sandhills on to the beach. Diving into the wildly rolling surf we were tossed about in the swell, shrieking with delight while the dog scampered about madly on the sand. Exhausted and bedraggled after that first night's fantastic swim on Britain's holiest island, we felt cleansed: this had been our ritual baptism into Northumberland.

Holy Island is the site of the ancient monastery, built entirely of wood, that St Aidan of Iona founded in the seventh century. The monastery became the centre of Christian learning in England and was the birthplace of the celebrated, exquisitely illuminated Lindisfarne Gospels. From here St Cuthbert set sail to the nearby Farne or 'retreat' islands to live in a cell and commune with the seals on the seashore.

The great king who helped the monks re-introduce Christianity to the region was King Oswald of Northumbria. His impressive castle, Bamburgh, lies just a few miles to the south, past the silvery glimmer of Ross Bank Sands and Budle Bay. It sits on a high basalt bluff rising out of grassland and moor. The current superbly fortressed building, a predominantly Victorian rebuild, was constructed around Saxon and Norman ruins. Its chain rooms, from where wrecks were regularly hauled in to land, are a reminder of the vicious nature of the sea hereabouts.

The stunning beach below Bamburgh stretches for three miles. It's a great place to have fun in the breakers but there is also a string of more sedate natural swimming pools to the north among Harkess Rocks. A local map displayed on the cliff helps identify some of them: Half Moon is crescent-shaped and warms up quickly on a sunny day; Gun Pool and Spark Plug Pool are narrow channels into which the swell charges; Egg Pool – large, oval and deep depending on how much sand has been washed into it – was the best place to learn to swim, according to older residents. Look north to Holy Island Castle and south to Bamburgh Castle and marvel at the seemingly endless sand and dunes between. Come here to wallow in the breaking rollers and watch the storm clouds pass by.

Bamburgh Castle Sands

136 Coves Haven, Holy Island

Grid ref.	NU127439
Postcode	TD15 2SJ
Walk	30 mins, mod
Train	Berwick-on-Tweed, 26km
Cycle	Route 1

Little known sandy bay on N side of atmospheric and spiritual Holy Island (Lindisfarne). Dunes, crags and castles. Where the monks came to stand and seek inspiration above roaring seas.

Turn L to Holy Island off A1, 18km S of Berwick. Continue 8km, across the tidal causeway and into Holy Island village. The causeway is not passable 2hrs either side of high tide (www.northumberlandlife.org/holy-island). Turn L 50m after the Ship Inn 🍴 (01289 389311), head to end of lane (300m) and proceed on farm track 1km. At field end head out on to dunes keeping same bearing due N to come to Coves Haven. Best sand is at N end of beach. We slept out on the grassy heath above the cove. On return stop at the delightful churchyard of St Mary and adjacent priory ruins. Visit castle and admire upturned boat sheds on the harbour bay.

137 Bamburgh Castle Sands

Grid ref.	NU180356
Postcode	NE69 7DD
Walk	5 mins, easy
Train	Chathill, 12km
Cycle	Route 1

Superb beach with dunes in front of iconic castle. Rock pools beyond.

12km S of turning for Holy Island, beyond Belford, turn R on to B1342, dir Bamburgh. Continue 5km, past magnificent Budle Bay L, to descend into charming Bamburgh village with massive castle. Turn L after village green down Wingdings, towards golf course. After houses on R (300m) find two car parks for beach.

A Continue along golf course road further 300m and park in lay-by (R). Posters by lighthouse explain the names of the **Harkess Rock Pools** – natural LT plunging pools. Continue on 200m to dip and test them (NU172361). Depths vary according to the amount of sand blown into the pools by storms. Temperatures reach their warmest during the afternoons LT. Continue on 500m to **Budle Point** sands.

138 Ross Bank Sands

Grid ref.	NU147377
Postcode	NE70 7EN (2km E)
Walk	30 mins, easy
Train	Chathill, 19km
Cycle	Route 1

Between Holy Island and Bamburgh. A spectacular stretch of pristine dunes and white sands. 4km S of Holy Island turn L, dir Elwick. Over level crossing, continue 3km and turn L at telephone box. Park on roadside (L) before Ross Farm (self-catering, 01668 213336). Follow track through farm and over grassland 2km to beach. 1km S leads to **Budle Bay** sands.

139 St Aidan's Dunes

Grid ref.	NU211329
Postcode	NE68 7RD (500m N)
Walk	10 mins, easy
Train	Chathill, 19km
Cycle	Route 1

S of Bamburgh 4km find St Aidan's dunes and Monk House Rocks on L. Continue on to **Seahouses** 1km for **Farne Island** boat trips (01665 721088) and well-loved Olde Ship 🍴: real ales and cosy rooms (01665 720308).

141 Dunstanburgh Castle, Embleton Bay

South Northumberland: Beadnell, Embleton and Druridge

Our Northumberland cycle expedition picked up again beyond Seahouses at a tiny pub on the edge of empty Embleton Bay. The salt spray blowing in on a light midsummer breeze added the perfect seasoning to our lunch of crab sandwiches and ale.

The Ship Inn, low-beamed and cosy, sits in a whitewashed square of eighteenth-century fishermen's cottages at Low Newton. Anchors and seafaring memorabilia adorn the houses and a little green runs straight down to the fine sands. The offshore rocky reef had given us an opportunity for some swimming, despite the big rollers. In calmer seas this bay is also very good for snorkelling. After our excellent lunch we walked up to Newton Point and swam again in the wonderful secret cove, Football Hole. No one could explain the origin of the name, but we were so taken with it we had an impromptu kick-about with some jetsam anyway.

Afterwards we lay in the meadows for a while, surrounded by pink sea thrift and giant daisies, watching black-backed gulls soar and dive in the wind and listening to the song of willow warblers. From this point Beadnell Bay lies to the north and Embleton Bay to the south; both are owned and protected by the National Trust. We cycled to Embleton and explored the fantastic fourteenth-century Dunstanburgh Castle – the largest ruin in Northumberland – a squat, impressive hulk with a huge gatehouse perched on an outcrop above the beach.

140 **Football Hole**

141A

141B

Wide grass downs link Dunstanburgh to Craster. We explored the rocks on the way, finding a large plunge pool, its water deep and purple-tinted. This is a good place for jumping. There are flat rocks for sunbathing and you can collect big, tasty mussels from the low-tide rocks. Nearby Craster is said to produce the best kippers and oak-smoked salmon in the north, and connoisseurs recommend the seafood at the the Jolly Fisherman. As evening fell, we pushed on and camped a few miles south under the trees at remote Sugar Sands. The moon rose over a calm sea as we made a small fire to bake our freshly caught shellfish, cooking them quickly among the embers. The next morning we washed in the brook before making for Warkworth, where a fabulous Plantagenet castle stands above the village. The castle mound is at the bend of the pretty River Coquet, which is a good size for swimming. Its clean, clear water meanders around an interesting outcrop where you'll find a hermitage with a series of rooms and a tiny chapel hewn by hand from solid rock. Here, a poor hermit prayed day and night for the Earl of Northumberland, for which he was paid £15 and a barrel of fish per year. You can swim over to the hermitage on the far side of the river or pay the ferryman to row you across and show you the interior.

We spent our last afternoon and evening exploring Druridge Bay, probably the loneliest of Northumberland's wild beaches and a stopping-off point for thousands of migrating birds. There we collected shiny black ingots of sea coal that had been washed up on the shore from the open coal beds that lie on the seabed. The distant chimneys of the Alcan aluminium works glowed on the horizon, the last vestiges of the region's once-thriving mining industry. Following the colliery closures of the 1980s the signs of deprivation are clear: vandalised housing estates that sit isolated among the fields, a nearby prison complex, and, more worryingly for us, a set of throwing knives lying on the sand, miles from anywhere.

Our driftwood and sea-coal fire kept our spirits up that night as we huddled under a star-filled sky. At one point a police helicopter buzzed down, its giant floodlight searching the desolate expanses and fixing on our camp. But the night passed without incident and the next morning, fire resurrected and sausages browning nicely, I sprinted down over dewy grass and soft sand flats to roll around in the bright white surf, the empty bay extending for miles into the bluest mid-morning sky.

142 Wild and isolated Druridge Bay

South Northumberland: Beadnell, Embleton and Druridge

140 Football Hole

Grid ref.	NU241256
Postcode	NE66 3EW (1km N)
Walk	25 mins, easy
Train	Chathill, 10km
Cycle	Route 1

Hidden sandy cove between two spectacular sandy bays – Beadnell and Embleton. Traditional fishermen's cottages in square now owned by NT.

9km N of Alnwick on A1 turn R on to B6347 (dir Christon Bank), then after 4km straight on to B1340 and after 2km, R across B1339, on to lane. Continue 2.5km, bearing R down hill to old fishermen's hamlet of Low Newton with Ship Inn 🍴 (01665 576262). Pub offers sandwiches, real ales and live folk music. Swim from beach outside pub – several rocky reefs make for good snorkelling and also shelter the beach. Follow coast path L (NE) 1km out to Newton Point and 700m around to Football Cove.

A Continue on from Football Cove 1km N to beautiful **Beadnell Bay** and tiny Beadnell harbour 3km (NU234286). Or walk S to **Embleton Bay** and Dunstanburgh Castle.

141 Dunstanburgh Castle

Grid ref.	NU247225
Postcode	NE66 3DT
Walk	2 mins, easy
Train	Chathill, 9km
Cycle	Route 1

Wide sandy Embleton Bay beneath dramatic Dunstanburgh Castle ruins.

From Newton take B1399 S to Embleton (2km) and turn L on last road opposite church (dir Craster) then L after 300m to Dunstan Steads and park at end near beach. Continue 2km S of Castle across rolling grassland to **Craster**, for Robson's kippers and oak-smoked salmon (01665 576223) and the Jolly Fisherman's 🍴 crab sandwiches (NE66 3TR, 01665 576461).

A 500m before Craster look out for small rocky inlet L off path with LT **plunge pool** (NU259206).

B 4km S of Craster on coastal path, between Howick and Howdiemont sands find **Sugar Sands** wooded sand cove with stream and pool (NU259163). Or on road via Longhoughton (B1339, 6km S of Embleton), lane L opp church then 300m N.

142 Druridge Bay, Hadston

Grid ref.	NZ274981
Postcode	NE61 5BX (1km S)
Walk	10 mins, easy
Train	Widdrington, 6km.
Cycle	Route 1

Perhaps Northumberland's most remote beach, partly a nature reserve.

5km S of Amble (A1068), pass Hadston and the Druridge Bay Country Park (good freshwater lake for swimming) and after 1km take next L down dead-end road, 1.5km, and park. A path leads to the R through dunes on to the middle of Druridge Bay (500m) with a low dune hill to the R.

A 6km N **Warkworth** is an outstanding medieval castle with riverside hermitage (rowing boat access or swim) 1km upstream and good beach 1km downstream (NE65 0XB, NU257064).

B 5km further N **Alnmouth** also has an excellent beach (NE66 2RJ, NU251107).

C 4km S of Druridge come to **Cresswell** beach (NE61 5LA, NZ29496) with home-made ice cream, try the 'blue cloud' flavour!

Scotland

The beaches of many of the Hebridean Isles wouldn't look out of place in the Seychelles, so fine and white are their sands. The west coast sports spectacular mountain and island backdrops, from Wester Ross right up to Cape Wrath in the far north. On Skye and along parts of the Aberdeenshire coast, volcanic rock has formed caves, rock pools and arches that are absolutely perfect for adventure swims.

Cape Wrath

A

164

B

A

B

163

Durness

Loch Laxford

Isle of Lewis

B

A

162

Loch Assynt

B

158

Ullapool

A

159

B A

160

A

South Harris

161

A

Gairloch

157

Dunvegan

154

The Quiraing

A

155

Portree

156

A

Loch Torridon

B

Applecross

Isle of Skye

153

B

Cuillin Hills

152

A

South Uist

Lossie

Inverness

Rum

149

151

A

Eigg

Arisaig

148

150

A B

Ardnamurchan

Coll

147

A

Tiree

Mull

Oban

144

A

143

B

A

C A

A

146

Jura

145

Islay

Glasgow

Edinb

Mull of Kintyre Arran

roats

165

The Hebrides

6 A B

Banff A 167 Fraserburgh

169

Peterhead

168

Newburgh A

Aberdeen

Stonehaven A

171

170

h

172

Berwick

A

A 175

143 & 146 The south-west coast of Mull has some of the best icing-sugar coves in Britain, yet few people know about them.

144A Giant Fingal's Cave on Staffa island is an awe-inspiring amphitheatre of towering basalt columns into which you can jump and dive.

148 Sanna Bay is the western-most point of the British mainland and its white-sand beach overlooks the isles of Eigg and Rum.

151 The famous beach scenes in the film, *Local Hero* were shot here, at Morar.

152A Delve into Spar Cave on Skye's coast to find the deep Mermaid Pool.

154 The coral beaches near the Isle of Skye's fairy castle are made from the twisted shapes of petrified algae.

156 This waterfall at remote Applecross cascades through plunge pools into the sea.

158 Swim overlooking 'Anthrax Island' – Gruinard Island – now safe and decontaminated.

159 At Luskentyre, the Outer Hebrides' most famous stretch of white sands, the water glows azure blue even on overcast days.

163A A four-mile walk leads to Sandwood Bay with its giant stack. Many make the pilgrimage to this, Scotland's wildest beach, though other stunning beaches lie nearer.

164 Looking out towards the arctic on the far north coast, Smoo Cave is a large sea cavern with a range of dramatic coastal arches and pools.

165 Papa Stour off Shetland has sea-cave tunnels that stretch under the island, from one side to the other.

168 Visit the ruined church in the Sands of Forvie – all that remains of this 'cursed' village. The rest still lies buried after a nine-day sandstorm.

144A Fingal's Cave, Staffa

Mull, Iona and Argyll

Mystical Mull has perfect white sand and swimming coves galore, yet few people ever find them. You can also snorkel into the cathedral-like vaults of Fingal's Cave and visit tranquil, sacred Iona – one of the sunniest places in Scotland.

My first experience of wild swimming was at Fidden campsite. Tufted grass ran down to an islet-studded bay and the dying sun seemed to be setting the distant archipelago on fire. I took a shallow dive into this great iced cocktail and swam down to touch the rippled grooves of sand along the shallow seabed. That night we made a fire in the dwindling half-light and sang songs under the stars on the beach.

Fidden is a perfect base for exploring the best beaches of the Ross of Mull. The uninhabited island of Erraid is accessible at low tide by a sandy causeway and has a beautiful cove on its south side. It was used as the shore station and stone quarry for the building of one of Scotland's most impressive lighthouses, Dubh Artach, 16 miles offshore. Life for the lighthouse keepers was harsh: living conditions were cramped and the sea was fierce, with 100-foot waves a regular occurrence, even in summer. One keeper became so desperate to escape that he even attempted to swim ashore. Robert Louis Stevenson, Scottish author and son of the famous lighthouse-building brothers who engineered Dubh Artach, visited Erraid several times and his heroic Scottish novel *Kidnapped* is set here.

To the east of Fidden an old road leads through birch and willow scrub, and past one of Mull's oldest oak trees to Tireragan, an abandoned

146 **Kilvickeon and Garbh Eilean**

143A **Traigh Gheal**

146 **East of Uisken**

settlement where crofters collected seaweed, and where you'll find several very remote white beaches. This is a perfect place for wild camping. There are many more coves along this multi-coloured shore where the granite is pink, the sand looks like white icing-sugar and the water is duck-egg blue. Uisken's steep crimson outcrops provide diving platforms for plunging into sandy-floored channels of luminescent turquoise water, while Garbh Eilean, the 'rough isle', is a beautiful dome on a perfect arc of sand.

For many, though, Iona is the main attraction. From this sacred island settled by St Columba in AD 563, Christianity spread throughout much of Scotland and northern England. Its ancient abbey, destroyed by Vikings in 794, was rebuilt as a Benedictine Monastery in 1203 and pillaged again during the reformation. It is the burial place of many early Scottish kings. Iona is a place for quiet reflection, with sweeping views of the ocean and the great Ardmeannach escarpment.

From Iona there are regular boat trips to Staffa, an uninhabited island composed of giant basalt columns similar to those at the Giant's Causeway in Ireland. It is the site of the famous sea cave, Fingal's Cave, or Uamh-Binn – 'the melodious cave' – in Gaelic. Inside, the hexagonal stones rise up like organ pipes to the ceiling and plunge down into incredibly clear depths. The acoustics in this natural sound chamber inspired one of Mendelssohn's overtures and the cave attracted visitors from Wordsworth and Turner to Queen Victoria.

After several days on the Ross of Mull and Iona we followed the spectacular mountain coast north, skirting Loch Scridain, rising over Ben More and dropping perilously into Loch Na'keal. We stopped to bathe and swim at Eas Fors, a series of plunge pools that cascades down through rowan-clad glades over a dramatic waterfall to the sea loch below. Finally we arrived at Calgary, a great bay by a tiny settlement with a superb farmhouse restaurant and hotel. The sands here are white and the water is shallow. It's a place where, on sunny days, children can learn to swim in safety among shoals of tiny fish. A little further round on the coast path you'll find the abandoned quay, constructed from giant pink granite blocks and a good place for jumping as long as you check the depth of the water.

144 Traigh Bhan on Iona, to Eilean Annraidh

Mull, Iona and Argyll

143 Fidden

Grid ref.	NM302215
Postcode	PA66 6BN
Walk	1 min, easy
Train	Oban, 59 km + ferry

Spectacular west-facing bay overlooking archipelago and Iona.

Turn L (S) before the pub at Fionnphort and find simple beachside campsite ⛺ after 2km – small fires on beach with sunsets over Iona (01681 700427).

A Turn L at Fidden farmhouse and continue down lane 3km. At large barns before Knockvologan farm gate see small 'walks' sign and leaflets. L. Leads 4km through reclaimed woodland to abandoned **Tireragan** village and remote wooded cove of **Traigh Gheal** (NM340173).

B Walk through Knockvologan farm, down track 500m to sandy bay and islets and LT crossing W to Stevenson's **Erraid** with Traigh Gheal to S (1.5km, NM295195).

C Bushwhack 1km S, around headland from Knockvologan to tiny **Traigh a Mhill** (NM313185) with dunes.

144 Traigh Bhan, Iona

Grid ref.	NM294261
Postcode	PA76 6SW (1km N)
Walk	30 mins, easy
Train	Oban, 59km + ferry

White sand beach on northern tip of Iona. Follow main road N to abbey and continue 1.5km, bearing R through gate by the basic hostel (01681 700781). Also **Camas Cuil an t-Saimh** ('Bay at the Back of the Ocean/NM263243) on W side, by golf course, with coves to N.

A Fingal's Cave (NM324351). Great jumps from basalt columns. 3hr ferry trips from Iona/Fionnphort (01681 700358). △

145 Kilbride Bay, Bute

Grid ref.	NR960669
Postcode	PA21 2BW (3km S)
Walk	20 mins, easy
Train	Gourock, 41km + ferry

Remote, mystical, wide and shallow bay overlooking Arran. Take Ardlamont road S of Millhouse. After 3km, before white house, take track on R turning L after Lochan, 1km. (Near Kames, A8003, B836 from Dunoon.)

146 Uisken

Grid ref.	NM398188
Postcode	PA67 6DT (800m E)
Walk	20 mins, diff
Train	Oban, 51km + ferry

From Fionnphort turn R in Bunessan. 4km leads to sleepy Uisken. Bushwhack E over headland to discover five sheltered coves.

A Turn R 700m after Bunessan (Scoor House). Continue 3.5km, past loch, up track, parking near ruined church. Track R over and down to superb **Kilvickeon** beach (NM411187) and Garbh Eilean.

147 Calgary Bay

Grid ref.	NM373513
Postcode	PA75 6QU
Walk	1 min, easy
Train	Arisaig, 67km incl. ferry

White sands and old granite jetty 1km along N shore for jumping. Wild camping area and toilets. Farmhouse Hotel 🍴 with rooms and smart meals (01688 400256).

A 15km S on B8073 stop for swim at spectacular cliff-top plunge pools **Eas Fors**, (NM445423, 3km N Oskamull).

202 Sanna Sands with Rum on the horizon

Ardnamurchan, Morar and Eigg

The breeze whistled through acres of dune grass as we followed the stream to the beach. We stripped off and swam in the gently lapping water, giving thanks for the sunshine and blue skies, and then scampered around on the sand like excited dogs as we shook the salty water off our skin.

Sanna Bay, the most westerly point of the British mainland, was bathed in bright morning light. Shells were strewn along the sand, and rocks covered with yellow lichen linked shallow blue pools. Most of the Ardnamurchan Peninsula shoreline is fringed by stony coves, but here it is as if the rocky claws of this far-western promontory have sifted out the seaweed and gathered in the pure white-shell sand, creating inlets with beautiful views to the Small Isles of Eigg, Muck and Rum.

We had crossed from northern Mull by ferry and after detouring to Sanna, we were heading inland via the single track road to Acharacle. Following a visit to the legendary Bakehouse for some of Helen Macgillvray's fantastic pasties, we swam at the ruins of Castle Tioram, situated on its own island with a shingle swimming cove. There's also an ancient stone shelter near the shore with a fireplace and a hole in the roof; you can change here or make a small fire and brew up some tea. Nearby Ardtoe is also worth a visit on a hot day – its pink basalt rocks form swimming ledges and small islands in the wide, shallow bay.

150

151

151 Camusdarach

If you are looking for a really wild beach and don't mind a good hour's walk (it's much quicker by bike), head for Camas an Lighe and its 'singing sands'. You hike past the flats of Kentra Bay and emerge through woodland to find a remote heather and birch-lined beach with grand views to the Small Isles (and there are further adventures to be had if you go east to the bays of Cul na Croise). To make the sands sing, shuffle across them with bare feet. Singing sands occur when sand grains are completely round and between 0.1 and 0.5mm in diameter. To generate the low frequency sound of about 450Hz they must also contain silica and have the right level of humidity. In dune systems they can be heard to roar or boom at certain wind speeds.

The most famous singing sands are those of Camas Sgiotaig, just 20 miles to the north. These are on the beautiful Isle of Eigg, purchased and saved by its community in 1997. It can be reached by day trip from Arisaig and there are spectacular views across to the towering 8,000-foot peaks of Rum, just 10 miles away. The island consists of the ancient remains of one of many volcanoes that erupted along this coast when the landmasses of Scotland and America were breaking apart. Arisaig is also the first stop for exploring the famous 'Sands of Morar', a string of beaches made famous in the widely acclaimed 1983 film, *Local Hero*. The plot centres on the frustrations experienced by a Texan oil giant (Burt Lancaster), who is negotiating to buy a small west coast village for development. Meanwhile, Marina, a wild-swimming marine biologist is under the impression that the beach is to become a nature reserve.

Despite recent tourist developments south of Arisaig along this short coastline, and the new A830 road bridge to the north at Morar itself, the original *Local Hero* beach location remains undeveloped. You can watch the sun setting over Rum and Skye and experience the magical Northern Lights here on summer nights. Camusdarach is the actual location of the chapel and beach-shack scenes from the film, but my favourite swimming cove is the little-known bay to the north, Rubh'an Achaidh Mhoir. Here the headland forms a smooth peninsula with perfect diving ledges. You can also keep walking around and up the magical river estuary of Morar, the shortest river in Britain, to find more white sand, oak groves and caves reaching right down to the water's edge.

Singing sands on Isle of Eigg, overlooking Rum

Ardnamurchan, Morar and Eigg

148 Sanna Sands

Grid ref.	NM448693
Postcode	PH36 4LN (6km N)
Walk	10 mins, mod
Train	Locailort, 72km

Most westerly point on British mainland. Stunning bay of coves and rocky islets. Views to the Small Isles. 10km from Tobermory (Mull) by ferry. Stop at the tourist centre with café 🍴 at Kilchoan (01972 510222). Go through village (dir Portuairk) but turn R after 1km to Sanna. Good sand and coves at Portuairk, too.

149 Singing sands, Eigg

Grid ref.	NM471900
Postcode	PH42 4RL (3km N)
Walk	10 mins, mod
Train	Arisaig, 2km + ferry

Tiny, vibrant, welcoming Eigg can be visited on a day trip from Arisaig via M.V. Shearwater (01687 450224). Hire bikes from the pier (01687 482432), take the minibus (01687 482494, £2) or walk the 6km to Camas Sgiotaig (singing sands) on N of island. Great views of Rum.

150 Singing sands, Kentra

Grid ref.	NM613690
Postcode	PH36 4LE (4km E)
Walk	60 mins, mod
Train	Locailort, 32km

Singing sands of remote Camas are set in cove lined with birch trees, with further coves to E. Views of Small Isles.

Take A861 from Salen, pass through Acharacle (pasties at The Bakehouse 🍴 01967 431484), turn L B8044 dir Kentra, Ardtoe, and L again after 1km to Arivegaig. From car park go through gate and follow clear track 2km, hugging shore, bearing R past Gorteneorn House, then into forest. After further 2km, bear R at sign for beach.

A At **Ardtoe** (NM628710, PH36 4LD) beyond Kentra find an enclosed cove with great rocks for snorkelling. Shame about the outflow pipe.

B Follow R Shiel by taking second L after Acharacle (signed **Castle Tioram**). Great river swim by footbridge (100m on L) or continue 5km to swim from cove below ruins on N side of tidal island (NM662725). You can make a fire in the small hut. △

151 Achaidh Mhoir, Morar

Grid ref.	NM662923
Postcode	PH39 4NT (2km N)
Walk	20 mins, diff
Train	Morar, 5km

Isolated beach at N end of Sands of Morar, next to *Local Hero* beach at Camusdarach. Good campsite.

From Arisaig follow old coast road (B8008) past caravan parks. After golf club (3km) find good swimming at next car park (500m) or continue on 2km, past the Camusdarach campsite 🏕 on L (01687 4502210) and after another 1km turn L into small car park. Walk down path by stream 500m. The *Local Hero* beach is to the L with further coves to L around headland. But continue on R side of stream and go round Achaidh Mhoir headland (NE) to find the diving rocks and wild beach. Continue on to explore estuary sands and caves.

A From Morar village take **Loch Morar** road past church. Many wooded islands with sandy coves (NM697932). See sign with telephone number – call this and someone will come down and hire you out a canoe!

155 Looking south from the road above Leac Tressirnish

Swimming from rocks just beyond the coral beaches

Isle of Skye

Many would say that Loch Coruisk, in the heart of Skye's highest mountains and at least a day's walk from the nearest road, is one of the wildest places in Britain. The peaks of the Black and Red Cuillins tower above it into the mist and gabbro slabs plunge into crystal-clear, jade-green water.

Here, among all the natural wonder, is a tiny shell-white beach at the head of Loch nan Leachd, one of the only sand beaches on Skye. You can reach Coruisk by taking one of the regular boat trips from Elgol and, if you're having difficulty finding the beach, just ask for the 'Bad Step' – the notorious slab of rock that hangs over the sea and is traversable only via the deep fissure across its face.

From Elgol you can also enjoy another very different wild-swimming experience in the deep Mermaid Pool within the Spar Cave. When Skye was one of the stops on the 'grand tour' of Britain, many artists of the Romantic school visited this cave, including Sir Walter Scott, who alluded to it in the *Lord of the Isles*, published in 1814 to raise money for a new house he was building. The huge vaulted structure is 50 yards long with a flowstone staircase and columns that look like marble. In places

153

152

155 **Leac Tressirnish harbour**

'The mermaid's alabaster grot,
Who bathes her limbs in
sunless well
Deep in Strath-aird's
enchanted cell...'

Sir Walter Scott alluding to Spar
Cave in *The Lord of The Isles*

the roof has been discoloured by the candles and torches of the visiting Victorians, who also removed most of the stalagmites and stalactites. A door once blocked the entrance so that an admission charge could be levied, but it was blown out by a yatch's cannon following a dispute. Few people come here today. On the north side of the Cuillins you can find Talisker Bay. The beach is made up of stratas of silver and black sand that alternate in bands down to the shoreline. There's a great waterfall cascading down the cliffs to the right and a giant rock stack to the left, surrounded by dark, shallow rock pools that are decorated with jet-black pinnacles and grotesquely contorted volcanic shapes.

No trip to Skye is complete without visiting the Quiraing and the Old Man of Storr, but few know about the dramatic coast that lies just below. There are great waterfall plunge pools at the shingle cove of Inver Tote, but the real local treasures are the caves, natural arches and natural harbour at Leac Tressirnish, a dramatic shoreline far below the cliffs accessible only by a scramble down a steep grassy slope. The harbour is a strange hook-shaped formation that forms a great platform of rock and is a perfect place for diving and jumping into deep water. You can also scramble round it and swim into several sea caves, some with roof openings.

The famous coral beaches of Skye are at its north end, just beyond Dunvegan where the castle displays the famous Macleod 'faerie flag'. This is no tropical coral, of course, but Scottish coral composed of the large fragments of billions of bleached skeletons of the red algae, *Lithothamnium calcareum*, that grow at the bottom of the ocean nearby. We arrived on the day of a wedding ceremony and the bridegroom explained that this was the couple's favourite place in the world. Thankfully, for them and us, the afternoon sun broke through the haze to illuminate the coral's milky glow. Cows lolled about on the beach sniffing at the seaweed and chewing the cud while we explored to the north to find a fabulous set of basalt columns that formed steps down into the sea. The island of Islay shimmered offshore like a backdrop to a Greek play as we dived, swam and snorkelled in the clearest waters I have ever experienced.

Isle of Skye

152 Loch nan Leachd, Coruisk

Grid ref.	NG492193
Postcode	IV49 9BL (8km NE)
Walk	20 mins, mod
Train	Kyle of Lochalsh, 36km

Tiny white beach overshadowed by Cuillin mountains. Reached by boat or long walk. Near Loch Coruisk.

From the Kyle of Lochalsh turn L off A87 at Broadford (12km) and continue 20km to Elgol. The *Misty Isle* (01471 866288) and the original *Bella Jane* (0800 7313089) both make the 30min boat trip. On landing take path to stepping stones (300m) then main coast path E 300m. 8km coastal walk E leads back to Elgol, via Bad Step.

A Cathedral-like **Spar Cave** (NG538128) – LT only. From Elgol continue on lane E to Glasnakille (2km) to find ruined barn just S (R) of junction. Descend to inlet then bear L along LT foreshore rocks 100m, passing another inlet, then traverse around into Spar Cave canyon. Inside, the R passage diminishes but the L one bears R and rises in flowstone staircase, descending to deep Mermaid Pool. Bring torches. △

153 Talisker Bay

Grid ref.	NG315303
Postcode	IV47 8SF (1km W)
Walk	30 mins, easy
Train	Kyle of Lochalsh, 43km

Dramatic bay with waterfall and stack with LT rockpools. From Sligachan Hotel 🍴 (excellent bunkhouse and bar food 01478 650204) take A863 Dunvegan road and turn L (B8009) after 9km, then second L after 5km and L on to Talisker (not Glen Brittle and the famous Faerie Pools). Park by house, walk 2km to beach.

154 Coral beaches

Grid ref.	NG223551
Postcode	IV55 8WF (5km N)
Walk	40 mins, mod
Train	Kyle of Lochalsh, 80km

Unusual 'coral' beach, best at HT but with beautiful rocks at N end for swimming too. Pass Dunvegan Castle (end of A863) and turn L after 5km to car park. Walk down track and along coast 2km. Behind hill at north end of beach find basalt column rocks on water's edge.

155 Leac Tressirnish

Grid ref.	NG523577
Postcode	IV51 9JW (3km S)
Walk	20 mins, diff
Train	Kyle of Lochalsh, 75km

Hook-shaped, natural harbour rock formation for snorkelling and jumps plus two sea caves. Calm seas only. △△

7km S of Staffin (A855, between the Quiraing and the Storr) find long lay-by on L, set back parallel to road. Look down to see flat grass plateau with the Leac rock formation. Continue to end of track, cross gate and bushwhack 300m R steeply down slope. After Leac, descend to inlet 100m to N (L), climb on and traverse foreshore rock plateau L, 200m, to find open-topped cave and – a 50m swim N – another sea cave.

A 3km N of Leac find parking and path above **Lealt waterfalls**. Descend steeply at end to find pebbly cove or huge plunge pools beneath waterfall (NG521604).

B Seashore caves off E side of **Dunan an Aisilidh** isthmus, near Gedintailor, 10km S of Portree on B883 (NG535353). △

Waterfall north of Applecross, overlooking Rona and Skye

Wester Ross

Crossing Skye Bridge we returned to the mainland but were soon climbing high into the mountains again. We crawled up miles of twisting mountain road to the 2,000-feet Coire na Ba pass where stopped to watch the final rays of the day before descending cautiously to Applecross Bay.

It was dark by the time we arrived. The tide was in as we pitched up on the shadowy shores, bright stars reflecting on a glassy summer sea that was lapping on the beach. I waded out up to my waist and a faint milky glow trailed out in my wake. Time passed as, in raptures, I watched my fingertips make luminous streaks in the water, and when I dived down the swirling patterns were like underwater St Elmo's fire

I had only experienced phosphorescence once before in the sea at Norfolk one hot summer. It occurs in Britain in warm shallows, especially after days of bright sunlight. The bioluminescence is given off by accumulations of plankton, which are disturbed by motion. Most often seen glowing in the bow waves of boats at night, phosphorescence is a global phenomenon, particularly common in the tropics. For many creatures that inhabit the deep ocean it is the only source of light.

By morning the bay had emptied leaving rivulets of straggling seaweed and stone running down to the shore. We broke camp and headed north up the coast road, the eastern mountain range in shadow but fringed with a halo of celestial rays. We passed the little cove of Sand and a series of stunning waterfall cascades, where we bathed in the

156A

Shieldaig, Loc Torridon

157

deep freshwater pools that ran to the sea, jumping from the rocks and basking like seals as the sun broke over the hill with a flourish. At Cuaig we found a secret bay and swam with silvery elver eels near a ruined fisherman's hut. Long kelp strands waved in the bay, rising up like a forest, and we could almost imagine ourselves swimming with the little eels in their spawning grounds, the great Sargasso Sea.

From here the long road was utterly spectacular as it ran alongside Loch Torridon with its stony bays and tree-cloaked islands. Gairloch and the exquisite Redpoint beaches are a journey of only 5 miles by water but over 40 miles by road. At Gairloch, the giant peach-coloured pebbles are streaked with crimson ripples and the sand glows ochre in the dunes but deep purple on the seabed. There's a meadow-covered islet and a ruined fishing station with rusty anchors lined up along its walls.

If you follow the Gairloch road and head towards Melvaig you'll find an excellent pub and some of the most dramatic cliffs, rock arches and sea caves in Scotland. Pass through Melvaig then walk up the private road towards the lighthouse and outdoor centre at Rudha Reidh, and stop by the first bridge to venture down to the shore. Here you'll find a huge cave, a waterfall and a rock arch where you can swim if the sea is dead calm.

The beaches retain their reddish sand all the way up and around the remaining Wester Ross coast. Firemore near Poolewe has a rocky promontory perfect for snorkelling, while Mellon Udrigle offers sands and ancient hut circles with views over the Summer Isles. But the final set of beaches on Gruinard Bay are the spookiest of all. They overlook the original 'Anthrax Island', chosen by the British government during the bleakest years of the Second World War to test lethal bacterial spores. Gruinard Island was the perfect location: remote, unpopulated yet close to the big allied military base at Loch Ewe. The spores, thankfully, were never used in battle and from 1986 a determined effort was made to decontaminate the land by removing topsoil and then treating the ground with a vast amount of formaldehyde. Finally, a flock of sheep was transported to the island and, when they remained healthy, it was re-opened after 48 years of quarantine. Visit if you dare!

157 Redpoint Beach near Gairloch

156 Applecross waterfall

Grid ref.	NG695565
Postcode	IV54 8XL (1km N)
Walk	10 mins, diff
Train	Stracarron, 48km

Applecross Bay is stony and shallow (HT swims only) but the sheltered, remote coastline to the N has many gems and views to Raasay and Skye.

12km N of Applecross, between Callakille and Cuaig, park at viewpoint towards top of hill on corner L then walk back S 500m to river and follow it downstream to sea. In deep canyon find pools or swim from rocky shore. △

A 1.2km N beyond waterfall parking find stream running L to hidden **Cuaig** cove (NG704586). Follow path on L bank 1km to arrive at stepping stones. L bank continues on raised road to old croft with good swimming from rocks at HT. Cross stepping stones for sands that appear at LT. Very quiet, very remote. Snorkelling.

B 5km N of Applecross Bay find **Sand**, a pink, sandy cove (NG683487).

157 Redpoint beach

Grid ref.	NG728689
Postcode	IV21 2AX
Walk	10 mins, mod
Train	Achnasheen, 56km

Pink sands and dunes in two remote bays. Enjoy a waterside sundowner in the Badachro Inn on the way back.

From Kinlochewe/Loch Torridon turn off A832 road on to B8056 6km before Gairloch and continue 10km beyond Badachro (with gastro-pub 🍴 01445 741255), Opinan and Redpoint to reach car park at road end. Bear R towards dunes (500m) for closer beach or turn L through gate, to and through Redpoint farm, for furthest beach (1.5km) with island, fishing station and dramatic views of Applecross (NG734675).

A Gairloch itself has a quiet cove 500m beyond the turning for the harbour (Charlestown) or continue 15km on B8021, past **Big Sand** for the Melvaig Inn 🍴 (IV21 2DZ, 01445 771212). The **Rudha Reidh** lighthouse road has superb cave and arch coastline. Try below first river bridge (NG737882). △△

158 Gruinard Bay

Grid ref.	NG953908
Postcode	IV22 2NG (1km E)
Walk	5 mins, easy
Train	Achnasheen, 75km

Empty sands and coves opposite infamous but now decontaminated Gruinard Island.

From Gairloch continue on A832 (dir Braemore/Ullapool) 25km to Gruinard Bay. Explore to R 800m to find further coves and rocky wild-camping site on mini-headland. Small islets 300m beyond. Even more remote beach 3.5km further along A832, after river and forest and as road turns R inland. Drop down 100m to L at NG965932.

A From Gairloch after 7km on A832, turn L at Poolewe (B8057) and find **Firemore** beach after 6km (between Inverasdale and Cove) with central rocky promontory for snorkelling and diving at HT (NG817885).

B 14km after Poolewe turn L at Laide to find beach after 5km by telephone box at **Mellon Udrigle** (NG892959).

159A **Traigh Sheileboist looking to Luskentyre**

159A **From Hornais, North Uist**

Outer Hebrides

South Harris and Uist are places of pilgrimage for the beach connoisseur. Ribbons of snow-white sand drift down the islands' Atlantic coasts and collect in sweeping bays. Meadows covered in wildflowers provide the perfect backdrop and offer endless wild-camping potential.

May or June is the best time to visit, before the midges and when the 'machair' (beach meadow) has come to life. The grazing on this western fringe is especially lush owing to dustings of lime-rich sand, and there is a profusion of different grasses intermingled with buttercups, daisies and orchids. So fertile is the land here that its poor communities were among the first to be evicted, around 1824 – a period when landlords across Scotland were destroying crofts and turning instead to large-scale sheep-farming for profit. The highland clearances and village burnings began soon after.

The best way to explore South Harris, which is only 15 miles from end to end, is by bike. Our ride started at Losgaintir and Traigh Rosamol, probably the most famous of the Outer Hebridean beaches, an expanse of estuarine sands and dunes overlooking the Isle of Tarasaigh (Taransay). The intensity of the colours cannot fail to move you. Even on overcast days acres of white sand glow under turquoise shallows, with the mountains of Lewis and a scattering of tiny islets providing an amazing backdrop.

161

161A

160B

There's also good swimming to be had on the other side of the estuary, two miles along the coast road at Sheileboist and Niosaboist. From here you can look back in awe at the white estuary and dune expanse that you've just left. Between two coves, a tiny primary school alone on the machair faces sand and sea in every direction, while the Macleod stone stands sentinel on the hillock.

At every switch and turn of the coast road the colours of the ocean, the sense of space and the sheer energy of the place created a real emotional charge; the strong scent of ozone in the air adding to the overall sensation. The island was so small, however, that I feared we would finish the journey all too soon. So we stopped to swim in rolling surf at Traigh Mhor, then lounged for a few hours in an expanse of meadow behind Scarasta before visiting Cleabhaig, the wildest of the beaches, set beneath the hill of Ceapabhal and by a tiny ruined chapel. A storm played out on the horizon as the incoming swell tumbled our bodies. I felt as if I could swim forever, like a selkie – one of the shape-shifting seal fairies of ancient Hebridean folklore.

That evening the ferry manoeuvred through the complex labyrinth of offshore rocks and islets that leads to Uist. We camped down a narrow lane on the machair close to an ancient graveyard at Hornais. The white sandy shallows seemed to turn even more mauve as twilight descended – as if they had stored up the colours of the day – and we were drawn half-mesmerised into the luminescent waters. By morning, a mist had formed, but the mauve-tinted light still permeated everything.

The people of the Uists, islands so remote that even the Reformation did not reach them, remain deeply spiritual. Living on the edge, they experienced great suffering as a result of the clearances and the near-eradication of their Gaelic tongue. The Catholic Church here is one of the most active in Britain and all along the western seaboard tiny white chapels alive with hymns and prayers dot the prairie, mountains towering up behind them on the eastern skyline. Sabbaths on the Uists are still held sacred and the islanders' faith is tangible and strong. This is a place for retreat and purification; a place where you can walk the sands, lie in the meadows, contemplate the beauty of the world and bathe away the day.

Cleabhaig Cove beneath Ceapabhal hill

159 Luskentyre/Losgaintir

Grid ref.	NG064999
Postcode	HS3 3HL (1km N)
Walk	5 mins, easy
Train	Kyle of Lochalsh, ferry via Uig

The Outer Hebrides' most famous beach: shell-white sand, tropical turquoise seas, mountain vistas, freezing waters!

From Tarbert ferry (South Harris) turn L and follow A859. After 10km turn R down side of river estuary to Losgaintir, 3km. There are beautiful coves along the early stretch of this road, but parking is difficult. Continue to car park to swim at Rosamol beach with dunes and superb views.

A Back to main road and turn R continuing on A859 W for many more beaches. 4km on, just beyond school, **Traigh Sheileboist** is a long beach while the cove 100m to its W is sheltered for swimming with an offshore islet for snorkelling (NG058973, HS3 3HR).

B 1km further on **Niosaboist** (with parking and caravans) and **Iar** coves lie on E and W of the MacLeod stone hill.

160 Cleabhaig, South Harris

Grid ref.	NF980911
Postcode	HS3 3JA (2km NW)
Walk	25 mins, mod
Train	Kyle of Lochalsh, ferry via Uig

Wild cove beneath South Harris' highest hill and behind massive expanse of Scarasta machair.

Continue 8km on A859 through Scarasta/Sgarasta to turn R into Taobh Tuath (4km). Go past Seallam visitor centre (01859 520258) to park 1.5km at road end. Continue through gate on track for 1.5km to Cleabhaig and two successive coves leading to a ruined chapel (NF970913, HS3 3JA). If you have energy to spare, climb Ceapabhal /Chaipaval for impressive views.

A 3km after Niosaboist park by telephone box and post office and cut across fields for beautiful, wild **Traigh Mhor** (NG024943).

B A further 2km leads to long stretch of **Scarasta** beach with huge machair at back (delightful rooms and very good but pricey restaurant at Scarista House ☎ 01859 550238, HS3 3HX).

161 Hornais, North Uist

Grid ref.	NF872768
Postcode	HS6 5AY, 2km N
Walk	2 mins, easy
Train	Kyle of Lochalsh, ferry via Uig

Sand, sea, machair. Old cemetery and standing stone. LT bar to Lingay Island.

From Harris ferry (Berneray) turn L and L again on to B893. After 2km turn R on to lane. Pass Clach an t-Sagairt standing stone (300m on R), pass between two cemeteries (700m) and continue on track to beaches. Also try **Traigh Iar** (NF828787).Turn R at Greinetobht (A865 W), then 3km down track. .

A Continue 45km on A865 across Benbecula to South Uist. One long endless beach on W side but tiny **Tobha Mor** has traditional thatched crofts, hostel, chapel remains, mountain backdrop and ruined castle on nearby loch island. 12km S of supermarket, signed to R (NF750366). Just turn up for a basic bed at Howmore Hostel (white thatched cottage at end of road, part of the excellent Gatliff.org.uk foundation). Take the preceding R turn (1km) for the Loch and Eilein and Caisteal Bheagram (NF761371).

North West: Assynt and Sutherland

At the extreme north tip, from Ullapool to Cape Wrath and along the Sutherland coast to John o' Groats, the wild coastline harbours some of the most beautiful swimming beaches in Britain.

Sutherland, or southern land, is the most northerly coast of Britain; when you realise it was once part of the great Norse empire the name makes more sense. Neighbouring Assynt, meaning 'rocky when seen from afar', is a reference to the famed mountains of Stach Pollaidh and Suilven that rear up from the flat moor and stand like monuments over the sea. Between the two districts is Achmelvich, literally 'machair meadow and dunes'. It's a stunning beach and one of the most popular in this area, but you can easily escape the handful of summer tourists by walking to the second cove, a wedge of skin-pale sands set between igneous outcrops that form a turquoise swimming pool and suntrap.

From here you can also walk on to the hidden bay of Port Alltan na Bradhan, a deep, sand-lined natural harbour, with very sheltered swimming at the bottom of a vale complete with ruined mill and giant millstones. The stream here has a waterfall and the grassy hummocks between the rocks are an ideal place for camping and picnics. I rejoiced in an entire afternoon of swimming and paddling an inflatable dinghy in baking sunshine and under clear blue skies.

The B869 coast road that passes by Alltan na Bradhan is one of the most scenic in Scotland, winding through a wildlife-rich landscape that

162

163A

164A

is home to red deer, sea otters and even ospreys. Heading north on the A894 I stopped at Badcall Bay and swam out as a golden sun set over the archipelago of scattered isles. But the usual destination for anyone looking for a wild beach this far north is legendary Sandwood Bay. Owned by the John Muir Trust, this remote beach is 15 miles south of Cape Wrath and accessible only by walking for a distance of 5 miles. This red-sand bay, with dunes and grassy clefts perfect for wild camping, is more than a mile long and framed by cliffs and the ancient alien-looking sandstone stack of Am Buavhaille (the Herdsman). The recently enlarged car park is testament to Sandwood's popularity and the next day I counted 15 groups, all here to make the pilgrimage. The bay is big enough to absorb everyone but you might find fewer people on Oldshoremore and Phollain beaches, which lie just next to the car park. They're safer for swimming and also have beautiful rock formations.

Near Durness, 20 miles north, Balnakeil Bay is a celebrated arc of dune and sand with a wild north shore featuring sea caves and rock arches. Immediately south you'll find the enormous Smoo Cave, which lies at the head of a deep sea-canyon impregnated with caves and swimming ledges. Continue around to the north of the headland beyond Pocan Smoo to Bagh Geal and find my favourite bay, a complex of green and black rock pools with arched entrances, tiny islands and several small caves.

From Durness onwards the remote A838 coast road winds eastwards and every one of the empty beaches and coves that unfolds could win awards. Few are named, let alone visited. I had just one more day to explore before heading to John o' Groats and back south again, so I camped that last night at Chailgeag, a sweeping stretch of perfect sand with rock arches and cove inlets set under the ancient prehistoric remains of a village settlement. Between me and the Arctic Circle far to the north there was no land whatsoever. Early next morning I found a flat rocky ledge by the sea, not far from the beach, and marvelled at the sheer enormity of the landscape around me. After a saltwater shampoo and shave and still covered in soapsuds, I dived into the great blue ocean and swam hard down through the cool waters to the sandy bay floor, washing all the bubbles clean away.

164 **Rock pools at Pocan Smoo, near Smoo Cave**

North West: Assynt and Sutherland

162 Achmelvich Cove

Grid ref.	NC058252
Postcode	IV27 4JB (1km W)
Walk	10 mins, mod
Train	Culrain, 75km

Superb white-sand cove with granite outcrops; a short walk from car park.

From Ullapool take A835 then A837 to Lochinver. Or take scenic coastal lanes via Inverkirkaig and Achins book and coffee shop 🍴 (IV27 4LR, 01571 844262). After Lochinver (B869), turn L and L again after 2km. Walk R (E) from the small car and caravan park 500m to find hidden cove.

A Walk 2km N along coast to find Port **Alltan na Bradhan** (NC051262) a very sheltered sandy bay with waterfall and rocks for jumping. Or drive 3km further up B869 and park at first proper lay-by on R then follow stream path down past ruins.

B 20km N on A894 find **Badcall Bay**, a tiny fishing quay with spectacular sunset swims over archipelago (NC163415, IV27 4TH, Eddrachilles Hotel 🍴 01971 502080).

163 Oldshoremore/Phollain

Grid ref.	NC199585
Postcode	IV27 4RS (1km W)
Walk	5 mins, easy
Train	Lairg, 60km

Two connecting white-sand bays with island, ledges and rock pools between.

Continue N on A894, A838, then B801 L to Kinlochbervie and on to Oldshoremore beach (turn L down to beach car park) or less popular Phollain beach, next L after 1.5km. Walk via rocks between both.

A Continue on lane 500m to Blairemore and John Muir Trust car park and WC. A well-marked track begins over gate opposite, a 5km walk across moor to **Sandwood Bay** with stack (NC218653). Turn L at end of second loch. Beware rip currents in surf conditions. Wild camping. △

B A further 1km from Blairemore leads to **Sheigra**. Turn L to beach, past cemetery to excellent wild-camping spot on grassland at bottom. Tiny sand and shingle cove for early morning swims (NC182600).

164 Pocan Smoo

Grid ref.	NC423678
Postcode	IV27 4QA (1km NE)
Walk	20 mins, mod
Train	Lairg, 91km
	or Forsinard, 53km

Weird and wonderful rock pools with arches. Smoo cave and canyon swim. △

Continue A838 N to Durness and 2km on to Smoo Cave (signed). Descend to cave on path, climb up other side of inlet and go through gate/fence on to headland. See steep path L down to rock ledges for swimming in gorge, but continue 500m on to N foreshore to find main rock pool on L, cave to R, further formations beyond.

A Turn L entering Durness to **Balnakeil Bay** (2km). Explore spectacular cliffs and gulleys with dunes behind on far (E) side of Faraid Head (NC393708, 2km).

B Continue beyond Smoo 2km to **Ceannabeinne** lost village (roadside L). Follow main path via wall to stream, then stream gulley to cove (NC441658). Or main beach parking 500m E (**Traigh Allt Chailgeag**).

162B **Badcall Bay**

228 Bow Fiddle rock arch

North East: Shetland to the Moray Firth

The island of Papa Stour off the west coast of the Shetland Isles is widely regarded as having the most spectacular sea caves, arches and stacks in Britain.

One cave, the Holl a Boardie, stretches for half a mile under the Papa Stour and you can row all the way through it. Another, Kirstans' Hole, was once a loch that collapsed into the sea caves below during a violent stormy night, 30 years ago. Today, the most accessible of these wild-swimming wonders is Brei Holm, which has an impressive set of tunnels, grottoes and catacombs interconnected by multiple arches and sea bridges.

Bearing south again, for the mainland and John o' Groats, the dramatic stacks and cliffs of Duncasby have deep inlets and canyons, and the nearby sands of Sinclair Bay are worth a visit. But if you are looking for more adventure, head for Whaligoe Steps where 365 paved Victorian steps cut out of the sheer cliff-face lead down to a natural inlet and harbour. On a calm day it is possible to swim here.

This impressive stairway was constructed in 1808 to give around 35 local families access to the sea and enable them to earn a livelihood from fishing. Men and women would haul their creel pots 200 feet

165

167

167

up to the curing house on the cliff top, and you can still see the waist-high ledges built so they could rest their loads. Now only rusty winches and chain rings bear witness to a once-thriving industry.

During the nineteenth century the herring fishing boom extended all along the east coast and employed many of those crofters displaced from the west by the clearances. Sixty miles to the south, on the Moray coast, Portknockie is another run-down fishing village with extraordinary coastal features. Here the Bow Fiddle rock sits in a little cove to the rear of the town and the slanted rock strata have created a huge natural arch, heavily stained with guano. The swim out is easy and once underneath you can peer right down into the deep water below. You may even be lucky enough, as we were, to witness a pod of dolphins swimming close by.

Historically, the Moray coast was also a place of resistance. West from Portknockie, Preacher's Cave was one of several used as secret places of prayer when the Free Church was breaking away from the Church of Scotland during the nineteenth century. Much earlier, in the thirteenth century, Findlater Castle, east of Cullen, was an important coastal defence against the Vikings. Today, in this remote yet rural setting, you'll find Sunnyside Cove, one of Moray's best-kept secrets, with a fine sandy cove far below the rolling wheat fields.

A better-known beach is at Pennan, 20 miles east, beyond Banff. The village and its pub were also used as locations for the film, *Local Hero*, though you may be disappointed to discover that the famous pub seems to be closed indefinitely for refurbishment. While you are waiting why not visit Hell's Lum, a cave-and-cove complex on the far side of Pennan Bay. There is a dramatic series of deep plunge pools and inlets, perfect for jumping and snorkelling, and a great cavern on the right leads via a tunnel to tiny Cullykhan Bay. Hell's Lum itself is a gaping scar in the hillside on the left that leads through the hill to a sea cave at the bottom of the cliffs. The jet-black rocks and deep-blue water give this place a sublime feel and the interconnected caverns, beaches and pools – all overlooking beautiful Pennan – make this one of the best wild-swimming locations in north-east Scotland.

North East: Shetland to the Moray Firth

165 Brei Holm, Papa Stour

Grid ref.	HU189604
Postcode	ZE2 9PW (1.5km E)
Walk	20 mins, diff
Train	Aberdeen + 14hr ferry, then 40km

Spectacular subterranean passages, sea caves and stacks on island off Shetland Isles. Brei Holm is the most accessible location.

Ferries leave from tiny West Burrafirth, 40km W of Lerwick, N of Westside (day trips Fri/Sat, 01957 722259). From jetty walk 1km around Housa Voe bay to S headland. Tiny Brei Holm is connected by a tidal causeway with arches on E side. 200m swim in wetsuit but boat support recommended. △△ NB Fogla Skerry (by boat only) on W coast has sea-cave tunnels right through island.

A Sinclair Bay: 4km N of Wick. Parking at Ackergill Links club house (KW1 4RG).

B 10km S of Wick, **Whaligoe**/Ulbster (ND322403, KW2 6AB) has ancient steps cut down cliff-face to reach inlet. Turn off A99 at telephone box, walk L around house to cliff and steps. Calm seas only. △△

166 Bow Fiddle, Portknockie

Grid ref.	NJ494689
Postcode	AB56 4NN (300m E)
Walk	5 mins, easy
Train	Keith, 20km
Cycle	Route 1

Dramatic slanted rock with arch on edge of small town. Caves in nearby bay. △

From Elgin (A96) travel E and turn L at Fochabers on to A98 (Cullen). After 18km turn L on A492 to Portknockie. Turn R down to bottom of Admiralty St then R into Addison St. Park and follow track down valley, 300m, to arch. Or find rocky bay with Preacher cave 200m to L, below Patrol Rd. Kids jump from green castle cliff.

A Return to A98 and turn R through Cullen. After 3km see **Findlater Castle** signed L at staggered crossroads. Turn L again after 1km and park at farm. Castle is 800m through fields on cliff edge. Turn L and secret **Sunnyside Cove** is 1km further along footpath (NJ537674, AB45 2UD 2km NW). Or turn R to Sandend Bay.

B **Portsoy** open-air tidal pool, nicely sited 500m, E of harbour. (NJ584665, AB45 2QA).

167 Hell's Lum, Pennan

Grid ref.	NJ838663
Postcode	AB43 6JB (1km W)
Walk	10 mins, mod
Train	Huntly 40km

Sandy cove plus dramatic network of snorkelling inlets, caverns and tunnels. △

Continue beyond Banff (A98) then L on to B9031 coast road for 13km. 1.5km before Pennan, as descending hill, turn L down track for Cullykhan Bay and fort. Follow path towards headland. Descend to the beach on R, or drop down L to follow stream steeply to rocky inlets and caves at bottom (300m). The deep inlet offers excellent snorkelling and jumping. The scar to the L is Hell's Lum. Climb in and through cave tunnels to emerge at sea under cliffs W side of Lion's Head. The huge cavern to the R (across boulder field) has tunnel that leads though to beach. Afterwards visit the famous Pennan Inn 🏨 (01346 561201).

A Returning 3km W, just before Gardenstown, turn R, past school, and R to view quaint **Crovie**, cottages all bunched up against cliff wall (NJ807656, AB45 3JQ). Swims from quay.

Aberdeen and Dundee

Peering down into the deep abyss early that evening we wondered if we could ever find a way down to the beautiful lagoon. The cliffs were sheer but the still, sapphire and cobalt waters gleamed temptingly when the low sun shone in through the cave mouth.

The Bullers of Buchan is a massive collapsed cave with a 150-foot-high arched entrance and a deep internal pool. It's clearly impossible to get down to without serious climbing equipment, but it's not impossible to swim into, if the sea is calm. So we returned early the next morning and followed the overgrown path down into the adjacent cove, working our way along the right-hand side as far as we could go. We changed and swam across the small bay, then scrambled around the headland before diving in beneath the cave. Lifted up by gentle swell, we peered fleetingly into the depths with our goggles as the cathedral 'doors' of the huge chamber opened above us. The acoustics inside the cave were fantastic and we hummed and sang after landing on one of the tiny rocky islands that must have once formed part of the cave roof.

Coming into such close contact with these geological wonders is awe-inspiring, so we were excited when a sea-kayaking guide told us of another set of arches just down the coast from Stonehaven. The Garran is rarely visited and there is no easy path but a route along the cliff brings you down to a rock platform the size of a football pitch.

168

171A

171

It harbours three massive rock pools with ledges that form perfect diving boards. To the right is another bay with a deep pool connected to the sea via a natural arch, and to the left two giant caves gape in the nearby cliffs – their openings large enough to sail a yacht into.

This coastline must have a thousand stories to tell: certainly the superb ruins of Dunnottar Castle have seen much bloodshed. Dating from the ninth century, the castle sits on a narrow outcrop and is protected by the sea on three sides. During the Wars of Scottish Independence its entire English garrison was burned alive by William Wallace, but today the location is comparatively peaceful. Two shingle coves on either side are good for swimming at high tide and the daring might try to circumnavigate the castle via the various stacks; one of them is said to have a cave that reaches right up through the centre like a chimney.

Cliffs, caves and conflict aren't the only characteristics of this coast. It has softer features, not least some of the largest expanses of sand dunes in the country. North of Aberdeen, near Peterhead, ruined Kirkton church and graveyard stand behind sand hills that glow peach in the evening light. In the south, near Montrose, the Red Castle at beautiful Lunan Bay takes its name from the red sands set in a wide crescent before it. A few miles to the north you'll find the ruins of a fort-like limekiln beneath Boddin Farm, and the Elephant rock arch a little further on. To the south is the tiny cliff-top village of Auchmithie, true home of the famous Arbroath 'smokie' – haddock smoked over hardwood until it takes on a burnished gold colour – and also But and Ben, one of the best family-run restaurants in Scotland.

The prize for the best sands in Scotland must, however, go to Forvie, a national nature reserve with extensive dunes and four miles of foreshore with marram grass, pennywort, crowberry and creeping willow. A village and its church once stood amid these dunes but the entire community was overwhelmed by a sandstorm in 1413, allegedly the result of a curse uttered by three sisters who were put out to sea in a leaky boat. The church ruins have been excavated but the rest of the village lies silently under the sand, still waiting to be found.

Sand dunes behind Kirkton ruined church

Aberdeen and Dundee

168 Bullers of Buchan

Grid ref. NK110381
Postcode AB42 0NS (200m E)
Walk 20 mins, diff
Train Aberdeen, 43km

Spectacular collapsed cave among dramatic cliffs and stacks. Deep lagoon accessed via swim through rock arch. △△

Turn L off A90 6km S of Peterhead on to A975 dir Cruden Bay. Park in large lay-by on L after 1.5km. Inspect arch and lagoon then descend to cove on R (S) side and scramble along cove edge 100m as far as possible (swimming gully if necessary). Swim across cove, scramble around headland, then swim in through arch. Calm seas only. Good walk N to North Haven bay. **Cruden Bay** (2km S) has a beautiful undeveloped beach.

A Continue 16km on A975 from Cruden Bay, past Collieston to car park L, opp river, for **Sands of Forvie**, huge dune system with cliffs behind. Take path 1.5km to ruined church and village then bear L along coast 1km to swim at beautiful Hackley Bay (NK028271, AB41 6AB).

169 Kirkton church and dunes

Grid ref. NK119509
Postcode AB42 3EN (1.5km E)
Walk 10 mins, diff
Train Aberdeen, 56km
or Inverurie, 44km

Remote dunes and beach accessed via ruined church. 4km N of Peterhead on A90, between Hallmoss and St Fergus, turn R by white post and opposite Inverquinzie Cottages. Park by cemetery and pass round to R, over rabbit warren and fence to dunes. Continue on road 1km to St Fergus to find main beach car park.

170 Lunan Bay

Grid ref. NO693515
Postcode DD11 5ST (200m E)
Walk 3 8mins, easy
Train Arbroath, 10km

12km N of Arbroath on A92, 2km after Inverkeilor, turn R to Lunan and beach. Space for wild camping. Limekiln and arch at Boddin Farm (NO714534, DD10 9TD) 4km N, below Dunninald. Visit Auchmithie, for smokies, But and Ben 🍴 for great family fare (DD11 5SQ, 01241 877223), 9km S.

171 The Garran

Grid ref. NO877789
Postcode AB39 2UL (1km NE)
Walk 25 mins, diff
Train Stonehaven, 8km

Sea arch and lagoon, huge rock pools and giant sea caverns along little-known coast. Excellent seafood pub. Nearby cliff castle with beach. △

Follow A92 from Stonehaven past Dunnottar Castle and turn L signed for Catterline and Creel Inn 🍴 (seafood gastro-pub 01569 750254) after 5km. Find primary school and cross into field behind playground and walk to far end of second field, beneath farm, about 1km. In final 300m note lagoon behind rock arch, then LT rock pools on rock platform and sea caves beyond (N). Drop down to rock platform at far end via difficult scramble and explore and swim.

A Swim from rocky bays on either side of **Dunnottar Castle**, located on its rocky headland, or swim right around. Castle Haven (shingle) on N side is good at HT in calm seas (NO881839). △

Seacliff beach – tiny harbour overlooking Tantallon Castle

Fife and East Lothian

When the bell rang out in the village of Elie, its inhabitants knew that Lady Jane Anstruther was bathing naked off the headland. You can still see the remains of her eighteenth-century bathing tower complete with changing hut built into the rocks below, from where she could plunge into the deep inlets.

Climb up above the Ship Inn and pass Ruby Bay, where they say garnets lie in the sand, to reach the tower. Below, at low tide, there is a variety of gulleys and pools. There are fantastic views, too, and you can imagine sitting in here by a warming fire on a summer evening – a fine place to dry off and watch the colours of dusk fade across the sea.

At about the same time Lady Jane was building her tower at Elie, Alexander Selkirk, the inspiration for Daniel Defoe's *Robinson Crusoe* was setting sail from neighbouring Lower Largo in the galleon *Cinque Ports* and heading for the southern oceans. After many months at sea the vessel dropped anchor at the uninhabited archipelago of Juan Fernández, off Argentina, to collect fresh water but Selkirk was so worried about the state of the ship he decided to stay on the island in the hope of being picked up. The *Cinque Ports* did indeed sink so Selkirk lived alone on the island for the next four years and four months and wasn't visited by a single ship. All he had brought with him was a musket, gunpowder, carpenter's tools, a knife, a Bible and some clothing. For the first year Selkirk stayed on the beach and camped in a cave, fearing the sounds of wild animals in the

174 **Canty Bay**

172A **Lady's Tower**

175A

interior of the island. Eventually hordes of raucous mating sea lions forced him to go inland where he survived by eating feral goats. Selkirk was finally rescued by a British boat and returned home to Lower Largo where he lived out his days alone with his cats.

If you'd like your own small adventure then try the Elie's chain walk, just three miles east of Lower Largo. The UK's only *via ferrata,* this series of chains and footholds takes you on a difficult scramble over a black volcanic landscape of pools, inlets and caves at Kincraig Point, a brilliant place to swim in calm seas at any tide. Apparently it was built to help the lighthouse keeper reach the cliff-top. To the north, the famous East Neuk coastline extends through several pretty villages; artists' colony Pittenweem with its cottage-lined foreshore and archaic tidal swimming pool was my favourite. Past Crail you'll come to sweet Cambo Sands, the beautiful beaches of St Andrews and the wild dunes of Tentsmuir Forest.

To the south, on the opposite side of Edinburgh and the Forth, the East Lothian coast is superb. The best beach in the area is at Seacliff with inspiring views to Tantallon Castle to the left and to great guano-iced Bass Rock straight ahead. You'll also find a tiny harbour inlet here, hewn from the stone – a wonderful place to swim and jump with the castle in view. A few miles before Tantallon we also found Canty Bay, a secret cove just visible beneath the coast road.

Other good beaches along this stretch include those around the John Muir Country Park, near Dunbar. The park commemorates Scotland's pioneering wilderness-lover, who established the Yosemite National Park in America. Peffer and Ravensheugh Sands to the north, though, are less crowded. Further south the aptly named Cove has an old track leading to an abandoned harbour quay with a long tunnel built through the cliffs. Here you can snorkel and jump off the quay on a calm day; there's also a rock arch on the far side of the bay. But the greatest attraction on this coast is St Abb's Head with its deeply folded red, green and yellow-coloured cliffs. If the sea is flat the most beautiful place to swim is from the rock pools and coloured slabs in Horsecastle Bay. Otherwise make for Pettico Wick shingle cove and marvel at the extraordinary power deep within the earth that must have created such elaborate formations.

174 Rock pools at St Abb's Head

172 Elie chain walk

Grid ref.	NT466996
Postcode	KY9 1HB (1km SE)
Walk	30 mins, diff
Train	Markinch, 22km or Springfield, 16km

Unusual 1km scrambling route with chain holds around dramatic Kincraig Point.

From Earlsferry at the W end of Elie Bay head W past golf course, along beach to find first of eight chains. Inlets, caves and ledges for swimming in calm seas. Best on a falling tide. △△

A From the convivial bay-side Ship Inn 🍴 in Elie (KY9 1DT, 01333 330246), turn R and R again up hill to headland and visit **Ruby Cove** and **Lady's Tower**. Bathe in narrow inlet below (NT499994). △

B Pretty beach and art galleries in front of cottages in **Pittenweem** village 6km E of Elie. Poorly maintained concrete tidal pool 1km W over headland (NO543022).

C Cambo Sands 10km E of St Andrews 1km off A917 at Kingsbarns. Walk 1km N for best sands (NO595136).

173 Tentsmuir

Grid ref.	NO501242
Postcode	DD6 9PF (3km SE)
Walk	10 mins, easy
Train	Leuchars, 6km
Cycle	Route 1

Forest, dunes and sands 15km N of St Andrews. From A919 turn R into Leuchars at roundabout and bear L out of village at church. Turn R after 2km, then 2km to toll.

174 Seacliff Beach/Tantallon

Grid ref.	NT603848
Postcode	EH39 5PP (500m N)
Walk	10 mins, easy
Train	North Berwick, 6km

Woodland beach overlooking Bass Rock. Tiny harbour inlet for jumps. Views of Tantallon Castle. 4km E of N Berwick (A198). Turn L at corner, 1km after Castle, signed Private Rd to Seacliff, £2. Also **Canty Bay** below road 1km before Castle, after golf course. Tricky parking (NT583854).

A Continue 5km S on A198, take second L after Whitekirk for **Ravensheugh/Peffer Sands** (L), **Tynes Sands** (R) (NT627809).

175 St Abb's Head

Grid ref.	NT918686
Postcode	TD14 5QF (1km N)
Walk	25 mins, diff
Train	Berwick-upon-Tweed,18km

Dramatic cliff formations, rock colours and marine wildlife at St Abb's Head. △△

St Abb's is N of Eyemouth on A1107. Take R on to B6438, past turning to Coldringham (good sandy beach), and 2km on to park at the NTS visitor centre/ café 🍴. Follow path past Starney Bay to Horsecastle Bay (1.5km) where wall starts, below loch. You can enter water from the stony beach but better to scramble on to flat, slanted, coloured rocks on L (N) side of bay. If HT, access from hill above through gate and drop down. Rock pool 'tubs' at LT.

A 13km SE from Dunbar on A1, take the second exit at the first roundabout (Cockburnspath) then down Pease Bay road. Turn L after 200m into **Cove** (NT786717, TD13 5XD). Park and follow track down to harbour quay and steps for swimming. Tunnel leads to E side of cove and to the rock arch. △

Ideas and Inspiration

From seashore foraging to swimming with dolphins, camping on the beach to exploring sea grottoes, wild swimming by the coast opens up new worlds of adventure and discovery.

Beach with the Kids

If you're spending a day at the beach with family take some ideas for games and activities, especially those for warming up everyone before or after a swim.

Wet sand makes a great Olympic arena so why not prepare a 100-metre sprint, a long jump and a hurdling course? Older kids might try javelin throwing with sticks, or the shot put with stones – ideally at a distance from everyone else! Beach 'musical chairs' is also fun: everyone lies down on the sand outside a large perimeter circle and when the sign is given they must race in to grab a stone or stick – except there's always one less than the number of people taking part.

Scavenger hunt competitions are a great way to explore a new beach – and do some litter picking at the same time. Send pairs out to collect by colour, or even by letter of the alphabet. Arrange the returns in a rainbow or use them to make a crazy golf or croquet course. Or why not build an obstacle course, with things to climb under and through at speed?

Boules with pebbles is a classic beach game: the aim is to see who can get their stone closest to the marker. Beach tennis is also fun. Start by marking out a large rectangle for the court and dividing it into three so the middle becomes the 'net' into which the ball must not fall. Use a beach ball and bat it with your hands, or use a picnic rug – get each team to hold it by the corners and use it to catch and bounce the ball.

Make an open fire and cook supper as night draws in; what could be more delicious? Then bed down under the stars to be lulled to sleep by the gentle sound of the waves. Only make fires below the high-tide line. Where fires are prohibited, create a warm glow with candle lanterns: put tea lights in white paper bakery bags weighed down with sand. If you're sleeping out, even on a dry summer night, you'll need an insulated ground mat and a good sleeping bag to keep you warm. You could use a tarpaulin, made from lightweight tent material; prop it up with sticks and anchor it with guy ropes to large stones or driftwood stakes.

Beach arts and crafts

- Build a fairy house and garden from seaweed and driftwood.
- Make a mosaic from collections of shells, sea-glass, stones and fossils.
- Have a sand-building competition – make castles, animals or cars. Or dribble wet sand to make Gaudi-esque spires and towers.
- Build a network of ponds and moats and race miniature boats made from discarded cuttle-fish 'bones'.
- Use a driftwood rake to make a Zen garden with sand patterns – or make a huge sand maze.
- Balance stones on top of each other to make a stone cairn or a statue. Take care!
- Make a heart splash in the water with your hair and see if you can catch it on camera (see below, centre).
- Go rock-pooling with a bucket, net and identification guidebook.
- Make a kite and see whose can fly the highest.
- Teach your dog some new tricks.

Bladderwrack and laver

Seashore Foraging and Food

The seashore offers a surprising variety and abundance of delightful wild foods and many can be sustainably harvested. Get yourself a good guide book – John Wright's *Edible Seashore* is recommended – light your fire, and get cooking!

Seashore green plants include sea-beet, sea holly, sea kale and sea-pea. One of my all-time favourites is **marsh samphire** (glasswort) found near sand dunes, sand flats and marshes above the high-tide mark. It has succulent, cactus-like stems that point upwards in clumps, about 20cm tall. Nip off stems at the base, boil for five minutes then eat with butter, using your teeth to strip the salty flesh from the stem.

Seaweeds are packed full of vitamins and minerals. No seaweeds are poisonous but some taste better than others. All can be eaten raw, after washing and dicing, and work well as an addition to salads, dressed with soy sauce. They're also good dried and used as a snack or condiment, particularly in a seafood soup. Harvest the tender young shoots by hand at low tide or at higher tides while snorkelling. **Bladderwrack**, one of our most common seaweeds, grows on rocks and has long fronds with a mid-rib and little flotation bladders along each side. It's best eaten dried.

Samphire, cockles and sea beet

Laver is boiled for four hours to yield a purée known as laverbread that is traditionally served with fried bread and bacon in Wales. When young the plant is green, but later turns deep purple. Its thin membrane-like leaves are often bunched and layered on rocks, like wet hankies, and it can be found quite high up the tide line. Tasty **sea lettuce** is similar but is a much more intense emerald-green colour. **Dulse** is another classic edible seaweed. It is purplish-red and its branched leaves have lots of tough flat fronds with blunt ends. Cook it with hash browns and other potato dishes. On the west coast of Ireland dulse is known as 'dillisk' and is usually sold dried as a snack food – often alongside winkles – on stalls in seaside towns.

Kelps are the traditional flat seaweeds you may have seen dried in Japanese supermarkets or served with sushi. Forests of plants sway

Marsh samphire

Spider crab

Red dulse

Tips for cooking on the beach

- Make your fire below the high-tide line.
- Dig a small fire trench and lay a grill on top.
- Let wood burn to glowing embers before grilling.

about in deep water off rocky coasts. Furbelows has lots of parallel strap-like, brownish and leathery fronds held to the rock floor by one strong central stem. Sugar kelp (also known as sea belt or oarweed) has only one frond but has fancy crinkled edges.

Blue Mussels are the classic forager's food and are delicious boiled or barbecued with butter. The largest are found in deep water offshore – a great excuse for a long snorkel around sea stacks and rocky islets at low spring tides. Mussels are filter feeders and can concentrate toxins, so if you are suspicious about water quality leave your mussels to soak for 24 hours in fresh water to clean them, rejecting any that are open. Boil for 20 minutes to cook and then discard any that remain closed. Never collect mussels where there might be sewage outflows or red algal blooms. As an extra precaution in built-up areas, avoid summer months when bacterial levels can be higher.

Cockles have a distinctive scallop-shaped shell. You can find them buried in wet sand on low-tide flats and marshes, sometimes up to 1,000 per square metre! They tend to hide about 15cm below the sand. Professionals use rakes to unearth them, but bare feet and toes also work. Be quick because these shellfish burrow very fast once they are disturbed. Soak cockles in fresh water overnight then boil or barbecue. Clams, dog whelks, oysters, razor clams, winkles and sea urchins can also be collected; **large limpets** can be eaten in survival situations, though they are tough and rubbery. Knock them sharply and swiftly to surprise them before they clamp on hard. Cut off the black sack then cook shell-side down on embers, or kebab them on a stick.

Crabs have delicious meat and four main species are found in the UK: the spider crab (with long legs); the edible crab (brick-red in colour); the common crab (also known as green crab); and the velvet swimming crab (with back legs like flippers). All are good to eat and the spider crab has the sweetest meat. They can be baited with some raw meat on the end of a two-metre line or string. Wait until they bite then pull them up slowly, net them and store them in a bucket. Alternatively, take a net with you when snorkelling as you may find one hiding under a rock ledge or in the seaweed. It is possible to pick a crab out of the water with your hands, but not recommended. Hold them at the back between thumb and finger. Crabs take 5–15 minutes to cook in boiling water, depending on size.

Swim with Dolphins and Other Beasties

One of the delights of swimming off the wilder areas of our coastline is the chance to see and experience amazing animals at close quarters.

Bottlenose dolphin

Dolphins and porpoises are cetaceans – small, toothed whales – highly intelligent and inquisitive mammals. Travelling in pods of up to 10, they breathe through lungs – relying on air from the surface – and communicate via a large vocabulary of sounds and echo-location. Dolphins and porpoises have outstanding vision both in and out of the water. They sleep by taking catnaps at the surface for a few minutes. The main British species of dolphin is the bottlenose, so-called because of its pointy nose. Sometimes dolphins are confused with their more reserved relative, the porpoise, which has a flatter nose, a shorter dorsal fin and never jumps above the water. Porpoises keep a low profile, making them difficult to spot unless the sea is dead flat.

Grey seal

Seals and walruses are also mammals with four flipper 'legs' but no real tail. The common seal tends to be found along southern and eastern British coastlines and loves to bask on sand banks (particularly in Norfolk and Lincolnshire). The grey seal (part of its Latin name, *Halichoerus grypus,* means 'sea pig') frequents the rocky western shores of Britain. Tamer and more curious than common seals, grey seals tend to practise 'bottling' – the endearing habit of standing upright in the sea to have a good look around. Their pups are white and furry and remain on land for several weeks. Common seal pups swim with their parents right from birth.

Basking shark

Seals are very fast swimmers and are confident in the water. They may well approach you and are known to nip snorkellers' flippers in play. However, never approach seals when they are on land and never approach seals with **pups** (early summer for common seals, winter for grey seals). Also be wary when exploring very remote coves, inlets and sea caves in case you surprise them.

Places to see dolphins in the UK

- The Moray Firth coastline, Scotland
- North Wales, particularly Harlech and Criccieth
- Pembrokeshire and Cardiganshire: Mwnt and Strumble Head
- Durlston Head, Purbecks, Dorset
- Prawle Point, Devon
- Penwith coastline, Cornwall
- Gairloch, Wester Ross, Scotland

Silver mullet

Kelp forest

Wrasse

Basking sharks are the most heart-stopping and other-worldly of the large British sea creatures. This shark may be just a fish, but it can grow as big as a bus and has a gaping, terrifying mouth. Despite its fearsome appearance, it's actually a harmless filter feeder that sifts plankton from the water. There are more basking sharks in Britain than in any other country; global numbers are threatened by the high value placed on their fins and livers in Asian countries. These sharks can be found close to the shore along remote Cornish coasts during the summer, though most are now heading north because climate change is causing our seas to warm.

Seaweeds and fishes inhabit the silent, underwater world and snorkelling is a great way to see them. Porthkerris on the Lizard, in Cornwall, and Kimmeridge Ledges in Dorset have well-known skin-diving centres, but almost anywhere in this book offers opportunities, especially in calm seas when visibility is higher. The most beautiful seaweeds include carpets of pink coral weed, vibrant blue rainbow wrack and impressive stands of golden thongweed and japweed. Rocky reefs provide cover for all manner of crustaceans, including the red-eyed velvet swimming crabs and even the occasional lobster.

Favourite fish to look out for include shimmering shoals of silver sand eels, mackerel – often striped and colourful – and the most vivid, almost tropical-looking fish of all: the ballan and corkwing wrasse, which builds seaweed nests in late spring. In summer, shallow-water bays such as Kimmeridge are usually a degree or two warmer than the open sea and make ideal nursery areas for juvenile fish such as pollack, bib and mullet. Why not buy yourself a pocket photographic guide to the seashore – Chris Gibson is my recommendation.

Phosphorescence is quite magical. The tiniest creatures – plankton – are also spectacular and can produce amazing displays of summer phosphorescence, or more accurately bioluminescence: a chemical reaction that causes them to emit light when they are disturbed. Norfolk is one of the better-known coasts for experiencing what local people call the 'burning', when the night sea becomes milky and glows in the bow waves of a boat or around the moving legs of a swimmer. But these conditions can occur throughout Britain in shallow, warm seas after prolonged sunlight – go night-swimming and you may just get lucky!

Boats and Boards

There are now a whole range of small, portable, easy-to-use boards that are great fun if you want an introduction to surfing. You can also buy entry-level canoes and kayaks that are perfect for exploring more remote parts of the shore.

Body or boogie boards offer an excellent introduction to surfing and are easy to carry with you to coves and secret beaches. The cheapest are about £5–15 from a beach-side shop. They're made from polystyrene so are light and quite rigid, but can break easily when used by adults. For £20–50 you'll get a rubber-plastic composite that is stronger but bendy, making it difficult to control. Ideally there should be a thick layer of plastic on the bottom, known as a 'slick', to make the board more rigid. You can also hire full-size boards and wetsuits in most resorts. For beginner's tips on surfing visit www.britsurf.co.uk.

Adults may prefer to wear **fins** (short flippers) to help pick up speed when catching waves and make the most of short boards. They cost about £20–40 but use them over neoprene 'socks' to minimise the cold and blisters. Aim for shorter, stiffer fins for efficiency and cross-cut fins if you're keen to ride 'drop-knee' rather than on your belly. Of course, it's also possible to **body surf** in big waves, especially if you pick up a bit of speed before the wave arrives. **Skim-boarding** is fun when the surf is down completely. The boards are flat and thin like a tray and are used to skate over very shallow water on the shoreline.

Some places now offer the opportunity to try **sea kayaking**. These long, thin craft have good handling as well as speed, and can cover long distances, but they require skill and a good knowledge of currents and rescue techniques. For calm seas and local trips **'sit-on-top' kayaks** are great fun for the beginner and prices start at about £300. They are stable, unsinkable and you can get in and out of them at sea so they're perfect for swimmers, snorkellers or scuba divers.

Inflatable kayaks also have potential though they can be slow. They may also be blown off course by wind and currents, and can split on sharp rocks. Make sure your kayak is double-skinned with multiple chambers, and don't plan long, complex expeditions. Finally, some people have a lot of fun visiting remote beaches in small **sailing dinghies**. Toppers are about the cheapest type (£500 second-hand).

Coasteering

One of Britain's fastest-growing adventure sports, coasteering is a mixture of swimming and exploring along the edge of the water, including climbing into caves, playing in the swell and jumping into pools.

If you want to try some simple coasteering yourself then this book will give you plenty of inspiration, but don't attempt it at rocky and very exposed locations unless the sea is really calm. You need to be a strong swimmer, confident when clambering about over rocks, and understand the basics of tidal flows (particularly if you are outside the protection of a cove or bay: *see* p.252). You'll need adequate footwear, such as trainers, and a wetsuit if you plan to be in for more than 15–20 minutes. Make sure you know how to get off the foreshore and on to the land if you get into difficulty, and how to summon help quickly.

Learn to deal with swell and rocks by building up your skills and confidence first in calm seas and sheltered areas. Once in the water, assume a squat or armchair position with your feet out in front as the main form of defence, and your hands ready to push off the rocks. As you approach your exit rock, work with the moving swell, riding it up and down, letting it launch you up to your chosen rock-hold but letting go and dropping back down again if you fail to get a strong enough hand-hold. Never haul yourself out on to rocks on your stomach – you'll only be dragged back down and suffer grazes. Remember that swell is intermittent so wait for a lull and beware of large ferries and tankers, which can create a large wake even at a mile's distance.

Exploring sea caves and swimming through them is a magical experience but even a light swell can suddenly strengthen as a cave narrows. Sudden high swell can also dump you on the rocks below, or knock your head against the ceiling. Take particular care if waves start breaking on the rocks.

'Deep Water Soloing' will definitely appeal to climbers. It's a new sport that specialises in locations above deep water, which means no ropes are required. For more information visit www.dwsworld.com.

RIP CURRENTS
Break the Grip of the Rip!

Currents, Tides and Safety

Rip currents are offshore surface currents that re-circulate water out to the back of the surf breaks during high surf. They increase in strength as the surf increases and do not occur in calm seas. Rips tend to form in natural channels: between sand bars; in a river mouth or estuary; or along a pier, jetty, groyne or rock stack. In coves, rips tend to form along the edges. Look for a calmer, possibly rippled, channel between the incoming surf breaks. Sometimes the channel is deep green in colour, or may be carrying foam or debris, or stirring up sediment. The waterline at the shore will also be a little lower where the rip begins. Surfers often use rips to take them out beyond the breaks, so ask them for advice.

Escaping a rip is straightforward if you are a strong swimmer and remain calm. People drown from panic, followed by exhaustion, so never fight against the current. Keep an eye on a shore landmark to establish whether you are in a rip. If so, stand or wade if possible. If not, swim out of it at ninety degrees parallel to the beach for about 20m. Once out of the rip, head back towards the beach, using the waves to body-surf you back in. If you are too exhausted to swim, raise your arm to attract attention and lie on your back – or on a board if you have one – to conserve energy. Remember, rips only extend to the back of the surf, rarely more than 100m, often less. They also slow down as they get further from shore.

Cross-shore rips occur when surf is coming in at an angle to the coast and creating a current across the beach. They will not take you out to sea, but may take you out of your depth.

'Dumping' surf forms on steeply shelving beaches (particularly on the shingle beaches of the south and east coasts, such as Chesil or Dungeness). This type of surf breaks quickly and heavily, dumping you hard on the ground. An immediate and highly localised undertow then sucks the water back out again, making it difficult to stand up and negotiate the steep shelf, especially if you are tired. Aim to land behind the breaking wave or try to find a more gently sloping part of the beach.

Jumping is great fun, but the danger of death, paralysis or severe injury is obvious. Check depths thoroughly before every jump and never trust your eyes – water always looks deeper than it actually is. A high tide one week may be many metres shallower than it was the previous week. Winter storms can also move underwater boulders around. On entry, keep your legs together, your head up and your arms tight in, either straight down or crossed on your chest. Jumping from a height of more than five metres can be painful and dangerous. For more safety information visit **www.wildswimming.co.uk**

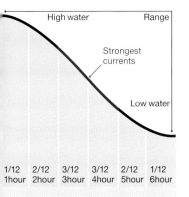

1/12 2/12 3/12 3/12 2/12 1/12
1hour 2hour 3hour 4hour 5hour 6hour

Rule of twelfths

If in doubt avoid the fastest flow in the middle hours of the tide. In the first hour of the tide, approximately one-twelfth of the water moves; in the second hour two-twelfths moves, during the third hour three-twelfths moves, and so on as the flow-rate decreases again.

What time is the tide?

Tide cycles repeat every 12 hours, occurring half an hour later each time. They occur about an hour later each day.

Spring tides

Contrary to popular belief spring(strong) tides occur every fortnight at new and full moons and are only partly affected by the season.

Find tides for the whole country at bbc.co.uk/ weather/coast/tides

Tides are created by the moon. The sea **floods** as the tide comes in and levels rise. It **ebbs** as the tide goes out and levels drop. The power of the tide varies from day to day and affects the tidal range (height) and the flow rate (current). Tides are predictable but are highly variable and localised. Determinants of the tide's strength include whether the water is slack, or in full flow (*see* Rule of twelfths, left), and how close it is to a spring or neap tide.

Spring and neap tides are respectively, strong and weak. At full or new moons the sun and moon are, astronomically speaking, in line. This creates the strongest gravitational pull on the sea and therefore strong tides, known as 'spring' tides occur, roughly every fortnight. At half-moons, sun and moon oppose each other, resulting in weak gravitational pull on the sea and creating weak tides, known as 'neap' tides. Spring tides might typically have a range of 5–6m, and 3–4 knots peak current. Neap tides are about a half to a third of that range. 'Springs' and 'neaps' always occur at the same time of day for a particular part of the coast. For Atlantic-facing coasts such as Cornwall, Devon and west Scotland, the peak spring high tides are always around 6am and 6pm – very handy for enjoying really low-tide beaches in the heat of the day!

The direction of flow is of vital importance for swimmers. Britain's south and west shores fill from the Atlantic up into the English Channel and Irish Sea, so tidal currents flow east in the flood and are progressively later as you go east to Dover or north to Liverpool. Britain's east and north coasts fill from the North Sea, with waters moving south in the flood and becoming progressively later as you go south down the east coast. The east Dorset coast has very small tides where the two flows cancel each other out.

Coves and bays are protected from tidal flows (though of course the sea levels will still change) but open coast is exposed to tidal currents. Currents strengthen around restrictions, such as headlands or islands (Portland Bill or Ramsay Sound) or at estuary or harbour mouths (Chichester Harbour or Blackwater Estuary). Remember that at an estuary or river mouth the current will be carrying you inshore as the tide comes in (relatively safe) but offshore when the tide goes out (potentially very dangerous).

Surfing in the sunset at Crackington Haven

Wild Swimming: Coast
(1st edition)

Written and photographed by
Daniel Start

Additional Photography:
Chris Parker

Publisher: **Jonathan Knight**

Project Manager: **Nikki Sims**

Editor: **Anna Kruger**

Proofreader: **Leanne Bryan**

Publishing Assistants:
**Sophie Dawson,
Catherine Greenwood**

Design and artwork:
**Paul Hamilton,
www.oneanother.ltd.uk**

Production:
**Sophie Dawson, Catherine
Greenwood, Paul Hamilton**

PR: **The Farley Partnership**

Published by:
**Punk Publishing Ltd
3 The Yard, Pegasus Place
London SE11 5SD**

Distributed by:
**Portfolio Books
Suite 3 & 4, Great West House
Great West Road, Brentford
Middlesex TW8 9DF**

Front cover: © Oliver Strewe/Getty Images

**All photographs © Daniel Start except the following (all reproduced with
permission):** Back cover, p5 top & middle, p194-5, p200 top, middle, bottom,
p204 bottom, p216-217, p220 top © Chris Parker; Back cover middle © Emma
Bradshaw; p1 © Thomas Magnusson; p8 top left © Emma Bradshaw; p12 bottom
© Hugh Spicer; p20, p26 middle & bottom, p45 © Seb de Gange; p22 middle ©
Sharon Meredew (www.smerredewphotography.co.uk); p23 © John Jamieson
(UtterlyFabFotos.com 020 8133 2413); p24 © John Such (www.suchgoodpictures.
co.uk); p28 © Justin Tiltman; p34 middle © Robert Slack; p38 middle © Phillip Rees;
p49 © John Palmer; p50 © Joseph Brooks; p61 © www.tunnelsbeaches.co.uk /
Neville Stanikk; p64 © Dave Croker; p72 bottom © Paul Ashton, p99 © Charlotte
Macpherson; p106 © Michael Rogers; p126 middle © Nick Cobbing; p128 & 131
© Martin Turtle (www.turtlephotography.co.uk); p130 © Jonathen Harty; p132 ©
Nick Cobbing; p159 top © John Powell; p159 middle © Aaron Jones; p 173 © Jim
Krawiecki (www.jimski.eu); p182 © Tony Sinton; p198 © Petra Kjell; p202 © Niall
Corbet; p205 © Lasse Andersson; p210 middle © Douglas Wilcox; p218 © Martin
Third; p224 middle © Ray Green; p230 © Jim Taylor; p243 bottom middle © Flickr
Ben; p243 bottom right © Entienou; p244 bottom & p245 middle © Sion Roberts;
p245 bottom & p246 bottom © Seb de Grange; p246 top © David Safanda, p246
middle © Arrow Studios; p247 top © Nick Free; p247 middle © Paule858, p247
bottom © QLDian; p248 top middle © Susan Stewart; p248 bottom middle © Ian
McDonnell; p249 right middle © Douglas Wilcox; p251 top © Flickr Ben; p251 bottom
right © Aloha Innovations.

Author acknowledgements: Special thanks to the friends and colleagues who helped
find, test and photograph all these swimming holes, come rain or shine, particularly
to: Emily Walmsley, Ciaran Mundy & Liquorice, Petra Kjell, Carl Reynolds, Chris
Parker, Seb de Grange, Charlotte Macpherson, Nick Cobbing, Briony Greenhill, Jack
Thurston, Charlie Cory-Wright, Anthea Lawson, Catherine Howarth, Chloe Kinsman
and the Flickr, Geograph and Panoramio community of photographers. The dedication
and commitment of the Punk editorial and production teams has, as ever, been truly
inspiring: Jonathan Knight, Anna Kruger, Paul Hamilton, Nikki Sims, Sophie Dawson,
Carol Farley, Catherine Greenwood, Marcus Freeman and Leanne Bryan. Also thanks
to (South West) Christopher Somerville, Douglas King-Smith, Emma Bradshaw, Alfie
and Bella, John Such, Seb de Grange, James Heath, Luke and Amanda Hudson,
Chloe and Ben Fletcher, Polly Braden, Catherine Howarth, Sam Williams of Cornish
Coast Adventures, Diana Evans and Caroline Andrews, Sophie Howarth, Fiona Gerrans
and Angus, Amy and Sabrina Lee, Naomi and Suna Nightingale, Joanna Johnston,
John Start. (South and East) Lucy and Jon Rouse, Tom Currie and Tor Udall, Charlotte
Macpherson and Pete, Rae and Flora Durgerian, Redge, Sophie and Anna Hurpy,
Natalie Start, Ralph, Caroline and Mishka Taylor, Alison de Braux, Maria Glauser and
Seth Reynolds, Mit Fitzgerald and family, Ben Fletcher and family, Marcus Freeman,
Jessica Lack & Zac, Sarah and David Boyle, Jessica Williams, Cosmo and Toby,
Charlotte and Philip Hampson and family, Donna Fry and family, Sara Reeves and family,
Harry Cory Wright and family, Joshua, Romeo Phillips and Stiffkey friends, Joanna
Adams and family, Kate Grange, Ed Gillespie, Chris Knight, Rachel and Piers Mahon,
Sarah McGeehan. (Wales) John and Caroline Walmsley, Mungo and Ishbel Amyatt-Leir,
Fiona Smith, Leanda Thomas, Rosie Jones and Toby, Janine Bonnet, Martin Turtle,
Tom Bullough. (North and Scotland) Jack Thurston, Roma Backhouse, girls at Boggle
Hole, Tom Walmsley, Nell Boase, Sue and Gavin King-Smith, Kat Jones, Jake and Isabel
Willis, Katy Marks, Tom Alcott, Tom Crompton. With final thanks to all the local wild-
swimmers and secret cove-hunters we met who shared their knowledge so generously.
Please explore sensitively and respect the local countryside.